THE ESSENCE OF

DATA STRUCTURES USING C++

THE ESSENCE OF COMPUTING SERIES

Published Titles

THE ESSENCE OF

DATA STRUCTURES USING C++

Ken Brownsey

Prentice
Hall

An imprint of **Pearson Education**

Harlow, England · London · New York · Reading, Massachusetts · San Francisco · Toronto · Don Mills, Ontario · Sydney
Tokyo · Singapore · Hong Kong · Seoul · Taipei · Cape Town · Madrid · Mexico City · Amsterdam · Munich · Paris · Milan

Pearson Education Limited
Edinburgh Gate
Harlow
Essex CM20 2JE
England

and Associated Companies around the World.

Visit us on the World Wide Web at:
www.pearsoneduc.com

First published 2000

© Pearson Education Limited 2000

The programs in this book have been included for their instructional value.
They have been tested with care but are not guaranteed for any particular
purpose. The publisher does not offer any warranties or representations
nor does it accept any liabilities with respect to the programs.

Many of the designations used by manufacturers and sellers to distinguish their
products are claimed as trademarks. Pearson Education has made every
attempt to supply trademark information about manufacturers and their products
mentioned in this book. A list of the trademark designations and their owners
appears below.

ISBN 0-139-48886-3

British Library Cataloguing-in-Publication Data
A catalogue record for this book can be obtained from the British Library

Library of Congress Cataloging-in-Publication Data
Brownsey, Ken.
    The essence of data structures using C++ / Ken Brownsey.
      p. cm. -- (The Essence of computing series)
    Includes bibliographical references and index.
    ISBN 0-139-48886-3 (alk. paper)
    1. C++ (Computer program language) 2. Data structures (Computer science) I. Title.
II. Series.
QA76.73.C153 B79   2000
005.13'3--dc21   00-025355
                                                   CIP

10 9 8 7 6 5 4 3 2 1
05 04 03 02 01 00

Trademark Notice
Delphi is a trademark of Borland International, Inc.
Eiffel is a trademark of Nonprofit International Consortium for Eiffel (NICE).
Java and Modula-2 are trademarks of Sun Microsystems, Inc.

Typeset by 43
Printed in Great Britain by Henry Ling, at the Dorset Press, Dorchester, Dorset

Contents

Series Preface

As the consulting editor for the *Essence of Computing Series* it is my role to encourage the production of well-focused, high-quality textbooks at prices which students can afford. Since most computing courses are modular in structure, we aim to produce books that will cover the essential material for a typical module.

I want to maintain a consistent style for the Series so that whenever you pick up an Essence book you know what to expect. For example, each book contains important features such as end of chapter summaries and exercises, and a glossary of terms, if appropriate. Of course, the quality of the Series depends crucially on the skills of its authors and all the books are written by lecturers who have honed their material in the classroom. Each book in the Series takes a pragmatic approach and emphasises practical examples and case studies.

Our aim is that each book will become essential reading material for students attending core modules in Computing. However, we expect students to want to go beyond the Essence books and so all books contain guidance on further reading and related work.

The study of data structures, and associated algorithms, is a core component of the computing curriculum and this book provides a comprehensive introduction to the subject. The reader is assumed to have a basic knowledge of C++, as any practical study of data structures requires a reasonable level of proficiency in programming. However, an important additional feature of this book is that it illustrates a disciplined approach to writing C++ programs which is applicable to a wider range of programming activities. The book develops the understanding of data structures via practical examples and there is extensive supporting material, including many substantial programs, accessible via the Web (`www.booksites.net/brownsey`).

Computing is constantly evolving and so the teaching of the subject also has to change. Therefore, the Series has to be dynamic, responding to new trends in computing and extending into new areas of interest. We need feedback from our readers to guide us – are we hitting the target? Are there 'hot' topics which we have not covered yet? Feedback is always welcome but most of all I hope you find this book useful!

Ray Welland
Department of Computing Science
University of Glasgow
(e-mail: ray@dcs.gla.ac.uk)

Preface

The background to this book

My experience of teaching data structures, in a modular course, over the last nine years, is that we have two main 'extreme' groups. One group of people are keen on designing and building systems. The others do not like programming but take the module because it is compulsory, their intention being to take all non-programming modules, where possible, and then get a job as a non-programming manager. Between we have a range of people who are not averse to programming but just want the tools to get the job done.

Ironically, it is sometimes the keener programmers who find the material a little baffling at first. Because they can already quickly write programs that produce results, they often get impatient with the apparently ponderous progress towards a full working system. Fortunately most come to appreciate the idea that we are engaged in building complex systems out of simple components, which calls for precise specification and design.

On the other hand, those with an allergy to programming tend to find that if they think in terms of *abstract data types*, almost the essence of the essence of data structures, as presented here, rather than the programming problem, then the programming, when it comes, is neatly defined and circumscribed. You still need to program but instead of a massive misery of a problem you have a collection of little problems, each much more tractable on its own.

I feel that the application of data structures extends beyond the 'traditional' domain of building systems in general-purpose programming languages. To take an example, I believe that when it comes to designing and implementing websites, then students with data structures backgrounds have a much greater grasp of the potential for creating and navigating around non-linear structures. They are thus in a much better position to let their imagination loose at an earlier stage. Perhaps they have no taste themselves for producing the Java code for dynamic linkage of pages, for example, but they know it can be done.

This book is not entitled 'Data Structures for Dummies' or 'Data Structures made Simple'. If students consider themselves dummies they must buy another book. I have tried to make things simple by presenting, as the title suggests, the essential features of data structures, but this does not make it easy. It is intended that a student who has passed the indicated prerequisites, which are reviewed here, and who puts in the work, should get a good grasp of the core material and get a competent pass on the data structures exams that I set, which I guess are not so very different from many others.

The material here is based on our module Data Structures and other courses at Oxford Brookes University. I would also like to acknowledge the influence of the excellent units produced for the Open University M353, Programming and Programming Languages course, on which I was a tutor for six years.

Who is this book for?

Modular course students

The main audience for this book is students taking a course in data structures, who will have had little or no experience in the use of pointers for dynamic data structures. In particular, I have in mind students taking a modular degree in computer science, information systems or software engineering. Typically there is a module called Data Structures or something similar, which runs over a term or perhaps a semester.

As mentioned above, some students are keener than others on programming, and as all lecturers on programming courses know, some are extremely reluctant programmers.

And at the other extreme, we might describe students as perhaps 'over keen', in that they want to rush into code.

This book is for both these groups as well as all the others in between.

I intend that the reluctant will be able to see how through the careful approach described here, one can put together programs by stages that do just what they are meant to do. Much reluctance comes from the misery of trying to find out why big cobbled together programs don't do as they are meant to.

I urge the 'over keen' to also consider this approach. It might take much of the excitement out of life not to have to sit up the night before the assignment is due, trying every possible 'hack', 'fix' and 'patch' that you can think of, but perhaps that might be replaced with the air of quiet satisfaction of having worked through systematically to a result that 'looks right' in the same way as a well-designed piece of machinery 'looks right'. You might have more time for things like hang-gliding to make up for the lost excitement.

Lastly, but not least, the ones in between, who have a reasonably good idea of what structured programming is, and why it is important, should find a clear and concise description of how to move on to the next stage of programming.

Individual students

As long as you have a computer with a C++ compiler, and at least occasional access to the World Wide Web to get hold of the code, you should be able to use this book for self study. But please note that this is not an introduction to programming. Ideally you will have taken a course like the Open University M205, or a module in structured programming. If you are going to teach yourself from scratch then you will need to study something like *The Essence of Programming Using C++* by Douglas Bell (Prentice Hall 1997).

What will you get out of this book?

I am occasionally informed by well-meaning students that there is no real need to worry about all these data structures and pointers and things. There is a package for this and a package for that. I have no qualms about using packages. However, packages are designed with a particular problem class in mind, and for many problem classes they can offer, at best, approximate solutions. A programmer who is familiar with a general-purpose programming language such as C++ has the technical ability to produce tailored solutions. Perhaps more fundamentally, he or she will have the confidence, ability and imagination to see that such a solution can be found with a general-purpose programming language. Even those who go on to become non-programming computer professionals will benefit from the realisation of what can be done, although perhaps not by themselves.

A related comment by others keen to make my life easier is that the new general-purpose languages and environments, e.g. Java and Delphi, provide data structures, such as the linked list, in class libraries e.g. the Java Vector. I am grateful for this intelligence and indeed do use the Vector in programming for my research. But I still need to understand the nature of a dynamic sequential data structure. Furthermore, I need to build quite complex data structures, which I am certain have never featured in any data structures textbook, just like most buildings have never featured in any architecture textbook. I know how to put together simple data structures to make more complex ones. In this I rely on the abstract data type approach.

There is no end to the charity shown towards me. Pointers, I am told, are 'out'. Java does not have them. All that miserable fiddling with pointer switching has gone the way of the motor car starting handle. But I find that I need to build dynamic structures, such as trees, in Java. Strangely enough I find I am reference switching. The semantics of Java equality seem not as simple as those of C++. But I remember that I must not confuse the pointer with the thing it points at, and similarly I must not confuse the reference with the thing it refers to, the *referent*. Then a problem turns up when I need to change the value of a reference, not the referent, passed as a parameter. Oddly I can see why the problem occurs due to my previous experience with pointers. The truth is, of course, that Java references are just pointers and that Java restricts the programmer by not allowing access to the address of any variable, reference or primitive. I am not saying this is a bad thing. But a sound grasp of what references, addresses and pointers are is a good deal more useful than perhaps some Java textbooks suggest.

I hope that these little homilies indicate what I hope that you will get from the book. You should understand that, within the limits set only by the nature of the primitive building blocks of records, arrays and pointers, you can build a data structure as intricate as is required. You should appreciate how the abstract data type approach makes the implementation of that intricacy tractable. You should be able to reuse the data structures supplied by the environment, fellow programmers or yourself from a previous project. Even if you intend to rise rapidly to the dizzy heights of being above mere programming, you will have sufficient understanding to be able to discuss possibilities and solutions with the hewers of code.

Why C++?

Data structures is a language-independent discipline, in the same way as learning to drive is a car-independent discipline. Both statements are true but in practice your motivation and learning experience will depend on what language or car you choose for your practical work. The choice can be controversial.

C++ is a popular programming language. That does not mean that it is the best. Eiffel is a far better object-oriented language. However, many, if not most, new programmers will program in C++. One aim of a programming course which observes best practice is to ensure that the tools and techniques of software engineering are understood well enough to help the students make up for the deficiencies of a language as far as that is possible. So, on the assumption that the largest group of readers will have used C++ in their first course, and will probably use it in further courses or work, the author and the publisher have chosen C++.

Having said this, I guess that many C++ programmers are actually C programmers using a C++ programming environment. This view has been confirmed by a large, ongoing but rather unscientific survey of colleagues from my own and other universities, as well as freelance and salaried programmers. And it is particularly true of beginners. There is nothing wrong with this, but it posed for me the question of where to start, what, if anything, new of C++ to introduce along the way and where to stop. I decided to start where *The Essence of Programming Using C++* leaves off. This means that students have a clear reference as to what is expected. It also means that students with a reasonable background in introductory programming using Pascal or Modula-2 can get up to speed fairly quickly on the C++ I use. They should start mainly by observing syntactic differences, although I would advise them to do this before their Data Structures course begins. I decided to introduce structures because they are clearly essential. I decided not to go into classes. These are important but are language support for abstract data types once the student has a grasp of abstract data types and the data structures that implement them. I must emphasise that this approach is not one of teaching a programming language, rather one of introducing those features of a language which are directly relevant to the theoretical and practical work of data structures.

Finally...

I welcome comments and questions on this text. *Please* let me know of any mistakes you think you find. I hope and intend that there should be none, but even something being technically correct and yet leading a reader to believe that a mistake has been made indicates a shortcoming that needs looking at.

Ken Brownsey
Oxford Brookes University
`kwb@brookes.ac.uk`

Acknowledgements and dedications

For what I have learned over the past 13 years about data structures and their uses I am greatly indebted to three groups of people. First, there are those who taught me as a mature student. Then there are my colleagues, past and present, who extended that learning process. Last but not least there are those students whose questions and diligence have led me to new insights, make corrections and see other ways of doing things. Well done and thank you everyone!

I am also very very grateful for all the work and help from editors Jackie Harbor, who started the whole thing off, and Kate Brewin, who made sure it got completed. Well done and thank you.

This book is for Jane, Lucy and William (alphabetical order). Well done and thank you too!

Introduction

The silken thread

Connoisseurs of old black and white movies may recall the Robin Hood film in which our hero shoots an arrow, attached to a long silken thread, up through the open windows of the imprisoned Maid Marian's boudoir. Either by design or good fortune the arrow misses the lady and embeds its head in a handy oaken chest. Attached to the silken thread is a long cord, so that the heroine, no shrinking violet, can haul up the thread to get hold of the cord. To the cord in turn is attached a long rope, which she gets hold of in the same way. It is then but the work of a moment for the feisty female role model to tie the rope to a secure wall fixture, and then abseil[1] down the castle wall to join the ranks of the Saxon Liberation Movement.

This little story is intended to indicate the approach taken in this book. The 'silken thread' is the essence as promised by the title of the book and the series of which it forms a part. If you can manage what is here, over a period of about three months, then, as the need for using different data structures or algorithms crops up, new problems call for new approaches, or you find references to more advanced related topics on other courses, then, in most cases, you should, with a little hard work, be able to pull up the 'cord' and then the 'rope'.

I have just pulled down a rather thicker book on data structures. In the contents list I see references to B trees, the implementation of which I have forgotten all about, and to AVL trees, which I never did know about. However, with the core of data structures that I do possess, I know that it will not take long to get back to grips with the B trees, as indeed I shall probably have to in the next month with some programming I have to do for a research project, and that the AVL trees are just a matter of time and concentration. What I have put into this book are those things that you need to remember, or at least have close to hand, in order that you can revise old forgotten topics and learn new ones.

The plan of the book

The book is almost linear – that is, each chapter presupposes knowledge of the previous one, except that Chapters 10 and 11 can be read in either order, with

---

[1] Actually I don't think she did abseil but if they made the film now then I'm sure that she would.

minor reference problems. However, complete knowledge of the previous chapter is not always assumed. For example, understanding simple recursion is essential for Chapter 7, on the binary search tree, but a complete grasp of the Hanoi problem or the simplified knapsack problem is not.

Example code has been supplied in the examples sub-directory of the appropriate chapter directory. This is an integral part of the book and so you must copy this from `www.booksites.net/brownsey` as soon as you can.

Chapter 1 discusses data and types, before introducing the record (`struct`), array and pointer as the three primitive building blocks of data structures, and looking at the technique of using a key/address record. In Chapter 2 the concept of an abstract data type (ADT) is introduced, using a draughts board example. The `Sequence_T` ADT is specified and then implemented based on an array in Chapter 3. Chapter 4 introduces linked lists and shows how the `Sequence_T` can be reimplemented using a linked list. Another linear data structure, the `Stack_T`, is introduced, specified and implemented as a specialisation of the `Sequence_T`, and then directly, in Chapter 5. An application of the `Stack_T` is given, and the `Queue_T` is specified for implementation. Chapter 6 introduces recursion and examines its role in problem solving and investigates the conversion from recursion to iteration in examples. The `BST_T` (binary search tree) is specified and implemented in terms of the `BT_T` (binary tree) in Chapter 7. In Chapter 8 the `BT_T` itself is implemented, the traversing of the `BT_T` and `BST_T` investigated, and the `BST_T` reimplemented, first procedurally and then non-recursively. The `Iterator_T` ADT is specified and implemented in the first part of Chapter 9, with the second part examining the implementation of a complex data structure using several `BST_T`s and a variety of key values. Searching and sorting are dealt with in Chapter 10, looking at algorithms on arrays and linked lists and relating these to algorithms on the `BST_T`. Also examined in Chapter 10 are heuristic searching and hashing. Chapter 11 is a case study, looking at the implementation of the `Graph_T` based on the `Sequence_T`, `Stack_T` and `BST_T`. Chapter 12 reviews what has been done and makes suggestions for further reading.

Exercises

Exercises are put in wherever it seems useful to get some practical experience or at the ends of chapters or long sections to consolidate material. Many refer to incomplete code, usually in the exercise sub-directory of the appropriate chapter directory from `www.booksites.net/brownsey`. In many cases solutions are provided in the solution sub-directory, but you will not grow as a data structurer or person if you just look at the solution. Try the exercise, maybe take a quick peek for a clue, but be resolute in working out as much as you can yourself.

CHAPTER 1

Data, types, structures and references

1.1 Introduction

The purpose of this chapter is to establish some preliminary ideas about real world entities and their representations as *structured data* in both paper and electronic form.

We first look at the nature of data in the real world, in terms of types and structure. A C++ language-specific description of the use of macros to define constants is given. Then we see how C++ provides language support for representing such types and structures in our programs. This includes some detailed material on pointers. A method for storing data separately from its referencing key is introduced. This is to be used elsewhere in the book. Finally we look at some operations on types and structures in a set of programs, which form the basis for practical work on this chapter.

1.2 Data in the real world

Commercial, organisational and engineering problems involve a great number of *data items*. Each individual data item is an atomic piece of information containing a *value* about some aspect of the problem.

1.2.1 Data typed in the real world

A data item has a *type*, that is a set of values from which it takes its own value. For example, the data item 'number of children' has the type 'non-negative integer', and the data item 'bank balance' has the type 'real number'.

Some types are just other types reused. For example, the type 'student number' is really just an integer, except that we do not usually do arithmetic with student numbers.

Other types are very much derived from the constraints of the real world. For example, the possible value of a day is restricted to one of seven – that is Sunday, Monday, ..., Saturday.

1.2.2 Data structured in the real world

Most solutions to commercial, organisational and engineering problems in the real world are provided by processing sets of data into other sets of data. For ease of processing and storage, data items are *structured* together. Consider the following examples concerning storage, structure and access of data.

Example 1

If you fill in a university application form then there are items of data such as your surname, your year of birth, your address and the courses you are applying for.

When the forms are received at the university then they are kept together in a *file*, which is a structure to hold a set of records. Each has been given an application number. The fact that your form is next to that of John Brown of 23 Acacia Avenue, Sometown, does not necessarily say anything about any real world connection between you and said John Brown, except that you have both applied. The connection is one imposed by the university admissions, who have given you application number 99284356 and John Brown application number 99284357. These numbers are instances of the *key* given to the file to order the records. A key is a specified item of data used to identify a particular record and is used for searching and sorting the data. In this case the keys say nothing about you or John Brown, except perhaps that you both applied for 1999 entry, but this is usually secondary to their main use in structuring the vast number of forms.

In this first example there are two sorts of structure. The form is a *record* holding together many individual but linked items of data, of various types, about a single entity, the student. The file is an *array* holding a set of records of similar types. These structures can be nested. In the example the 'courses applied for' field will be an array of elements, each of type 'course applied for'.

We also see two types of data here. One is concerned with the *real world problem*, that is students and their applications. This is *real world data*. The other is about how the real world data is to be stored and accessed. This is *structural information*. If we had no structural information, we would have no structure in which to store and access real world data. The key is an item of structural information, although it may either be derived from real world data – e.g. surname – or come to be real world data as well as having its structuring role – e.g. student number.

Example 2

A student taking Modern Literature has an exam about the book *Moby Dick*. She needs to be pretty familiar with the story and so on, and has made a number of notes, with page numbers on, to help her revise. However, the fact that she forgets every page number when it comes to the exam has no effect on her ability to pass the exam. The page numbers are purely structural information to make it much simpler to get the information she really needs.

Example 3

This is perhaps a little less obvious but may help you to understand a future topic. Suppose that you want to find out something about the medieval philosopher St Thomas Aquinas. You ring up a philosophy lecturer at your local university. He doesn't know the answer to your question, but he gives you the number of a philosopher at another university, who you phone. She doesn't know either but she gives you another number and so on, until you phone a philosopher who does. The series of telephone numbers you get are nothing to do with the answer to your question about Aquinas, but they help you to find it by providing a structure through which you can search. The telephone numbers are structural information, each acting as a *pointer* to the next piece of real world data.

1.3 Use of macros: #define

This section is not strictly about types or structures. It introduces a further feature and an account of how I use it to overcome a deficiency in C++.

Convention

I like to use macros to indicate explicitly the use of a Boolean type. In C++ the Boolean value 'true' is any non-zero value and 'false' is 0. The result of applying any relational operators, such as > or ==, is 1, if the relation holds, and 0 if not. However, Booleans are a primitive type and should have explicit language support, as they do in most other third-generation languages. Note that the type boolean is primitive in Java for example. Thus I usually set up the following

```
#define TRUE    1
#define FALSE   0
#define BOOLEAN int
```

This makes the code easier to read. Strictly speaking, this is not setting up a Boolean type, it is more in the way of in-line documentation, but I find it helps immensely. In all the programs used in this book, this declaration is found in my_const.h. The only drawback to this is that if any identifier or string literal contains any of the substrings TRUE, FALSE or BOOLEAN, then these too will be translated into 1, 0 or int at compile time. The overhead of checking that this is not so is far outweighed by being able to use clearly what should be a primitive type. I do not make any macros for ! (NOT), || (OR) or && (AND), because these are straightforward synonyms rather than the use of another type.

Constants are implemented in different ways in different languages. In C++ we use the macro facility. Suppose that we want to put people who owe too much in a special class. Then we could introduce a constant monetary value, such that anyone who owes more than that is a bad payer! Here is how we do it.

```
#define DebtLimit_C    2000
```

This says that everywhere the compiler comes across the text DebtLimit_C, it can replace it by the text 2000 before getting down to the serious business of compiling. The advantage of doing this is that if the authorities change the debt limit then we need change only this one statement and then recompile. If the debt limit value were to be used many times and we had explicitly written 2000 in each case, then we would have to find each occurrence and change it.

1.4 Language support for typing data

Most languages provide support for developing a type system in our programs that reflects that in the real world problem. Here we shall look at how C++ provides support for this over and above the direct typing of variables such as, for example

```
int Count;
char NextOption;
```

already dealt with in *The Essence of Programming using C++* (pages 9–19).

1.4.1 Synonyms

Suppose you are writing a payroll package. Wages would figure a lot in such a package. Wages are usually real numbers, for example £232.23. Presumably variables for wages pop up all over the place. Using typedef we can create a type for wages, which is just a *synonym* for float.

```
typedef float    Wage_T;
```

We can then define and use variables of this type.

```
Wage_T    TotalWages,
          NextWage;
.................
TotalWages = TotalWage + NextWage;
```

Convention

All my user-defined types have identifiers that end in _T. This makes the code easier to read and understand.

1.4.2 Enumerated types

An *enumerated type* is a type defined by the programmer as a (finite) list of values.

```
enum  Day_T {Mon, Tue, Wed, Thur, Fri, Sat, Sun};
```

It can then be used to declare variables of that type;

```
enum Day_T DayOfLecture;
```

and to do things with that variable

```
DayOfLecture = Mon;
```

Comment

What is really happening is that the type is an int in disguise. Unless otherwise stated, the first value is 0, the second 1 and so on. For example Fri has value 4. So why bother? Well it is much easier to understand and reason about your programs if the names of types and values are meaningful, just as with variables. Depending on your compiler, you can do all sorts of weird and wonderful things with enumerated types, and, in most cases, you shouldn't. It makes sense to use the fact that it is *ordinal* – that is has an ordering – to index an array, but don't do anything unnatural, like explicitly assigning an int value to a Day_T variable, for example.

1.5 Language support for structuring of data

All modern programming languages provide support for structuring data in the three senses mentioned above.

1.5.1 Arrays

It is assumed that you are familiar with simple arrays in C++. It is often useful to declare a new type based on an array. Suppose that we know that we shall be using integer arrays of size `MaxSize` in a number of places in a program and we already have a macro for `MaxSize`.

```
#define MaxSize  5;
```

This is set deliberately small for testing and demo purposes. Then

```
typedef int IntArray_T[MaxSize];
```

sets up the new type `IntArray_T` and we can declare variables of this type

```
IntArray_T Nums;
```

We can pass them as parameters

```
void
Read_In_Values(IntArray_T IntArray) {
  int Index;

  for(Index = 0; Index < MaxSize; Index++) {
    cout << "\nPlease type in an integer ==> ";
    cin  >> IntArray[Index];
  }
}
.................
  Read_In_Values(Nums);
```

as well as all the other things we did with the primitive types. `ch1\examples\udt_arr.cpp` demonstrates user-defined array types.

Comment

You will also see that the procedures are documented with *pre-* and *post-conditions*. For example

```
// PRE TRUE
// POST prompts for and reads values into IntArray
void
Read_In_Values(IntArray_T IntArray) {
```

This will be discussed more fully in Chapter 2, but briefly you must check that the pre-condition of a procedure is TRUE before calling it, and then the post-condition is guaranteed, by the procedure implementor, to be TRUE after the procedure has been implemented.

1.5.2 Records

Most (but not all) third-generation languages provide support for records. In C++ this is done with `struct`. Suppose that we have already defined the following types

```
typedef enum Dept_T {Toys, Food, Clothing};

typedef int InvNum_T;
typedef float Balance_T;
```

Together with `typedef`, we can define a new type as follows

```
typedef struct {
  InvNum_T    InvoiceNum;
  Balance_T Balance;
  enum    Dept_T Dept;
} InvRec_T;
```

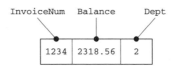

Figure 1.1 The variable `NextInvoice` of type `Invoice_T`, with fields `CustomerNumber`, `InvoiceNumber` and `Amount`, an example of a `struct` in memory.

The physical layout of this type is illustrated in Figure 1.1. We can then access the fields of the records thus, and treat them like the individual variables they are – it is just that they go around together in a bunch.

```
cout << "\nInvoice Number ==> ";
cin >> InvRec.InvoiceNum;
cout << "\nBalance ==> ";
cin >> InvRec.Balance;
cout << "\nDepartment ";
InvRec.Dept = Read_Dept();
........................................
if (Rec.Balance > HighBalance) {
........................................
```

See `ch1\examples\inv_rec1.cpp`. Note the following points:

- There are two procedures, `Read_Rec` and `Write_Rec`, for In/Out (IO) operations on this particular record type.
- Because `Dept_T` is an enumerated type we need two procedures, `Read_Dept` and `Write_Dept`, for IO operations on this type.

- These extra IO procedures take time to write and test but what we are doing is extending our library of IO operations from those just given us in `<iostream.h>`, rather than having to 'inline code' them every time we need them.
- This is the first program with a loop for user options using a switch statement, so examine the structure carefully, noting how there is a top-level breakdown into `Initialise`, `Loop` and `Finalise`, which will be a common pattern in this book.

Exercises

1   Compile and run `ch1\exercise\int_arr.cpp`. Note that if at least one value has been read in, then when you choose the e option to remove a value, previously entered, you get a silly message. Do not believe it when it says that it has deleted the selected value! You are to design and implement the body of `Delete_Val`. Note that the type declaration for `IntTable_T` has a record type (`IntTable_T`) containing an array type (`IntArray_T`).

```
#define Max 5

typedef int IntArray_T[Max];
typedef struct {
  IntArray_T  Nums;
  int         NextVacancy;
} IntTable_T;

IntTable_T Table;
```

Look at `Initialise` and `Add_Val` to work out the role of `NextVacancy`.

Comment

Note that reading in a new value happens at two levels. First, `Read_NewVal` is called, which does some interaction with the user, calls `Q_Full` to check if the table is full, and, if not, then calls `Add_Val` to actually add the value. Why have these two levels? The answer is that `Q_Full` and `Add_Val` are members of a set of primitive operations on the `IntTable_T` which may be used by a number of higher-level operations like `Read_NewVal`. `Read_NewVal` is really an interface procedure and its purpose is to check that adding a new value can be executed, getting the data if it can and so on. I call a procedure like `Read_NewVal` a *wrapper* procedure, since it wraps around the procedures that actually deal directly with the data.

Here is a pictorial clue.

```
NextVacancy is 4
```

23	45	12	88	37

```
NextVacancy is 3
```

23	12	88	88	37

2 Records can contain records. To see the beginning of a demonstration of this compile and run `ch1\exercise\inv_rec2.cpp`. There are a number of changes to be made so that the `Date_T` record is fully functional. You have the type 'declarations' so all that is required is the code in the relevant procedures.

1.5.3 Arrays of records

We can hold any type of variable in an array, including other structured types. That is, we can have an array of records or an array of arrays. Similarly records may contain arrays. For example, we can define a type `InvoiceArray_T`, which contains invoice records. These are of type `InvRec_T` as before.

```
typedef InvRec_T InvoiceArray_T[Max];
```

Exercise

1 Compile and run `ch1\exercise\inv_arr.cpp`. Once again there are changes to be made if we are to have a properly functioning database of invoice records. Design and implement these changes.

1.5.4 Pointers and memory management

We now turn to a nuts and bolts topic underlying most data structures used in computer program solutions to complex real world problems. The following account of *pointers* builds on that in *The Essence of Programming using C++* (pp. 118–25).

Locations, addresses, variables and values

It is useful, and not so far from the truth, to return to a picture of the main memory of your computer as a very long array of *locations*, each location having an *address*. Data, and indeed the program itself, are stored in these locations. The

type of data being stored determines the size of the location. So, from the
following declaration

```
char Mode,
     Dept;
int Number;
int Mods[3];
```

we might get the set-up in memory shown in Figure 1.2. The chars take one
byte each, the int takes two bytes, and the array of ints takes $3 * 2 = 6$ bytes
altogether.

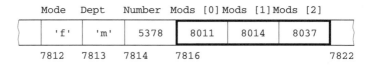

Figure 1.2 Memory and types.

The addresses are shown underneath. Of course, these are just figures I made
up, and there is no reason why the locations have to be next to one another, but
this picture will do fine. An address references a *byte*, the usual fundamental
symbolic level of our computers, though the unit of *information* is the *bit*.

Thus we have three attributes associated with a variable. There is the name we
give the variable, e.g. Dept; there is the value of the variable at any time, e.g. 'm';
and there is the address of the variable, e.g. 7813.

Pointers

A *pointer variable* is a variable whose values are the addresses of other variables.
Here is an example, where we declare and assign a value to a pointer variable.

```
int *Bill_Ptr;
.................
Bill_Ptr = &Number;
```

Translated this says 'Bill_Ptr is a pointer to something of type int' – this is
achieved by use of the *indirection operator* * in front of Bill_Ptr – and
'Bill_Ptr becomes equal to the address of Number' – this is achieved by the
use of the *address operator* & in front of Number.

Convention

All my pointer variables have names ending in _Ptr.

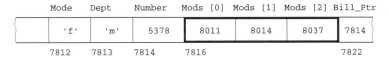

Figure 1.3 Assigning values through pointers.

This results in the following arrangement in memory, shown in Figure 1.3. Here we take it that a pointer variable takes up four bytes.

Most of the diagrams that we shall use are not too concerned with just how much memory is allocated to different types. Figure 1.4 shows the style of pointer diagram I normally use. Note that there are no numbers indicating addresses, just a pointer link from the pointer variable to the thing it is pointing at. There is no need to know the values of the addresses, with the exception of the NULL value, indicating that the pointer is not pointing at anything.

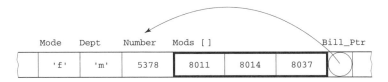

Figure 1.4 A typical pointer diagram.

Allocation and de-allocation

As a programmer you do not know what a freshly declared pointer variable is pointing at. This situation must be resolved without delay, as the chances are that it is pointing right in the middle of your beautifully designed code! Fiddling around here may produce interesting results but it is not programming. So you can make it point at a variable of the right type, *or* you can allocate some memory for a variable of the right type, *or* you can initialise it to be a NULL pointer. The NULL pointer will have to wait until Chapter 4. Here is an example to demonstrate the first two alternatives, where lines of program code are interleaved with diagrams to show what is going on.

```
#include <iostream.h>

main() {
  int *New_Ptr;
  int Tom,
      Hold;
```

All three variables contain rubbish.

```
New_Ptr = new int;
```

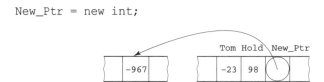

The operating system gives `New_Ptr` a previously unallocated location in memory to point at. This location is just big enough for an integer. Note that the only reference to this location is through `New_Ptr` – that is *indirectly*.

```
cout << "\nType in a new integer value ==> ";
cin  >> Tom;
cout << "\nand another new integer value ==> ";
cin  >> *New_Ptr;
```

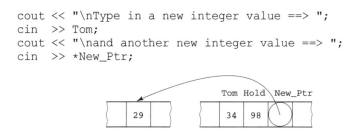

Assuming that we type in 29 and 34 this is what happens.

```
cout << "\nValues are "
     << Tom
     << " and "
     << *New_Ptr;

cout << "\nNow we swap them over";

Hold = Tom;
Tom = *New_Ptr;
*New_Ptr = Hold;
```

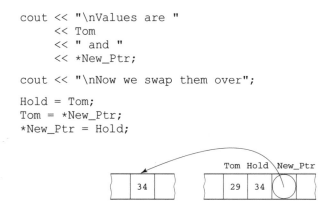

Using `Hold` as a midway place, we swap the two input values in memory.

```
cout << "\nSo values are now "
     << Tom
     << " and "
     << *New_Ptr;
delete(New_Ptr);
New_Ptr = &Tom;
```

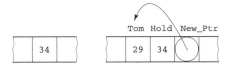

delete lets the operating system have back the memory pointed at by New_Ptr. The value of New_Ptr remains the same until the address of Tom is assigned to it. After using delete, never try to access what the pointer was *referencing* (pointing at) until you give it a new reference (address) which does point at properly allocated memory.

```
    cout << "\nFinally values are "
         << Tom
         << " and "
         << *New_Ptr;
}
```

And this is what the whole interaction looks like.

```
Type in a new integer value ==>34

and another new integer value ==>29

Values are 34 and 29
Now we swap them over
So values are now 29 and 34
Finally values are 29 and 29
```

This example is the program ch1\examples\ptr_swap.cpp.

Arrays, strings and pointers

In C++ array variables are pointers. This means that if you want to pass an array to a procedure to be changed, as we shall do in sorting, then you do not need to pass the address of the array, since the array variable contains the value of where the elements in the array start. Rather than go into examples here, we shall wait until the sorting examples in Chapter 10.

Strings are pretty essential to most computing applications. As in most languages, C++ supports strings as arrays of characters. The end of the string in the array is shown by the \0 null end-of-string character. There is a special library <string.h> to provide support for string processing. Thus string variables are pointer variables to chars. The following common problem illustrates the relationship of pointers to char, string variables and arrays of char. When we refer to 'the string variable X', what we really mean is 'the array of chars whose first element is referenced by X'. Usually there is no confusion, but do remember this. The following example will help to clarify this, particularly in the diagrams.

Suppose that we know that all the strings we shall get will be less than 200 characters. This means that we can read them into an array of 200 characters, the extra character being for the end-of-string marker. However, we also know that almost all strings will be much less than 199 characters in length. If we store hundreds of thousands of such arrays in memory, a lot of memory will be wasted. Fortunately we can allocate enough memory at run time as long as we know how big the string actually is.

Here is a solution, in the form of the function `Read_String()`, which returns the next string read from the keyboard.

```
char
*Read_String() {
  char *Result;
  char Buffer[200];

  cin >> Buffer;
  Result = new char(strlen(Buffer) + 1);
  strcpy(Result, Buffer);
  return(Result);
}
```

Here is a text and diagram explanation of how `Read_String()` works.

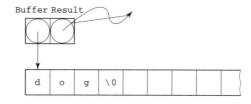

Figure 1.5 The string 'dog' is read into `Buffer`.

`Buffer` is declared as an array of `char`s, which means that it references the first element in such an array. It is a *temporary* array set up by the function call. `Read_String()` first reads the input string into the array thus referenced by `Buffer`, as shown in Figure 1.5.

Figure 1.6 shows how just enough memory is allocated for the string and its end of string marker. `strlen` is a function from `<string.h>` which counts the characters up to and excluding the first end-of-string marker in its argument. So, if 'dog' was in the array referenced by `Buffer`, it would return 3. After

```
Result = new char(strlen(Buffer) + 1);
```

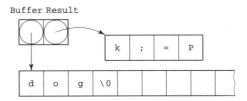

Figure 1.6 4 (= `strlen('dog')` + 1) bytes are allocated and referenced by `Result`.

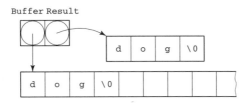

Figure 1.7 The string 'dog' is copied from the array referenced by `Buffer` into the array referenced by `Result`.

new allocates room for $3 + 1 = 4$ chars, and returns a pointer to this space, which is assigned to `Result`. `Result` then references an array of chars of length $3 + 1 = 4$.

`strcpy` copies the string from its second argument, here the array referenced by `Buffer`, into its first argument, here the array referenced by `Result`, putting an end-of-string marker at the end. Figure 1.7 shows this. Because the array referenced by `Buffer`, as well as `Buffer` itself, are temporary variables, whose lifetime is that of the execution of the function `Read_String()`, the memory they take is released back to the system when `Read_String()` terminates. However, the memory allocated to the array referenced by `Result` has been dynamically allocated and remains allocated until explicitly released by the program, using `delete`. The *value* of `Result`, a pointer, is passed back and, here, is assigned to `New_String`, in the `main()` procedure of `str_demo.cpp` as follows.

```
New_String = Read_String();
```

`New_String` now references the allocated block of memory, referenced in the `Read_String()` function by `Result`.

See `rd_str.cpp`, `rd_str.h` and `str_demo.cpp` in `ch1\examples` for a demonstration of this `Read_String` function. Note that this is your first multi-file program to compile and link so you must find out how your environment does this.

This demonstration of string handling also shows how pointers can point at structures, such as arrays. In the next section we shall see pointers used to point at record structures. As we shall see later, this contributes to information hiding.

Pointers and records

For a number of reasons it is useful to have pointers to records. This will be seen in the next section of this chapter, and in the next chapter, where we look at opaque types. In this section we shall look at the technical aspects.

This is demonstrated by srecdemo.cpp, which uses data.cpp and data.h as well as rd_str.cpp, rd_str.h, all from ch1\examples. Since we want to develop some generic approaches to storage independent of the type of data being stored, we have put all the details of dealing with the data record, here about students' details, in data.h/.cpp. Here are the declarations in data.h.

```
typedef enum StudyMode_T {FullTimeMod, PartTimeMod,
FullTimeNonMod, PartTimeNonMod};

typedef int StuNum_T;
typedef char *Name_T;
typedef StuNum_T Key_T;

typedef struct {
  StuNum_T StuNum;
  Name_T Name;
  enum  StudyMode_T Mode;
} SRec_T, *SRec_Ptr_T;
```

Note that we also have the synonym

```
typedef SRec_Ptr_T DataRec_T;
```

This serves to mask the fact that the main program, srecdemo.cpp, is dealing with pointers and provides a certain degree of genericity in dealing with data records in data.h/.cpp. The details of storage are hidden from other files that 'use' data.h/.cpp. This idea will be exploited more systematically in the next section. The radically new feature here is StudentRec_Ptr_T. Variables of this type are pointers or references to variables of StudentRec_T.

Convention

My pointer type names usually end in _Ptr_T. But if I wish to hide the fact that a type or a variable is a pointer type or variable then I leave out the _Ptr. This is the case with DataRec_T and DataRec, used by srecdemo.

DataRec_T DataRec

A struct of type
SRec_T which
is accessed as
*DataRec

Figure 1.8 SRec_Ptr_T, alias DataRec_T, variable called DataRec points
at a SRec_T variable.

This is shown in Figure 1.8, where the DataRec_T synonym of SRec_Ptr_T is
used in the declaration

```
DataRec_T DataRec;
```

In order to access fields of the referenced SRec_T we have to dereference
DataRec. To 'get at' the name field of what DataRec is referencing we go in two
steps. First we dereference – *DataRec. – then we access the field using the dot
operator – as (*DataRec).Name. Brackets are for clarity. However, we have a
shorthand for this in C++. DataRec->Name means 'the Name field of the structure
referenced by DataRec' and is equivalent to (*DataRec).Name.

Here is the Read_Rec function from data.cpp to illustrate this.

```
// PRE   TRUE
// POST prompts user for student record
//       which is read into DataRec
void
Read_Rec(DataRec_T &DataRec) {

  DataRec = new SRec_T;
  cout << "\nNumber ==> ";
  cin >> DataRec->StuNum;
  cout << "\nName ==> ";
  DataRec->Name = Read_String();
  cout << "\nMode of study ";
  DataRec->Mode = Read_Mode();
}
```

We have also designated a particular field, StuNum, as the key field. To deal with
it as a key type Key_T we have the further synonym declaration

```
typedef StuNum_T Key_T;
```

Since keys are going to be an essential feature of much of our data structuring,
we shall have a generically specified function (Get_Key) to get the key value
of a record, as well as to read in (Read_Key) and write out (Write_Key) key
values.

Exercises

1   Reimplement data.h/.cpp so that they deal with pointers to the invoice
     record from ch1\exercises\inv_rec2.cpp. What changes need to be
     made to srecdemo.cpp to test your reimplementation? Perhaps a change
     of name to invptr.cpp, but what other changes do you think are
     required? The solution to this is in the ch1\solutions\invptr sub-
     directory. Why does it need to go in a separate sub-directory?
2   In the exercise in Section 1.5.3 we had an array of invoice records.
     Redesign and implement a similar system, with the difference being that
     the records are the invoice records you have used in invptr.cpp above –
     that is, what you will be manipulating is an array of pointers.

1.6 Storage, keys and locations

Data has to be physically stored somewhere. Often this will be in the form of a
very large record or perhaps a file. In manipulating data we are often not so much
concerned with changing it as much as reading it, reordering it and referring to it.
In this section we see how we separate out the concerns of *storage of data* and
reference to data.

1.6.1 Dealing with large records stored in arrays

A very straightforward way of dealing with records is to put them into an array
and refer to a particular record by the index of the array cell in which it is
contained. However, if we want to keep them in *key order* then we have to 'shuffle
up' half the array contents, on average, when inserting. This is shown in
Figure 1.9, where the numbers are the keys of the records. The whole record
may be very large of course. If so, then this can be expensive in terms of time.

What we really want to do is somehow keep the keys in order, move the keys
about and find records for the keys, as long as there is some link between the
keys and the array indices. The way to do this is to have a second set of records,

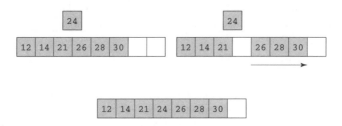

Figure 1.9 'Shuffling up' the array elements to insert a record with key 24.

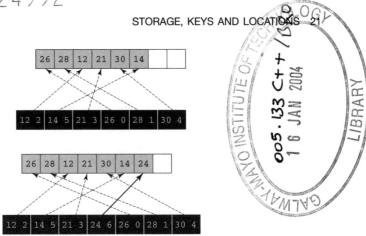

Figure 1.10 Moving small key/index records about instead of large data records.

each containing the key of a record and the index of that record in the array. Then all we need do is to keep these records in order in another array. This is much less expensive timewise because the key/index pair will take up two `ints` of space, in this case, whereas the original records may need many kilobytes of space. Of course we lose on space because of the extra two `ints` for each record but often it is space that we are happy to trade for time saving.

In Figure 1.10 the original records, shown in grey with black key numbers, are still in the same type of array except that new records are added in the first empty place. When this is done a new key/index pair record, shown in black with white key/index numbers, is created for the second array and inserted into place.

What we have done is to separate the two concerns of storing the data and structuring the data. As a result the data structuring has become less expensive.

Exercises

1   `par_arr.cpp` is the main file of a multi-file program in `ch1\exercise`. Find out what the other files are. *Hint*: trace through the `#includes`. Compile and link them all together, and then run the executable. `Add_Stud` needs to have its main body written. Note that the key/index records are to be kept in key order in the array, while a new main record just goes in the first available place. This involves finding where the key/index pair is to go and then shuffling up the records to make a 'hole' for it to go in. Look at Figure 1.10 and try it on paper first. Are there any special cases? For example, suppose the new key is bigger than any in the array? Or smaller?

2   There is nothing for deleting records in `par_arr.cpp`. Design, implement and test a `Delete_Stud` procedure together with a 'wrapper' procedure `Remove_Stud`. You may assume that deletions are not frequent so that it does not matter if you shift the main records around for this procedure.

3   Suppose that deletions were quite frequent. Outline, in high-level terms, how you would deal with this. You need to
    - identify the problem;
    - describe any new structures or types required;
    - describe changes to existing functions and procedures that might be required.

    Fully design, implement and test your proposed solution.

1.6.2 Storing images

The same idea helps if the data are for large images stored in files on a multimedia system. Each image has a catalogue reference, which acts as key, and a filename, containing the actual data for the image.

```
A232     fort1.bmp
A267     wall5.bmp
A289     fort3.bmp
A295     ox35.bmp
A312     wall1.bmp
A337     cf.bmp
B002     foss7.bmp
B121     horse3.bmp
```

1.6.3 Storing URLs

The uniform resource locator or URL of a web page is really just another filename, except that it is structured as a location. If you developed a web browser then you could design a sub-system to allocate key references to pages of interest and store them in much the same way as the images in the section above.

1.6.4 Storing records on disk

The records may be held on disk, in which case we have a disk address rather than an array index. The idea is the same, having a secondary array of key/address pairs by which we structure the data and then access any individual items we want.

1.6.5 Storing records using dynamic memory allocation

In many cases in the rest of this book we are going to store the actual data records – that is those that contain *real world* data – in memory that is dynamically allocated at run time and reference it through the use of a key field and a pointer value, its address. The basic idea is that

- the data record is read into a temporary record variable – i.e. a local variable in a procedure;
- the key of the record is extracted;
- sufficient memory is allocated for the record and the address noted;
- a key/address record is made up of the key and address and returned.

The returned record is then stored in some suitable structure. Here we shall use an array but in later chapters we shall be using a number of different structures. Before looking at the array of key/address records, let us just concentrate on a single key/address record in the program made of the files `data.cpp`, `rd_str.cpp`, `store.cpp` and the main file `stordemo.cpp` in examples. The purpose of `store` is to look after the type `KAPRec_T` (Key/Address Pair Record Type).

Here is the declaration in `store.h`.

```
typedef struct {
   Key_T    Key;
   DataRec_T *Address;
} KAPRec_T;
```

This means that I can use `KAPRec_T` with any data type, just so long as it has a designated key field and has the appropriate declaration to give it the synonym `DataRec_T`. Although this is similar to what we saw in the section on pointers and records above, there is an important difference. It is that the `DataRec_T` is the actual record and *not* a pointer. Rather we have a reference, through the pointer `Address`, to the actual `DataRec_T` record. The `StudentRec_T` is just such a type. There are just four operations specified on `KAPRec_T` and it is essential to understand each of them. The first is the most complex and is explained with diagrams and text. Look at the original code in `store.cpp` before working through this explanation.

```
// PRE   TRUE
// POST RETURNS a key address pair record
//       with key that of record and
//       address that of location where record is stored
KAPRec_T
MakeKAPRec(DataRec_T Rec) {
   KAPRec_T KAPRec;
   DataRec_T *Address;
```

Rec   Address   KAPRec

The parameter `Rec` is passed and the local variables `Address` and `KAPRec` set up by the function call.

```
Address = new DataRec_T;
```

An amount of store, big enough for `DataRec_T` is set up and referenced by `Address`.

```
(*Address) = Rec;
```

The contents of `Rec` are copied into the area referenced by `Address`.

```
KAPRec.Key = Get_Key(Rec);
```

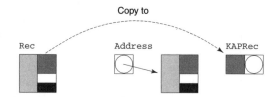

The key value of `Rec` is copied from `Rec` to the key field in `KAPRec`.

```
KAPRec.Address = Address;
```

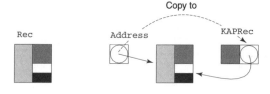

The value of `Address` – that is the reference to the new area of memory storing a copy of `Rec` – is copied to `KAPRec`.

```
return(KAPRec);
```

Copy of
KAPRec

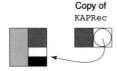

The value of KAPRec – that is a copy – is returned so that the calling procedure now has direct access to the key value and indirect access to the copy of Rec when it needs it. The memory for the parameter Rec, the local variable Address and the local variable KAPRec is all freed up when the procedure halts.

```
}
```

If you follow the Make_KAPRec function then the next two should be fairly straightforward.

```
// PRE   TRUE
// POST RETURNS key value of KAPRec
Key_T
Get_KAPRecKey(KAPRec_T KAPRec) {

  return(KAPRec.Key);
}
```

Get_KAPRecKey simply fishes out the key value and returns it.

```
// PRE   TRUE
// POST RETURNS record stored at address value of KAPRec
DataRec_T
Get_DataRec(KAPRec_T KAPRec) {

  return(*(KAPRec.Address));
}
```

Get_DataRec goes through the reference Address to get a copy of what Address is referencing – that is the DataRec_T stored – and returns a copy of it.

The last procedure physically deletes the data record referenced by the KAPRec_T. This will be needed in Exercise (1) below and elsewhere in the book.

```
// PRE   TRUE
// POST Memory taken up by record referenced
//      by address attribute is freed up
void
Free_RecMemory(KAPRec_T KAPRec) {

  delete(KAPRec.Address);
}
```

Exercises

1   ch1\exercises\arr_stor.cpp is the main file of a multi-file program,
    the others being data.h/.cpp, rd_str.h/.cpp and store.h/.cpp.
    Compile, link and run all the required files to make the executable
    arr_stor.exe. Clearly Add_Stud needs mending! Design, implement and
    test the amendments.

2   If deletion is to be done, then there are two steps. First, the actual
    data record needs to be deleted using the operation Free_RecMemory in
    store.cpp. Second, there is the deletion of the actual KAPRec_T to
    consider. Design, implement and test such procedures, together with all
    necessary 'wrapper' procedures and so on.

3   It may be the case that once the record is stored, the associated KAPRec_T
    has several copies, each held in a different structure. What difficulties arise
    for the deletion operation of (2)? Discuss possible solutions.

1.7 Summary

Now that you have read this chapter, you should have learned that:

- Programming languages should provide support both for representing
  structure within real world data and for further structuring for purposes of
  storage, access and reorganisation within the computer.
- Application data are data directly from the real world area.
- Structural information is data used to structure the data internally in the
  computer.
- C++ provides such support through arrays, records (structs) and pointer
  variables.
- User-defined types can be introduced through the use of synonyms,
  enumeration, arrays and records (structs).
- Pointer variables reference – that is hold the address of – other variables.
- Memory can be allocated for pointer variables to reference, by the new
  command, and can be de-allocated – released for further use – by the
  delete command.
- Records usually have a key value which is used for structuring the file of
  records.
- For ease of manipulation a record key can be kept separately from the
  main data record itself (and will be for most of this book) through the use
  of key/address pairs.

CHAPTER 2

Abstract data types (1): a draughts board example

2.1 Introduction

The use of *abstract data types* (ADTs) is practically essential for the systematic construction of correct programs, beyond the most trivial of applications. In this chapter we shall briefly define what is meant by an ADT and then look at an example of the specification and implementation of an ADT.

2.2 Some definitions

A *data type* is a set of *values* and a set of *operations* defined on those values. For example, the type integer in arithmetic has a set of values $0, \pm1, \pm2, \ldots$, and a set of operations including multiplication, addition, subtraction and division.

An *abstract data type* is a data type where the specification of the values, and the operations' effects on the values, is separated from the representation of the values and the implementation of the operations. For example, when arithmetic is implemented in C++, I suspect that I am like most programmers in having at best a hazy idea of how all the half adders and logic gates do their stuff. If I needed to I could find out, but I do not need to know. So when I type the line of code

```
Total = Total + NextItem;
```

I do not worry myself about how this will actually be implemented at the machine code level or at the machine level. I don't need to. All I need to know is how to write a line of code to do addition at the C++ level. Abstract data types are about keeping information on a 'need to know' basis.

2.3 A draughts board: an example of an ADT

I assume that you are familiar with a draughts (or checkers) set – that is an 8 by 8 board of alternating black and white squares, and 12 white counters and 12 black counters. Most of us have played draughts, but there are a number of other games that can be played with a draughts board and an unlimited set of counters of both colours. For simplicity I shall just consider those games where only a single piece or a double piece – a 'king' in draughts – can occupy a non-empty square. We want to be able to put pieces on both the black squares and the white squares for some games. So, for example, we could play 8 by 8 Othello or Go if we wished. Thus when I use the expression 'draughts board' I mean the board plus an unlimited number of counters of both colours.

Think carefully for a moment about what a draughts board is as a data structure. If you had no specially made set, you could scratch out a board in the sand, and use coins or bits of wood for the counters. You do not even need a physical board – each counter could have its board position written on it, in erasable crayon. This last option would be inconvenient, but the important thing is that it is not impossible. All the relevant information can be retrieved for processing. The question is what information do I need to be able to obtain and how do I need to be able to update it in order to provide the basis for playing a game? This is provided graphically and physically by the actual physical board and counters.

The board consists of locations on a rectangular grid. If rows go from left to right and columns from top to bottom, then a row number and column number specify a position. Given a position perhaps I want to know what is in that position. Or maybe I would like to replace what is in that position by something else – a white piece by an empty square for example. I may want to have the position of an adjacent square in a particular direction. And possibly I need to know if a particular position is a black square or a white square.

2.3.1 Types in a draughts set

I have four types here. The main type is the board type, where I am taking Board_T to have as values all possible configurations of the black and white counters and empty squares. Then there is a type I shall call SquareStatus_T, which has as values the five statuses of Empty (being empty), BlackPiece (having a black counter), BlackKing (having a black king), WhitePiece (having a white counter), or WhiteKing (having a white king). As well as this, we need to deal with positions of the squares, which is Position_T, whose values are all the possible ordered pairs of integers, one for the row and one for the column – e.g. (4, 6) refers to the position in the fourth row and sixth column. See Figure 2.1.

Finally we have directions, which we shall take from the points of the compass, N, NE for north, north-east, and so on. See Figure 2.2.

In the implementation the types are made known to potential users of the ADT in a header file board.h.

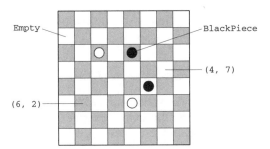

Figure 2.1 A value of `Board_T`, some values of `SquareStatus_T` and `Position_T`.

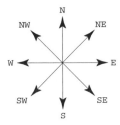

Figure 2.2 The values of `Direction_T`.

```
typedef enum SquareStatus_T {Empty, WhitePiece, BlackPiece};
typedef enum Direction_T {N, NE, E, SE, S, SW, W, NW};

typedef int Row_T,
            Col_T;

typedef struct {
  Row_T Row;
  Col_T Col;
} Position_T;

typedef void *Board_T;
```

Note that `Board_T` has all its details hidden away by use of the `void` pointer making it an *opaque* type, to be described later. Strictly speaking the details of `Position_T` should not be made known, but to hide it away with a `void` pointer would introduce rather more complex code at an early stage and, since it is a minor abstraction, I have not done anything about it.

If you think about it, this is a sort of 'ideal' way to handle the board and pieces. Perhaps you do not think of a move as being north-west, rather 'up and left' or something. And it is unlikely that you think of square status, instead of more obvious things such as 'a black piece is on that square'. However, the important thing is that the essential information or data about the game is caught in this set of linked types.

2.3.2 *What it does: specifying the ADT* `Board_T`

So we have identified four data types associated with the game. In fact we have also implicitly assumed the use of integers and Booleans, as we shall see. Now we need some operations on these data types. I am going to specify a set of basic or *primitive* operations which are sufficient to build any more complicated operations.

The *syntax* of the operations is given in the form of C++ *function and procedure prototypes*, which will appear with the type information above in the `board.h` *definition file*. A function or procedure prototype shows what types it takes and what type it returns, if any. The *semantics* are given in the comments showing the *pre-* and *post-conditions*. If the pre-conditions are TRUE, immediately prior to the operation commencing, then, after the operation is completed, the post-conditions will be TRUE. For example, the syntax and semantics, in this form, of `Get_Status` (second in the list of functions and procedures below) really just say the following:

> `Get_Status` takes a `Position_T`, say `Position`, and a `Board_T`, say `Board`, and returns the status of the square if `Position` is on `Board`.

For example, `Get_Status((3, 3), Board)` is `WhitePiece` and `Get_Status((4, 3), Board)` is `Empty`, where `Board` is the board in Figure 2.1. Before this operation can be applied `Q_OnBoard(Position)` must be TRUE – that is we should not try to find the status of a position that is off the board.

Note that the single quote on an identifier shows that we are talking about the variable value *after* the function has been executed. For example, see `Board` and `Board'` in `Set_Status`.

So we have the following:

A function to check if a position is on the board:

```
// PRE   TRUE
// POST IF Position is on Board THEN
//         RETURNS TRUE
//      ELSE
//         RETURNS FALSE
BOOLEAN
Q_OnBoard(Position_T Position);
```

A function to return what is in a particular position:

```
// PRE  Q_OnBoard(Position, Board)
// POST RETURNS content of Position on Board
```

```
enum SquareStatus_T
Get_Status(Position_T Position, Board_T Board);
```

A function to return the next position in a particular direction:

```
// PRE   TRUE
// POST RETURNS position in direction Direction from Position
Position_T
Get_NextPosition(Position_T Position, enum Direction_T
Direction);
```

A procedure to put a piece in a particular square or make the square empty. Note that Board' stands for the value of Board after the operation:

```
// PRE   Q_OnBoard(Position, Board)
// POST Get_Status(Position, Board') = Status
void
Set_Status(Position_T Position, enum SquareStatus_T Status,
Board_T Board);
```

A function to make up and return a position from the row and column values:

```
// PRE   TRUE
// POST RETURNS Position with first co-ordinate Row and
//     second Col
Position_T
Make_Position(int Row, int Col);
```

A function to check if a position is that of a black square or not:

```
// PRE   TRUE
// POST IF Position is that of a black square
//        RETURNS True
//      ELSE
//        RETURNS False
BOOLEAN
Q_BlackSquare(Position_T Position);
```

A function to check if two positions are the same:

```
// PRE   TRUE
// POST IF Position1 and Position2 are the same THEN
//        RETURNS TRUE
//      ELSE
//        RETURNS FALSE
BOOLEAN
Q_SamePosition(Position_T Position1, Position_T Position2);
```

A function to read in a new position:

```
// PRE   TRUE
// POST Prompts for and RETURNS a Position_T
Position_T
Read_Position();
```

A function to write out a position:

```
// PRE   TRUE
// POST Position printed in Cartesian co-ordinate format
//    to screen
void
Write_Position(Position_T Position);
```

A function to read in a direction:

```
// PRE   TRUE
// POST Prompts for and RETURNS a Direction_T
//       IF the Direction_T read is not valid
//          RETURNS(Invalid)
Direction_T
Read_Direction();
```

A procedure to write out a direction:

```
// PRE   TRUE
// POST Direction printed as string to screen
void
Write_Direction(Direction_T Direction);
```

A function to check that a direction is valid:

```
// PRE   TRUE
// POST IF Direction is a valid one
//          RETURNS TRUE
//       ELSE
//          RETURNS FALSE
BOOLEAN
Q_ValidDirection(Direction_T Direction);
```

A function to give a direction at random:

```
// PRE   TRUE
// POST RETURNS random valid Direction_T
Direction_T
Random_Direction();
```

The use of some of these operations may not be apparent. What you have to do is recall how you use a draughts board. You can see that a square holds a black piece, or where the next square in a particular direction is. We have to give the computer the simple operations to be able to do the same.

Those of a suspicious mind might object at this point that I said what these operations look like and what they do but have dodged the question of how they do it! To which I plead guilty, but if you are prepared to wait for a while, I hope to walk without a stain on my character. For now, treat these operations on Board_T and so on as you would operations on the integers. You are happy to use them but probably know little of the details of their implementation.

What we now have is the ADT Board_T. It involves several other types, which are themselves ADTs. It is an ADT because, in the form of C++ function prototypes and pre- and post-conditions, we have been told all that we need to know about it.[1] We know nothing of how it is implemented but can immediately write code using these operations. Of course this will not be much good unless someone does implement Board_T.

2.3.3 Building complex operations from the primitive operations

We can build more complicated operations, like finding the highest common divisor of two integers, out of the basic operations of addition, subtraction, multiplication and division on the integers. Similarly we can define more complicated operations on Board_T etc. The operations prototyped in board.h have been implemented in board.cpp, but we are not going to look at the details just yet. Another program checker.cpp is to use these operations. You can find all three files in ch2\examples. Compile, link and run them. The resulting executable checkers.exe is rather limited, allowing the user to place white and black pieces and move them, but it demonstrates how Board_T could be used for a real game.

Here are two examples of the more complicated operations from checker.cpp.

```
// PRE   Q_OnBoard(Position) AND Q_OnBoard(NextPosition)
// POST Get_Status(NextPosition, Board') =
//       Get_Status(Position, Board)
//  AND Get_Status(Position, Board') = Empty
void
Move_Piece(Position_T Position, Position_T NextPosition,
    Board_T Board) {
  Set_Status(NextPosition, Get_Status(Position, Board),
      Board);
  Set_Status(Position, Empty, Board);
}
```

---

[1] Or we hope that we have. If our specification phase has been carried out correctly then this will be true. A sloppy specification leads to things that are technically ADTs but do not correspond cleanly to the things that we wish to model.

Move_Piece just moves the piece from Position to NextPosition on Board, using the primitive operations Set_Status and Get_Status. In order to make sure that we specify exactly what we want, we use very formal pre- and post-conditions in terms of the primitives defined on Board_T. Recall that the use of the single quote, as in Board′, indicates the value of the variable after the operation, while Board by itself stands for the value of the variable Board before the operation. What it says here is if Position and NextPosition are proper board positions, then, when the operation is complete, the value of Board is what it was before, but with the value in NextPosition being that previously in Position, and Position is now Empty. Why not write it in English? Even for a relatively simple example like this, the unambiguous English text would turn out to be quite lengthy. We have a formal 'language' to talk about the ADT Board_T with – that is the set of primitive operations. So if we can describe the pre- and post-conditions using this language, then we are well on the way to the actual implementation. The initial overhead is that of getting used to thinking rather more formally than before but it pays dividends in terms of developing correct code more rapidly. In many cases we still use English, or a mixture of English and this formal language. See Make_Move below.

We then use Move_Piece in a larger procedure with user interaction called Make_Move. Informally this prompts the user for a position on the board, and, if it is a valid position, prompts for a direction. If it is possible to move in that direction then the move is made. Here are preliminary pre- and post-conditions.

```
// PRE   TRUE
// POST user prompted FOR board position
//    AND IF position on Board contains a piece,
//      user is prompted FOR a direction
//      AND IF piece can move in that direction
//          piece is moved in that direction
//      ELSE
//          appropriate error message
//      ELSE
//         appropriate error message
PROCEDURE Make_Move(Board : Board_T);
```

As a first step of design, we can refine the post-conditions as follows. Note that we use the available primitive operations where they are useful.

```
// PRE   TRUE
// POST
//    User is prompted for position
//    Position = Read_Position()
//    IF NOT Q_OnBoard(Position)
//      Error message
//    ELSE
//       IF Get_Status(Position, Board) = Empty
//          Error message
```

```
//      ELSE
//         User is prompted for direction
//         Direction = Read_Direction()
//         NextPosition =
//            Get_NextPosition(Position, Direction)
//         IF Q_OnBoard(NextPosition, Board)
//           AND Get_Status(NextPosition, Board) = Empty
//           Get_Status(Position, Board') = Empty
//           Get_Status(NextPosition, Board') =
//              Get_Status(Position, Board)
//         ELSE
//           Error message
void
Make_Move(Board_T Board);
```

Here is the pseudo-code for Make_Move. This should meet the post-conditions and provide the stepping stones to implementing the code. Instead of heavy nesting of the IF...ELSE... statements I have used a flag Q_OK. We need only one level of refinement.

```
1   Set Q_OK to TRUE
2   Prompt user and Read_Position(Position)
3   IF NOT Q_OnBoard(Position)
4     Error message
5     Set Q_OK to FALSE
6   IF Q_OK
7     IF Get_Status(Position, Board) = Empty
8       Error message
9       Set Q_OK to FALSE
10  IF Q_OK
11    Prompt user and Read_Direction(Direction)
12    IF NOT Q_Valid(Direction)
13      Error message
14      Set Q_OK to FALSE
15  IF Q_OK
16    Set NextPosition to
17        Get_NextPosition(Position, Direction)
18      IF NOT Q_OnBoard(Next_Position)
19        Error message
20        Set Q_OK to FALSE
21  IF Q_OK
22    IF Get_Status(NextPosition, Board) <> Empty
23      Error message
24      Set Q_OK to FALSE
25  IF Q_OK
26    Move_Piece(Position, NextPosition, Board)
```

Note that the actual code could be implemented in any procedural language at this point. We are using language-independent terms such as Set Q_OK to

FALSE, which should map neatly into one or more actual statements in the target language, which is here C++ of course!

```
void
Make_Move(Board_T Board) {
  int Row,
      Col;
  Position_T Position,
             NextPosition;
  BOOLEAN Q_OK;
  enum Direction_T Direction;

  Q_OK = TRUE;

  Position = Read_Position();

  if (!Q_OnBoard(Position)) {
    cout  << "\nSquare ";
    Write_Position(Position);
    cout  << " is not on the board";
    Q_OK = FALSE;
  }

  if (Q_OK) {
    if (Get_Status(Position, Board) == Empty) {
      cout  << "\nSquare ";
      Write_Position(Position);
      cout  << " is empty";
      Q_OK = FALSE;
    }
  }

  if (Q_OK) {
    Direction = Read_Direction();
    if (!Q_ValidDirection(Direction)) {
      cout  << "\n\nDirection is not a valid one\n";
      Q_OK = FALSE;
    }
  }

  if (Q_OK) {
    NextPosition = Get_NextPosition(Position, Direction);

    if (!Q_OnBoard(NextPosition)) {
      cout  << "\nGoing ";
      Write_Direction(Direction);
      cout  << " will move piece off board";
      Q_OK = FALSE;
    }
  }
```

```
    if (Q_OK) {
        if (!Get_Status(NextPosition, Board) == Empty) {
            cout << "\nBoard occupied to the ";
            Write_Direction(Direction);
            Q_OK = FALSE;
        }
    }

    if (Q_OK) {
        Move_Piece(Position, NextPosition, Board);
    }
}
```

This is a fairly lengthy procedure, mainly because of the interaction with the user. However, it also has to do a lot of work to check that the position given by the user is on the board, that it is occupied, that the direction is valid, that the next position in that direction is empty and not off the board. Only if all these are true will it finally call Move_Piece. A little thought shows that if it gets to calling Move_Piece, then the pre-conditions for Move_Piece must be TRUE, not just usually or 99% of the time or if we're lucky, but necessarily TRUE by the semantics of C++ and logic. In fact a number of other things are TRUE, like NextPosition being Empty, Position not being Empty, making the situation stronger than the pre-conditions, which is fine. If the pre-condition of your going out for a meal is having £15.00, then having £20.00 is a stronger condition, obviously making having £15.00 true.

In terms of *all* the code used to write Make_Move we have a very complex operation. However, precisely because we have first defined a set of operations on Board_T which can be used by Make_Move, we have *structured complexity*. This means we can deal separately with the Board_T operation components of Make_Move. Structured complexity isn't trivial but it's tractable. *Unstructured complexity* is known technically as a *mess*.

2.3.4 How it works: implementing Board_T

So far there has been no mention of how Board_T and so on are represented, or how the primitive operations are implemented. The case is that *if* they have been implemented according to the specification above, *then* Move_Piece and Make_Move will work perfectly. If William and Lucy had been working on this project, then once they had agreed the specification of the primitives, William could have gone away and implemented Board_T and so on with the primitives, and Lucy could have gone away and designed and written the code for a simple game, on the same level as Make_Move. She could have had a set of 'dummy' primitive procedures, which did nothing but helped to check that her code compiled. When they meet up a couple of days later, they can put their code together, compile and link it, and then test it all.

Here are some details of the implementation of Board_T, in board.h and board.cpp in examples.

In the header file board.h we have the following constant and type declarations, in addition to the function prototypes we have already met:

```
#define   NumCols 8
#define   NumRows 8

typedef enum SquareStatus_T {Empty, WhitePiece, BlackPiece};
typedef enum Direction_T {N, NE, E, SE, S, SW, W, NW,
    Invalid};

typedef int Row_T,
            Col_T;

typedef struct {
  Row_T Row;
  Col_T Col;
} Position_T;

typedef void *Board_T;
```

First note that we set up SquareStatus_T and Direction_T as enumerated types. Then see how Position_T is declared, using fields of types Row_T and Col_T, which are synonyms of int. Finally Board_T is declared as an opaque type. All we have is that it is a pointer but we cannot say from here what it points to. This is in contrast to Position_T, whose implementation is clearly visible.

In board.cpp we have the following:

```
typedef struct {
  enum SquareStatus_T Board[NumRows][NumCols];
} BoardStruct_T, *BoardStruct_Ptr_T;
```

This is where the 'real' structure of Board_T is described. We have declared BoardStruct_T to be a record containing a two-dimensional array, and BoardStruct_Ptr_T to be a pointer to this. We shall see how this is used to complete our implementation of Board_T as an opaque type.

```
typedef struct {
  Row_T Up;
  Col_T Along;
} Move_T;

Move_T Moves[8] = { {-1, 0}, {-1, 1}, {0, 1}, {1, 1},
    {1, 0}, {1, -1}, {0, -1}, {-1, -1}};

enum Direction_T Directions[9] =
    {N, NE, E, SE, S, SW, W, NW, Invalid};
```

Move_T is a type internal to the implementation. The programmer user of Board_T – that is the writer of checker.cpp – need know nothing about it, any more than the user of a television set need know about particular circuits.

Here are the implementations of two of the operations.

```
// PRE   TRUE
// POST RETURNS IF  Position is on Board THEN TRUE
//             ELSE FALSE
BOOLEAN
Q_OnBoard(Position_T Position) {

  return((Position.Row >= 1) &&
         (Position.Row <= NumRows) &&
         (Position.Col >= 1) &&
         (Position.Col <= NumCols));
}


// PRE   Q_OnBoard(Position, Board)
// POST content of Position on Board is Status
void
Set_Status(Position_T Position,
        enum SquareStatus_T Status, Board_T Board) {
  BoardStruct_Ptr_T Bd;

  Bd = (BoardStruct_Ptr_T) Board;

  Bd->Board[Position.Row - 1][Position.Col - 1]
        = Status;
}
```

The implementation of Q_OnBoard is clearly determined by the particular implementation of Position_T, while that of Set_Status is similarly determined by the implementation of both Position_T and Board_T.

So here are examples of the implementation of two procedure bodies, corresponding to two procedure prototypes in board.h. The 'user' – here the program checker.cpp – 'knows' how to call them and what their effects are, or rather the programmer of checker.cpp does. However, the 'user' has no idea of the implementation.

In the body of Set_Status, the opaque type implementation of Board_T is completed. Bd is a BoardStruct_Ptr_T, a pointer to a BoardStruct_T which, in the file board.cpp, we know all about. Any procedure calling Set_Status does so with a Board_T, which is a pointer, giving no information at all. Inside the implementation, however, it is as if a sort of 'map' was put over the 'fog' that Bd is initially pointing to. Using (BoardStruct_Ptr_T) superimposes the 'map', which is just the struct description BoardStruct_T. Now Set_Status can happily access elements of what Bd is pointing at.

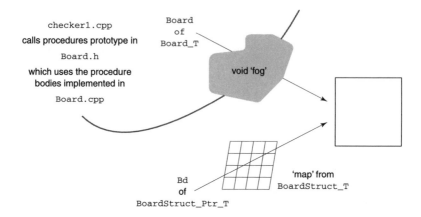

Figure 2.3 The 'foggy veil' of the interface between the public declarations in board.h and the private implementations in board.cpp, and how opaque types are implemented, using a cast to provide a 'map overlay' on the 'fog'.

The situation about procedure prototypes and their bodies, as used with opaque types, is summarised in Figure 2.3. The curved line is the interface boundary, a sort of 'foggy veil'. The user can send messages, of the right sort, into the fog, and get responses of information or action, but never see the details of how these responses are produced.

2.3.5 Alternative implementations

We have just seen an implementation of Board_T, based on the use of a C++ 8 by 8 array. However, there are any number of alternative implementations which fulfil the terms of the specification. Here are two other possible implementations.

Instead of the two-dimensional array, we could have a one-dimensional array of 64 elements. Here is a flavour of this alternative implementation.

```
typedef struct {
  enum SquareStatus_T Board[NumSquares];
} BoardStruct_T, *BoardStruct_Ptr_T;

typedef int Move_T;

Move_T Moves[8] = {-NumCols, -NumCols + 1, 1, NumCols + 1,
    NumCols, NumCols - 1, -1, -NumCols - 1};

// PRE   TRUE
// POST RETURNS Position with first co-ordinate Row and
//     second Col
Position_T
```

```
Make_Position(int Row, int Col) {
  Position_T Result;

  Result = (Row - 1)*NumCols + (Col - 1);
  return(Result);
}

// PRE   TRUE
// POST IF Position is that of a black square
         RETURNS True
       ELSE
         RETURNS False
BOOLEAN
Q_BlackSquare(Position_T Position) {
  int Row,
      Col;

  Row = Position / NumCols;
  Col = Position - (Row*NumCols);

 return((Row + Col)%2 == 0);
 }
```

Now that we have changed implementation a position is just an integer. This makes some things easier but others more difficult. So, for example, seeing if a square is black involves working out a relationship between the row and column represented by a `Position_T`.

Alternatively we could have four one-dimensional arrays of 64 elements. Each element is a `Position_T`. The first array contains the positions of all the white pieces, the second those of the black pieces, the third and fourth those of the white and black kings respectively. Further fields would be required to show how many white pieces there were, how many black pieces and so on. This is a more radical change than the previous suggestion because it goes from a board-centred representation to a piece-centred representation, even though we still use the same name of `Board_T`.

In this case I am just pointing out that there could be alternative implementations. If we use an alternative implementation of `Board_T` in our system we do not change the source code of the main program using it, we just recompile. See Figure 2.4, where we have two different games programs, `game1.cpp` and `game2.cpp`. Over a period of time `board.cpp` is rewritten to accommodate successive implementations of `Board_T`. But no change is made to `game1.cpp` and `game2.cpp` or `board.h`, the interface to `board.cpp` in its various versions.

In practice, it is usually the case that a new implementation is adopted because it is more efficient. ADTs are introduced at the design stage and are concerned with the correctness of programs – that is, do they perform as specified? ADTs are not concerned at all with run-time efficiency. Naturally run-time efficiency is another essential consideration. The reimplementation of an ADT will change

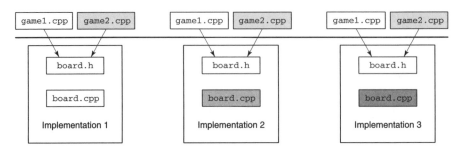

Figure 2.4 game1.cpp and game2.cpp both use the ADT Board_T, with no reference to its internal workings. Board_T may have several implementations over time as more efficient methods are developed, but the source code for the programs using Board_T remains the same.

the run-time efficiency. First, though, we have to make sure that we have the correct ADTs for the job. 'Get it right then get it fast' rather than 'Get it fast then get it right'.

2.4 A note on creating values of ADTs

You may have noticed that board.h also contained an operation, specified as follows:

```
// PRE   TRUE
// POST RETURNS an empty Board_T - i.e. memory allocated etc.
Board_T
Create_Board();
```

This had an implementation

```
Board_T
Create_Board() {

   return ((Board_T) new (BoardStruct_T));
}
```

So why wasn't this mentioned before? The answer is that specifying an ADT does not involve its implementation. In our specification we assumed that just declaring the existence of a board somehow presents us with a nice new shiny board. However, in implementation, there may be language-related issues to do with setting up the initial value of the ADT. In this case it is necessary to allocate memory for Board_T, using the new operation in C++. Thus we get the following line in checker.cpp:

```
Board = Create_Board();
```

This does the absolutely initial work of making sure that we have a safe space in memory to work with. The subsequent call

```
Initialise();
```

sets up the board by making squares empty. If it were for a draughts game, it would make sure that all the black and white pieces were on the right squares and so on. It's a little like the difference between building a house (Create_House) and getting it ready for people to move in (Initialise). In some ADTs the creation operation is a valid part of the ADT specification, as we shall see.

2.5 ADTs and language support

An ADT is a set of values and a specification of the operations on those values. They can be used in the design process regardless of the target language. However, the process of moving from design to implementation may be helped by language support for ADTs. The ability to define structures and operations on those structures as units is one form of support provided by high-level languages. The separation of function prototypes from their implementations using .h and .cpp files is further support, as shown in Figure 2.4. The most useful support in C++ is that of being able to define classes of objects. This will not be covered extensively in this book, for reasons already discussed, and it is also useful to understand ADTs as such separately from the full language support offered by object-oriented programming.

Exercises

The purpose of this set of exercises is to develop your understanding of ADTs. Even though it might be tempting to fiddle with board.cpp, for example, when the instructions say not to amend board.cpp, resist! You will be a better person for it.

1   Copy the files checker.cpp, board.h and board.cpp from ch2\examples. Compile and run them, with checker.cpp as the main program. Explore the functionality of this program.
2   Amend checker.cpp so that the pieces can move only diagonally. At present they can move in any direction. *Do not amend* board.h *or* board.cpp.

3 Specify, design and implement a new procedure `Jump` in `checker.cpp`. `Jump` is the procedure for jumping an opponent in draughts. Think about what must be the case. For example, there must be a piece to do the jumping, there must be a piece in a specified direction, of the opposite colour, to be jumped and an empty square beyond that. There must be user interaction to find out which piece is to do the jumping. *Do not amend* `board.h` *or* `board.cpp`.

4 Carry out the first alternative implementation of `Board_T`, based on a one-dimensional array of 64 elements. *Do not amend* `checker.cpp` *or the function and procedure prototypes in* `board.h`. You may wish to change the implementation of `Position_T` in `board.h`, depending on your design decisions.

5 Design and implement a program that allows two people to play noughts and crosses, taking turns to move. You will make only one change to `Board_T` to make it a 3*3 board. Take it that white pieces are noughts and black pieces are crosses. Then in the main program `o_and_x.cpp`, you will need procedures to allow players to place their pieces validly, to check if either player has won, if there is a stalemate etc.

6 `f_and_g.cpp` is the main file of a program using `board.h`/`.cpp`. This program lets you, the user, take the side of the geese in a game of fox and geese. For the benefit of younger readers I must remind you that there is a single fox, who aims to get from the north edge of the board to the south edge. He can move diagonally in any direction. A gaggle of four geese aims to pen him up by occupying squares such that he cannot move. Geese can only move north-east or north-west. The fox moves first. A goose can get stuck because there is nowhere for her to move to. A stalemate results if all the geese are stuck and the fox is not yet home. The purpose of this exercise is to play the game several times, to get a feel for it, and then to investigate the code for it, in `f_and_g.cpp`.

7 (Advanced) Taking inspiration from `f_and_g.cpp`, design, implement and test a program that will play noughts and crosses against a human player. Do this in two stages. In the first assume that the human goes first – i.e. is crosses. Then in the second version allow the user to choose either noughts or crosses.

2.6 Summary

Now that you have read this chapter, you should have learned that:

- An abstract data type (ADT) is a set of values and a set of operations specified on those values, where the specification is quite separate from the representation of the values and the implementation of the operations.

- In the example of a draughts board, the board is the main ADT and then a set of primitive operations, required for playing any game with draughts pieces and a board, is specified.
- Higher-level operations are specified and implemented in terms of the primitives.
- Alternative implementations of the ADT do not affect the coding of the higher-level operations.
- ADTs are used in design but there is usually language support to aid the implementation of ADTs.

CHAPTER 3

Abstract data types (2): definitions, container and application data ADTs

3.1 Introduction

An example of an abstract data type was introduced in Chapter 2 to give some feel for the concept and related matters. In this chapter the discussion is extended with further definitions and analogies before looking at two important sorts of ADT, the container and the application data ADT.

3.2 Definitions and analogies

The process of understanding the concept of an ADT usually works best by interleaving definitions, and repeats of definitions, with examples and analogies. Having given the basic definition of an ADT and the example of `Board_T`, we move on to further definitions and analogies.

3.2.1 Definitions

Recall the definition of an ADT from Chapter 2:

> An *abstract data type* is a data type where the specification of the values and the operations' effects on the values are separated from the representation of the values and the implementation of the operations.

For the `Board_T` we could specify what a value of `Board_T` would be – that is a set of values of `Position_T` associated with the black pieces and so on. Then we could specify the primitive operations such as `Q_OnBoard` and `Get_Status`. When it came to implementation we investigated a full implementation based on an 8*8 array, and two other implementations were briefly sketched. Some implementations are better than others in terms of criteria such as simplicity of design or run-time efficiency. But all must have the same *semantics* – that is, they must meet the same *specification*.

We could then specify more complex operations on `Board_T`, which could be implemented in terms of the primitives. That is, once we had the implementation of `Board_T` we could implement those complex operations. The `Board_T` example illustrates the meaning of several other definitions.

Data abstraction is the separation of the specification of a set of values for a data type from the implementation of that set of values. The abstraction is from the application domain, allowing us to talk, for example, of board positions, the status of squares and so on, before we even need think of what language to use.

Procedure abstraction is the separation of the specification of a set of operations on a set of values for a data type from the implementation of that set of operations. This is done with our syntactical and semantic specifications. Using pre- and post-conditions establishes a contract between William, the implementor of the `Board_T` ADT, and Lucy, the application programmer who is to use `Board_T`. If the pre-conditions of an operation are TRUE, then William must ensure that the post-conditions are TRUE after the operation has been executed. If Lucy uses an operation, then she must ensure that the pre-conditions are TRUE at the point in her program where the operation is to be executed. If something goes wrong but the pre-conditions were TRUE, then William can be sued! However, if the pre-conditions were not TRUE, then it's all Lucy's problem!

Information hiding is the concealment of how a set of values or a set of operations for a data type are implemented. How this is done depends on language support. For example, we were able to use opaque types, implemented using `void`, and `.h` and `.cpp` files to do this.

3.2.2 Analogies

Consider the term 'software engineering', used for the wider activity we are, or should be, engaged in when we write programs. Software engineers build structures and mechanisms with symbols and syntax, just as hardware engineers build structures and mechanisms with girders (or cogs or resistors) and connections.

Good engineers provide just the access needed to their structures and mechanisms and no more. A bridge builder will not suddenly decide that it would be rather good if cars could get on the bridge through any car-sized holes at the side of the bridge. Rather she will ensure that there is no access, on to or off the bridge, through any place except that as originally required. Makers of ovens do not usually let you have access to the wiring so that you can increase or reduce the temperature by popping a couple of resistors into a circuit, instead of using the control knob.

When engineers work in teams, perhaps spread across several companies, countries or continents, they are producing components to be fitted together to make a bigger structure or mechanism. They must have a specification of what their component is to do and where the connections (interfaces) are to be in order to fit in with other components. Imagine if Acme receives a widget from Ajax that doesn't fit in with the gadget they got from Perfect Products plc. Perfect Products might say 'Oh well, just lever the lid off and fiddle with the insides, bend the outward connections and see if that works'. Or Acme might then say to Ajax and Perfect Products 'Get your engineers in touch with each other and see if you can botch them together'. Would you like to fly on an aeroplane put together like that?

The ADT approach is the way by which we can work as engineers to produce vastly complicated mechanisms, such as web browsers and word processors, which work according to specification. Of course some programmers still think that this might deprive the customers of the excitement and expense of finding all the shortcomings in software for themselves.[1]

3.3 The ADT Sequence_T

An extremely versatile data structure is the *sequence*. Informally a sequence is a set of things coming one after the other. More formally we can characterise a sequence of elements as follows.

- A sequence has a first element and a last element.
- Each element, except the last, has another element after it, its successor.
- Each element, except the first, has one before it, its predecessor.
- If x is the successor of y then y is the predecessor of x.
- If the sequence is not empty then one element is picked out as the current element.

For example, the sequence (3, **4**, 7, 2) has first element 3 and last element 2, and 4 is the successor of 3, 7 the successor of 4, 2 the successor of 7, 7 the predecessor of 2, 4 the predecessor of 7 and 3 the predecessor of 4. 4 is the current element. The idea of the current element is that we consider only one element at a time, like reading only one page of a book at a time, or looking at one record in a database at a time.

The elements can be of any type but all the elements in a particular sequence are of the same type. So we can have a sequence of integers, a sequence of characters, or a sequence of accounts records. A sequence of groceries is called a shopping list.

Let us imagine that in the course of developing an application, a need has arisen for a sequence data structure. If this sounds too contrived let me reassure you that the need for just such a data structure occurs repeatedly in commercial and research applications, and that the specification and implementation I am basing this discussion on actually comes from my own programming on a research project about intelligent telephone answering systems.

---

[1] I think that it was Professor Tony Hoare who said that software engineering was the only profession where you get paid to rectify your own mistakes.

3.3.1 Specifying the Sequence_T *ADT*

Let's start off informally and then tighten things up. If we have a sequence, then we want to be able to go to the first element. If we are at any position in the sequence, we want to go to the next element. We want to be able to actually get the element in the current position where we are. We also need to be able to add elements to the sequence and delete elements from it. And we shall need to be able to start off with a sequence with nothing in it, the empty sequence. Notice that when we add elements to the sequence we need to be able to add an element before or after the current element. For example, in Figure 3.1(a), we want to insert a value 9 in between the 7 and the 2. One way to do this is to move the circle indicating the current element forward one place, so it is now 7, and then add 9 *after* the current element. Alternatively we can move it forward one more time, so the current element is now 2, and insert the 9 *before* the current element.

However, if we want to add 5 at the end, after the present last element, 2, then the only way to do it is to move the current position circle marker along so that 2 is in the current position, and then add the new element, 5, *after* 2, as in Figure 3.1(b). Similarly, there is only one way to put a new element at the start of the sequence, by making the current position the first and then inserting the new element *before* this.

That means that we also need some functions to tell us if the current element is the last in the sequence, because if we try to go to the next element at the end of the sequence, we will have a problem. Finally we need a function to tell us if the sequence is empty and another to tell us if it is full – assume that there is a maximum number of elements for the sequence.

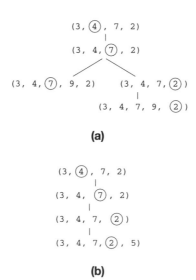

(a)

(b)

Figure 3.1 Illustrating the sequence.

Here are the more formalised syntax and semantics of the operations on Sequence_T. The type of the elements in a sequence is Element_T. In our exercises here, Element_T is just a synonym for KAPRec_T, whose address field references a record of DataRec_T. This could be a student record or an accounts record or any record with a key value. (We can take it that the example above was showing only the key values in the sequence.) Note that the Create_Sequence operation is explicitly specified here, as is another related operation Free_Sequence, which will be discussed in Section 3.7.

```
// PRE   TRUE
// POST RETURNS an initialised Sequence_T
Sequence_T
Create_Sequence();

// PRE   TRUE
// POST IF Sequence is full THEN
//         RETURNS TRUE
//      ELSE RETURNS FALSE
BOOLEAN
Q_Full(Sequence_T Sequence);

// PRE   TRUE
// POST IF Sequence is empty THEN
//         RETURNS TRUE
//      ELSE RETURNS FALSE
BOOLEAN
Q_Empty(Sequence_T Sequence);

// PRE   NOT Q_Empty(Sequence)
// POST IF current element last in Sequence THEN
//         RETURNS TRUE
//      ELSE RETURNS FALSE
BOOLEAN
Q_At_End(Sequence_T Sequence);

// PRE   NOT Q_Empty(Sequence)
// POST first element of Sequence' is the current element
void
Go_To_Head(Sequence_T Sequence);

// PRE   NOT Q_Empty(Sequence) AND
//       NOT Q_At_End(Sequence)
// POST current element in Sequence' is the one after
//      current element in Sequence
void
Go_To_Next(Sequence_T Sequence);

// PRE   NOT Q_Empty(Sequence)
// POST RETURNS current record
Element_T
Get_Current(Sequence_T Sequence);
```

```
// PRE   TRUE
// POST Sequence' = Sequence with NewRec added AND
//       IF Q_Empty(Sequence) THEN
//         current of Sequence' is first element
//       ELSE
//         NewRec is after current in Sequence'
void
Append_After_Current(Element_T NewRec, Sequence_T Sequence);

// PRE   NOT Q_Empty(Sequence)
// POST Sequence' = Sequence with NewRec added AND
//       NewRec is before current in Sequence'
void
Insert_Before_Current(Element_T NewRec, Sequence_T Sequence);

// PRE   NOT Q_Empty(Sequence)
// POST Sequence' = Sequence with current of Sequence removed
//       AND
//       IF NOT(Q_Empty(Sequence'))
//         current of Sequence' is first element of Sequence'
void
Delete_Current(Sequence_T Sequence);

// PRE   Q_Empty(Sequence)
// POST all memory allocated to Sequence is freed up
// NOTES Sequence will need to be re-initialised
//       with Create_Sequence() before being used again
void
Free_Sequence(Sequence_T Sequence);
```

Once again this is expressed in the format of function prototypes, which will make up (part of) the C++ sequence.h file. For the while do not concern yourself with the representation and implementation issues. Study the syntax and semantics and convince yourself that it captures all that was expressed more informally above. Note that we have specified that we can only insert into an empty list with Append_After_Current. We could have allowed for this with Insert_Before_Current as well, but didn't. However, we need to be able to use at least one of them to start off with an empty list.

3.3.2 Container ADTs and pure polymorphism

This is a good place to point out that Sequence_T has two related properties, which make it a little different from the Board_T ADT. First, it is what I call a *container type*. The term is a direct steal from the expression *container class* in object-oriented programming. All it means is that Sequence_T contains other types – Element_Ts – student records, accounts records, integers and so on. You have already met two container types, arrays and records (structs) at the language level in C++. Second, it is a *pure polymorphic type*. This is a functional programming rather than an object-oriented programming term, but I think it expresses the idea better. Sequence_T is a pure polymorphic type because it can hold Element_Ts of any other type, as long as all the elements are of the same type. So I can use Sequence_T in my student administration program to structure student records, then I can use it in my accounting program to structure accounts records, and in my arithmetic program to structure sets of integers, and so on. I need specify, design, implement and test Sequence_T only once and then use it in all these different programs. In some languages I can only have Sequence_T used with a particular Element_T *in a single program*, and this is how we shall use it here. This means that if I want sequences of student records and sequences of accounts records in the same program I would have to produce two lots of code, looking very similar, one for StudSequence_T and one for AccSequence_T. (This is what we shall be doing in Chapter 11 for our first implementation of the Graph_T.) More recent versions of C++ support the use of *templates* with classes, which overcomes this restriction, and all pure functional languages, such as Gofer or ML, positively revel in pure polymorphism, allowing you to implement Sequence_T once and then use it for sequences of student records, accounts records and so on. within the same program.

Note that Element_T will usually be an ADT. In our examples it is just KAPRec_T, which is more of a structural ADT because its role is to facilitate storage and rearrangement of DataRec_T. Of course KAPRec_T references DataRec_T, which is an *application data* ADT since its operations are operations on the data involved in the real-world application. These are mainly concerned with input and output, as well as selecting items such as key values. These are specified and implemented in separate pairs of files, namely data.h/.cpp and store.h/.cpp.

3.4 Testing Sequence_T

At this point we can draw up a test plan for Sequence_T. You might think this a little premature, since we haven't actually implemented it yet! However, in the design of the operations we shall be considering cases and it makes sense to consider how we shall test each of those cases. Furthermore, implementation can bias your testing! You may remember that you had a horrendous problem, which you overcame with great skill, and then emphasise the testing of the circumstances in which the problem arose to the neglect of others. Ideally, following specification, an independent person will draw up a test plan. Failing that, it is best if you draw up the test plan before you are knee-deep in pointers and things.

Often the specification is such that, having implemented several procedures, some testing can be done, rather than having to implement the whole set of procedures before testing. Most procedures will require others to be implemented before they can be tested. So we could test Append_After_Current, Get_Current and Go_To_Next together.

Let us take the example of drawing up the part of the test plan for Append_After_Current. In this case we might consider what happens if

(1) The sequence is empty.
(2) The sequence contains just one element.
(3) The sequence contains several elements and the current is the first.
(4) The sequence contains several elements and the current is the last.
(5) The sequence contains several elements and the current is neither first nor last.

The driver program for a test harness will allow us to perform the primitive operations through 'wrapper' procedures that will test the pre-conditions before calling the primitives, so we assume that we shall be able to append, move to next, print the current and so on.

There will be one test for each of the five conditions above and we restart the program for each test. Table 3.1 shows the test plan derived from the above

Table 3.1 The test plan for Append_After_Current.

Test	Option	Data	Expected	Actual
1	Append	Rec1		
	Print current		Rec1 printed	
2	Append	Rec1		
	Append	Rec2		
	Move to next			
	Print current		Rec2 printed	
3	Append	Rec1		
	Append	Rec2		
	Append	Rec3		
	Append	Rec4		
	Move to next			
	Print current		Rec4 printed	
4	Append	Rec1		
	Append	Rec2		
	Move to next			
	Append	Rec3		
	Move to next			
	Append	Rec4		
	Print current		Rec4 printed	
5	Append	Rec1		
	Append	Rec2		
	Move to next			
	Append	Rec3		
	Append	Rec4		
	Move to next			
	Print current		Rec4 printed	

conditions. It is assumed that we have four records ready to put in but the details of the records are not important here.

Note that with an operation that has a pre-condition that is not simply TRUE, then we do not, indeed should not, test for cases where the pre-condition is FALSE. For example, with Go_To_Head, there is no need to consider the case Sequence being empty, because the pre-conditions guarantee that, used legitimately, the Sequence will never be empty when Go_To_Head is called. By analogy, a pre-condition for a television to work is that it is plugged into the electricity, so no test plan would include the case where it was not plugged in.[2]

You should note down the actual results and store the completed test plan document with all the other documentation. If there is a problem, 'expected' and 'actual' are different, then you, or your successor as programmer, need this information if you are to solve the problem. Even if all goes well, the test documentation must be kept, because your successor may come across a bug and will need to see what cases you considered. Possibly he or she will be able to work out a case you missed and get a lead on what the bug is.

Despite taking this very careful ADT approach, mistakes can still be made. However, because we proceed in a structured manner, it is usually the case that we can reason about where the mistake is likely to be and rapidly isolate a small area of suspect code. With the unstructured approach all we know is that there is a mistake but we have very little idea of where to start looking.

3.5 Designing and implementing Sequence_T

A partial implementation of Sequence_T is given in ch3\exercises. This is in the files sequence.cpp/.h. The main program is stud_db.cpp. One of your tasks is to provide the full design and implementation. Here I shall just outline some of the details.

3.5.1 Types and data structures

As before we shall have an opaque type using void. So the following line appears in sequence.h, along with the function prototypes from Section 3.3.2.

```
typedef void *Sequence_T;
```

---

[2] You may feel that it is as well to check that the pre-condition has been observed. Formally this is OK, in that the post-conditions are undefined anyway if the pre-conditions are not TRUE. Pragmatically this is a bad idea. It leads to what Bertrand Meyer calls 'conceptual pollution'. The user of the operation should check the pre-condition, not the implementor.

Since the Element_Ts are just synonymed KAPRec_Ts, we also need to include the header for the KAPRec_T in sequence.h

```
#include "my_const.h"
#include "store.h"
```

and a synonym for Element_T

```
typedef KAPRec_T Element_T;
```

What information do we need to store about a sequence? Clearly we need the elements and some way of showing the successor relationship. Furthermore, we need to identify the current element. And we shall need to be able to find out how many elements it contains or where it ends – if we have one, then we can find the other.

Here is the actual data structure used to implement Sequence_T:

```
typedef struct {
  Element_T Recs[MaxElements];
  int  CurrentElement,
       NumberElements;
} SeqRec_T, *SeqRec_Ptr_T;
```

where we already have

```
#define MaxElements 8
```

(I know that 8 isn't many but it is enough to allow testing. You can increase it to whatever you want later!)

So we have an array that holds the actual Element_T records, and a cursor field, which indexes the current element, and a field showing how many elements have been entered. The whole structure is called a SeqRec_T and we shall be working with a pointer to it called Seq_Ptr_T. This is what the void pointer type Sequence_T really is. Recall how Board_T was really BoardStruct_Ptr_T. We can visualise an example as shown in Figure 3.2.

This can look quite complex, even alarming, especially if you have only just really started dealing with pointers in this book! However, one thrust of this book is to work out how to manage complexity rather than try to avoid it. In fact the management of the Element_Ts and their associated DataRec_Ts has been accomplished in Chapter 1. Only the Sequence_T is new. So we shall use a simpler diagram to help in our design process, as shown in Figure 3.3, where we only show the keys of the KAPRec_Ts.

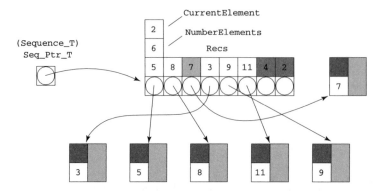

Figure 3.2 A `Seq_Ptr_T` points to a structure containing an array `Recs` of `Element_T`s. Because `Element_T` is a synonym for `KAPRec_T`, each has a key and a pointer to a `DataRec_T` which contains the key again and other information in the grey and dark grey rectangles. `NumberElements`, 6 here, is the number of valid elements in `Recs`, so the last two elements of `Recs`, keyed 4 and 2, are rubbish, heavily greyed. `CurrentElement` is in the range 0 to `NumberElements - 1`. Here it is 2 picking out the `Element_T` with key 7, lightly greyed.

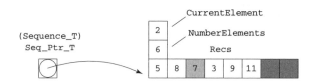

Figure 3.3 A simplified view of `Sequence_T`/`Seq_Ptr_T`.

3.5.2 Procedures

Here are the bodies of three sample procedures, with comments.

In `Q_Empty`, once again we superimpose the 'map', this time of `Seq_Ptr_T`, over the void pointer value passed across in `Sequence`. Note how we use the `NumberElements` field to establish whether or not `Sequence` is empty.

```
BOOLEAN
Q_Empty(Sequence_T Sequence) {
  SeqRec_Ptr_T Seq;

  Seq = (SeqRec_Ptr_T) Sequence;
  return(Seq->NumberElements == 0);
}
```

All that is required for `Go_To_Next` is to increment the `CurrentElement` field.

```
void
Go_To_Next(Sequence_T Sequence) {
  SeqRec_Ptr_T Seq;

  Seq = (SeqRec_Ptr_T) Sequence;
  (Seq->CurrentElement)++;
}
```

For `Append_After_Current` we can consider the same cases as we did for drawing up the test plan. Case (1) is where the sequence is empty. `NumberElements` is 0 and the value of `CurrentElement` is unimportant.

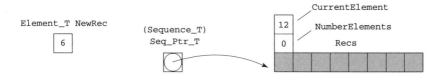

This is fairly straightforward. The value of `CurrentElement` is now important.

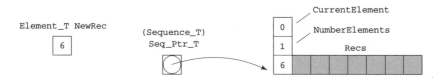

The remaining cases now seem to fall into two larger cases, distinguished by whether `CurrentElement` indicates the last element or not.

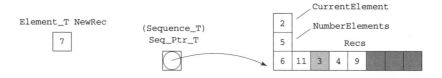

If it does not then we want to shift all the elements after the current element right by one.

```
if Seq->NumberElements > Seq->CurrentElement + 1;{
  for ( Index = Seq->NumberElements - 1;
        Index > Seq->CurrentElement;
        Index--) {
    Seq->Recs[Index + 1] = Seq->Recs[Index];
  }
  // Index = Seq->CurrentElement
```

Note my comment. It is useful to state what must be TRUE when a loop finishes.

We then slot NewRec into the 'hole' just created after the current element and increment NumberElements.

```
    Seq->Recs[Seq->CurrentElement + 1] = NewRec;
    (Seq->NumberElements)++;
}
```

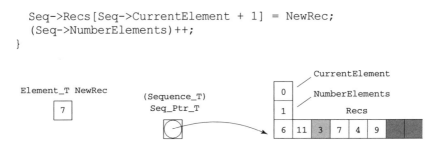

In the case where the current element is the last element we do not need to create the 'hole'.

```
else {
// NumberElements == Seq->CurrentElement + 1
```

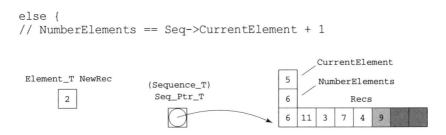

So we just slot in NewRec in the next position and increment NumberElements.

```
    Seq->Recs[Seq->CurrentElement + 1] = NewRec;
    (Seq->NumberElements)++;
}
```

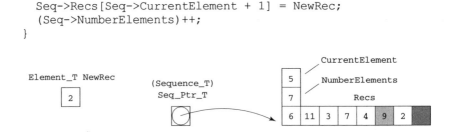

However, if it were TRUE that Seq->NumberElements == Seq->CurrentElement + 1, then, even if the code for the loop, in the previous case where the current element was not the last element, were encountered next, the body of the loop would not be executed, since the first value of Index is

```
Seq->NumberElements - 1 == Seq->CurrentElement + 1 - 1 ==
Seq->CurrentElement
```

This would not pass the continuation test

```
Index > Seq->CurrentElement
```

Control would drop through to the statements

```
Seq->Recs[Seq->CurrentElement + 1] = NewRec;
(Seq->NumberElements)++;
```

The result is that the code for the non-empty cases is more compact, as shown below.

```
void
Append_After_Current(Element_T NewRec, Sequence_T Sequence) {
  SeqRec_Ptr_T Seq;
  int Index;

  Seq = (SeqRec_Ptr_T) Sequence;
  if (Q_Empty(Seq)) {
    Seq->CurrentElement = 0;
    Seq->NumberElements = 1;
    Seq->Recs[0] = NewRec;
  }
  else {
    for ( Index = Seq->NumberElements - 1;
          Index > Seq->CurrentElement;
          Index--) {
      Seq->Recs[Index + 1] = Seq->Recs[Index];
    }
    // Index = Seq->CurrentElement
    Seq->Recs[Seq->CurrentElement + 1] = NewRec;
    (Seq->NumberElements)++;
  }
}
```

You can see the implementation of other procedures in sequence.cpp. Still others are left for you to implement in the exercises.

3.6 Higher-level operations on `Sequence_T`

The main program `stud_db.cpp` contains procedures to test the primitive operations of `Sequence_T`. Each of these uses the primitives in an obvious way. As well as that we have several other higher-level procedures which use the primitives to produce results. Here is one of them:

```
// PRE  NOT Q_Empty_Sequence(DataBase)
// POST RETURNS number of elements in DataBase
//      AND Q_At_End(DataBase')
// NOTES this is a function with side effects
int
Find_Size(StudentDB_T DB) {
  int Size;

  Go_To_Head(DB);
  for (Size = 1; !Q_At_End(DB); Size++) {
    Go_To_Next(DB);
  }
  return(Size);
}
```

The point to observe here is that we have defined our operation for finding the size of the `Sequence_T` in terms of the primitive operations and not on any special knowledge about the underlying implementation. It might turn out that we decide to implement `Find_Size` as a primitive later for reasons of efficiency but it will have the same semantics.

3.7 Freeing up an instance of an ADT

We shall discuss memory management issues at appropriate times throughout the book. Here is a good place to start with a little example. `Create_Sequence()` allocates enough space for the structure `SeqRec_T`, returning a pointer to the start of this space. When we have finished with our sequence, this memory is still allocated and cannot be used by anything else *unless* we explicitly free it up. Of course, we can do this with the C++ delete operation, which takes a pointer and frees the space for the structure it is pointing at. But at the ADT level we do not know what the structure is. In `sequence.h` it is hidden away behind a void pointer. So we need a special operation at the ADT level. Here is the specification and the implementation.

```
// PRE  Q_Empty(Sequence)
// POST all memory allocated to Sequence is freed up
// NOTES Sequence will need to be re-initialised
//       with Create_Sequence() before being used again
```

```
void
Free_Sequence(Sequence_T Sequence) {
  SeqRec_Ptr_T Seq;

  Seq = (SeqRec_Ptr_T) Sequence;
  delete(Seq);
}
```

The pre-condition is that Sequence is empty. So this cannot be called until that is true. I have extended the specification to NOTES. These are useful comments but should not be overdone, else they will obscure the specification.

Here is the current version of Finalise(), in stud_db.cpp.

```
// PRE   TRUE
// POST Clears up
void
Finalise(StudentDB_T DB) {
// for(;!Q_Empty(DB);) {
//   Delete_Current(DB);
// }
   Free_Sequence(DB);
   cout << "That is it !\n";
}
```

Some of the useful bits have been commented out! This is because one of your tasks is to implement a proper version of Delete_Current. See the exercises below.

3.8 Program structure and ADTs

There are two sample applications, stud_db and ord_db, both of which use Sequence_T, DataRec_T and KAPRec_T. The program structures for both are shown in Figure 3.4.

If we reimplement Sequence_T, as we shall in Chapter 4, then we need only 'unplug' the old sequence.h/.cpp files and 'plug in' the new sequence.h/.cpp files, recompiling only the files stud_db.cpp and ord_db.cpp, which depend on them. Alternatively the type of data may change, causing the code in data.h/ data.cpp to change. All the files will now need recompiling but no change to the source code in the other files is required.

Thus the program structure we have reflects the abstract data type structure we have employed. In a complex application there may be many ADTs and, as a rule of thumb, one ADT should be specified and implemented in one .h/.cpp pair.

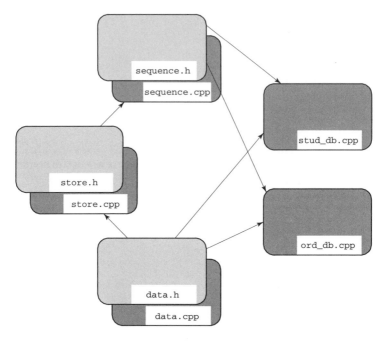

Figure 3.4 Program structures for stud_db and ord_db.

Exercises

1 Consider the remote control of a television set. Why is this like an abstract data type? List some typical operations with the input and output. How is this ADT implemented?

2 Why is a good building subcontractor like an ADT?

3 Q_At_End, Go_To_Head, Insert_Before_Current, and Delete_Current in sequence.cpp/.h all need fixing.
   (a) Work out a sensible order of implementation, so that you can test as you go along.
   (b) For each function to be implemented use the specification to draw up a test plan and a design. Use diagrams where helpful. Then implement and test them.

4 Using Find_Size as a guide, design and implement code for Print_All, specified as follows – a stub and silly message exists for this.

```
// PRE   TRUE
// POST IF DB is not empty all values are printed to
//    screen
//       ELSE message to say that DB is empty
void
Print_All(StudentDB_T DB)
```

5 `ord_db.cpp` is the main program for a simple database where the records are kept in key order. Well, it will be once you have fixed `Add_Stud`. From the specification draw up the test plan and design. *Hint*: look at `Q_Present`. Implement and test your `Add_Stud` function.

6 `ch3\Examples\Numbers` contains another application that uses `int`s as the `Element_T` for `Sequence_T`. Examine the code and see how only a small change is needed to `sequence.h` to make `Sequence_T` use `int`s instead of `KAPRec_T`s.

3.9 Summary

In this chapter we have covered the following:

- The ideas of data abstraction, procedural abstraction and information hiding have been introduced, through definition and analogy, and related to the definition of an abstract data type.
- The `Sequence_T` has been introduced informally and then specified as a pure polymorphic, container ADT, using the `KAPRec_T` and `DataRec_T` from Chapter 1.
- The role of a test plan has been explained, together with a discussion of when and how to design and draw it up.
- The design and implementation of `Sequence_T` has been introduced through diagrams relating the data structure to selected procedures.
- Further comments on memory management have been made.
- The relationship of program structure to the ADTs used has been discussed.

CHAPTER 4

Abstract data types (3): implementation of ADTs by dynamic data structures

4.1 Introduction

Chapter 1 was taken up with looking at the three structuring methods available to us, namely arrays, records and pointers. In Chapters 2 and 3 we looked at abstract data types as an element of the design process, and then their implementation principally using arrays or records. Pointers played a part. First, we used pointers in the key/address pair method of storing data records separately from the structuring method. Second, they were used for information hiding, by means of the void pointer. In this chapter we shall see how pointers can play a central part in the structuring method.

4.2 A linked list

The idea of referencing a structure is what underlines the key/address pair approach taken in this book. Suppose that we had a pointer referencing a structure, which contained a pointer, referencing another structure, of the same type, and so on. Such an arrangement is shown in Figure 4.1. It is called a *linked list*, or more specifically a *simple linked list*. A pointer variable references the first item in the list, called the *head*. Each item is called a *node*. Each node structure contains a pointer field, referencing the next item in the list. This is shown, as before, by circles with arrows coming out of them. The pointer is structural information. The greyed-in section represents the real-world data held. The actual position of a node in memory does not have to bear any relation to that of the node after it, or the one before it. The last item in the list has this value set to

Figure 4.1 A simple linked list, with head and other nodes, and the last node containing a NULL pointer.

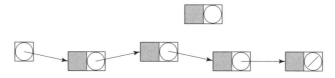

Figure 4.2 A new node is to be added.

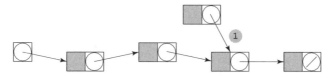

Figure 4.3 First, change the pointer field to reference the node which is to be the successor of the new node.

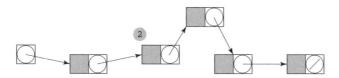

Figure 4.4 Second, change the pointer field of the node which is to become the predecessor of the new node to reference the new node.

NULL, indicated by the 'no go sign' of a diagonal line in a circle, showing that the end of the list has been reached.

By changing the values of the pointer fields we can add new nodes into the linked list or remove existing nodes from the linked list. For example, Figures 4.2 to 4.4 show how a new node can be added.

With an array we added data to or removed data from an existing static structure. Here we can dynamically create new nodes, at run time, using new, and add them to the structure, or remove existing nodes using delete. This is why a pointer-based linked list is an example of a *dynamic data structure*. The ability to expand and contract data structures dynamically opens up very natural programming solutions to a whole range of application problems. Precisely because they offer so much more flexibility than using static structures, dynamic data structures usually require more effort at the design and implementation stage. However, as we shall see, a careful, step-by-step approach enables programmers to achieve just what they want with dynamic data structures. Once implemented, dynamic data structures, and the ADTs based on them, can be used again and again.

The order in which we change the pointer values is crucial. What would happen if we tried change 2 before change 1? See Exercise (1) at the end of this chapter about this and other issues concerning inserting into and removing from a linked list.

4.3 A linked-list-based structure to implement `Sequence_T`

As has been stressed before, an ADT is a specification. The actual implementation may take a number of forms. We have implemented `Sequence_T` in Chapter 3 using an array as the central structure. Here we shall reimplement `Sequence_T` using a simple linked list as the central structure. This will demonstrate some fundamental ideas about programming with dynamic data structures, as well as underlining the nature of ADTs.

4.3.1 Diagrams

Figure 4.5 shows the overall structure. The difference from the list in Figure 4.1 is that we have two extra pointer variables alongside the head pointer and a pointer to reference this trio.

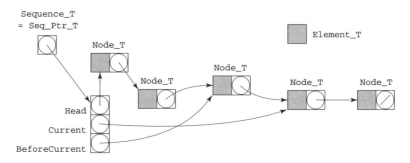

Figure 4.5 Implementing `Sequence_T` as a linked list.

The greyed square in each of the `Node_T`s is an `Element_T`. This could be an `int` or a `StudentRec_T` but in `ch4\exercise` it is a `KAPRec_T`. Recall that each of these contains a key value and also another pointer variable referencing the actual data record, but this is not shown here. With these added we would have a very complicated diagram, showing the actual complexity of the whole structure. Once again, the point is that through the ADT approach we have structured and managed complexity so we can deal with it.

The structure containing the three pointer variables `Head`, `Current` and `BeforeCurrent` keeps track of where the list actually starts (`Head`) and where we are currently in the list (`Current`). For reasons to do with insertion and deletion we also need to know where the node before the current one is (`BeforeCurrent`).

As with the previous implementation we want an opaque type, so `Sequence_T` is actually a `void` pointer, and the real way to reference the list is through a `Seq_Ptr_T` which just points at a `Head`/`Current`/`BeforeCurrent` trio structure.

4.3.2 Code for structures

Here is the code for the node structure.

```
typedef struct Node_Tag {
   struct Node_Tag  *Next_Ptr;
   Element_T  Element;
} Node_T, *Node_Ptr_T;
```

The node structure has to contain a pointer to reference another node structure of the same type. It is known as a *self-referential structure* and is the first example of a *recursive* structure we have seen. In order to do this we need a tag identifier, here Node_Tag, which is used only in the declaration. Node_T is the actual node structure type and Node_Ptr_T is a pointer to it. Node_T contains an Element_T field and the link to the next Node_T, Next_Ptr. In Figure 4.6 the solid node is referenced by the Next_Ptr field of the previous node, and references the next node with its own Next_Ptr field. The final greyed and dashed node has a NULL pointer as its Next_Ptr, indicating the end of the list.

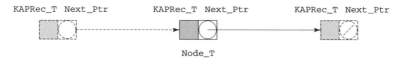

Figure 4.6 The Node_T structure.

Here is the code for the pointer trio structure. See Figure 4.7.

```
typedef struct {
   Node_Ptr_T Head,
             Current,
             BeforeCurrent;
} SeqRec_T, *SeqRec_Ptr_T;
```

This is not self-referential.

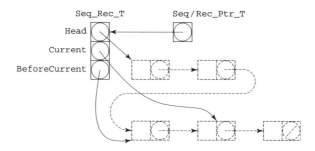

Figure 4.7 The SeqRec_T and SeqRec_Ptr_T structures.

4.4 Designing and implementing the operations on Sequence_T

In this section we shall work through the reimplementation of the three procedures we considered in detail in the array-based implementation of Chapter 3, namely Q_Empty, Go_To_Next and Append_After_Current. As well as that we shall also look at Create_Sequence.

4.4.1 Implementing Create_Sequence

For Create_Sequence we need to set up a new SeqRec_T and initialise all the pointers to NULL, before returning it. Figure 4.8 shows this.

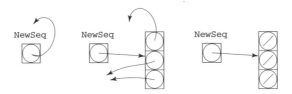

Figure 4.8 Create_Sequence builds an initialised SeqRec_T, NewSeq, which is returned.

From the diagram we can write down pseudo-code or, in this case, the C++ code directly. Note that we cast the result NewSeq to a Sequence_T in the return.

```
Sequence_T
Create_Sequence() {
  SeqRec_Ptr_T NewSeq;

  NewSeq = new SeqRec_T;
  NewSeq->Head = NULL;
  NewSeq->Current = NULL;
  NewSeq->BeforeCurrent = NULL;
  return((Sequence_T) NewSeq);
}
```

4.4.2 Implementing Q_Empty

The two cases for Q_Empty are shown in Figure 4.9. If a Sequence_T is empty then that means there is no head element, else there would be at least one element. (The BeforeCurrent would be NULL if Current were the first but the important thing is that Head is NULL.) So all we need to do is check if the Head pointer is NULL or not.

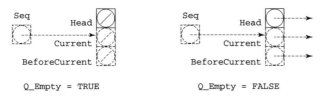

Figure 4.9 The two cases for Q_Empty.

Again it is straightforward to go from the diagram to the C++ code.

```
BOOLEAN
Q_Empty(Sequence_T Sequence) {
  SeqRec_Ptr_T Seq;

  Seq = (SeqRec_Ptr_T) Sequence;
  return(Seq->Head == NULL);
}
```

4.4.3 Implementing Go_To_Next

There are two cases for Go_To_Next. The first is the case where the current element is the first, as shown in Figure 4.10. In this case the current element becomes the next one along and the before current element becomes the old current element, as shown in Figure 4.11.

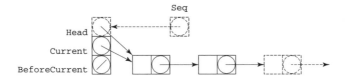

Figure 4.10 Before Go_To_Next where the current element is the first.

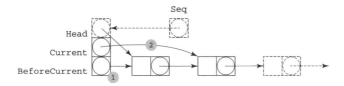

Figure 4.11 After Go_To_Next where the current element had been the first.

In the second case for Go_To_Next, the current element is not the first and so BeforeCurrent has a non-NULL value, as shown in Figure 4.12. As before, the current element becomes the next one along and the before current element becomes the old current element, as shown in Figure 4.13.

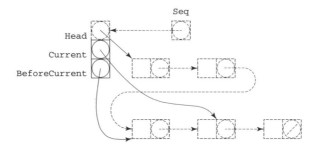

Figure 4.12 Before `Go_To_Next` where the current element is not the first.

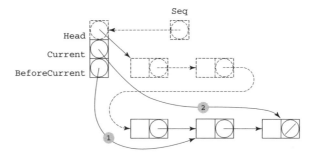

Figure 4.13 After `Go_To_Next` where the current element was not the first.

So, although the two cases seem different to start with, the actual steps in the operation are the same. This gives us the following code.

```
Go_To_Next(Sequence_T Sequence) {
  SeqRec_Ptr_T Seq; Seq = (SeqRec_Ptr_T) Sequence;
  Seq->BeforeCurrent = Seq->Current;
  Seq->Current = Seq->Current->Next_Ptr;
}
```

4.4.4 Implementing `Append_After_Current`

There were five cases for `Append_After_Current(Element, Sequence)` listed in Chapter 3.

(1) The sequence is empty.
(2) The sequence contains just one element.
(3) The sequence contains several elements and the current is the first.
(4) The sequence contains several elements and the current is the last.
(5) The sequence contains several elements and the current is neither first nor last.

Let us consider the cases in light of our chosen implementation and see if two or more cases reduce to the same thing. It is clear that (1) is all by itself, since we are going to have to change the value of Head. Figures 4.14 to 4.17 illustrate this.

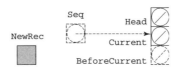

Figure 4.14 Before Append_After_Current for the empty list.

Figure 4.15 Creating a new node to Append_After_Current in the list.

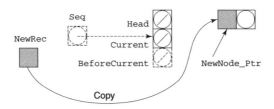

Figure 4.16 Copying the value of NewRec into the Element_T component of the new node.

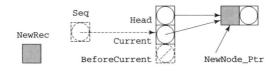

Figure 4.17 Setting the pointer values.

Once again we can write down the C++ code straight away from the diagrams.

```cpp
if (Q_Empty(Seq)) {
  Seq = (SeqRec_Ptr_T) Sequence;
  NewNode_Ptr = new Node_T;
  NewNode_Ptr->Element = NewRec;

  Seq->Current = NewNode_Ptr;
  Seq->Head = NewNode_Ptr;
  Seq->Current->Next_Ptr = NULL;
```

In the other cases either the current element is last or it is not. If so, then the value of the Next_Ptr field in the new node has to be NULL, but this is the same as the value of the Next_Ptr field in the current node at the start of the operation. Then the Next_Ptr field of the current node must change to reference the new node. This is shown in Figures 4.18 to 4.21.

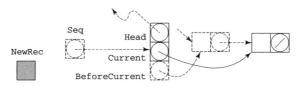

Figure 4.18 Before Append_After_Current for the non-empty list with the current element the last.

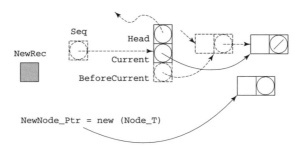

Figure 4.19 Creating a new node.

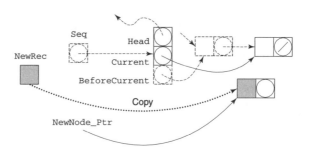

Figure 4.20 Copying the value of NewRec into the Element_T component of the new node.

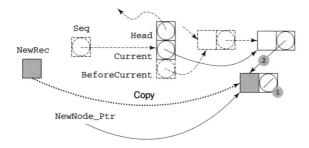

Figure 4.21 Setting the pointer values.

If not, then the value of the `Next_Ptr` field in the new node has to take the value of the `Next_Ptr` field in the current node, and the `Next_Ptr` field of the current node must change to reference the new node, as illustrated in Figures 4.22 to 4.25.

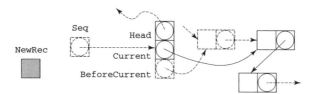

Figure 4.22 Before `Append_After_Current` for the non-empty list with the current element the last.

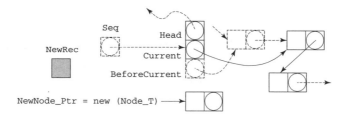

Figure 4.23 Creating a new node.

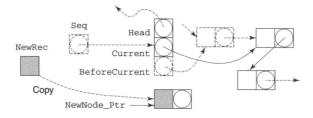

Figure 4.24 Copying the value of `NewRec` into the `Element_T` component of the new node.

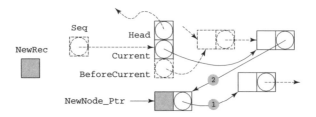

Figure 4.25 Setting the pointer values.

So, either way, the value of the `Next_Ptr` field has to be made equal to that of the `Next_Ptr` field, `NULL` or non-`NULL`, in the current node and the `Next_Ptr` field of the current node must change to reference the new node. So we have the following code:

```
else {
  Seq = (SeqRec_Ptr_T) Sequence;
  NewNode_Ptr = new Node_T;
  NewNode_Ptr->Element = NewRec;

  NewNode_Ptr->Next_Ptr = Seq->Current->Next_Ptr;
  Seq->Current->Next_Ptr = NewNode_Ptr;
}
```

Note that the three lines

```
Seq = (SeqRec_Ptr_T) Sequence;
NewNode_Ptr = new Node_T;
NewNode_Ptr->Element = NewRec;
```

occur as the *first* three lines of each branch of the if ... else ... statement. So they can be 'factored out' to a position just before the if, as shown below. Putting all this code together, with some data declarations and some brackets, we get the complete `Append_After_Current` procedure.

```
void
Append_After_Current(Element_T NewRec, Sequence_T Sequence) {
  SeqRec_Ptr_T  Seq;
  Node_Ptr_T    NewNode_Ptr;

  Seq = (SeqRec_Ptr_T) Sequence;

  NewNode_Ptr = new Node_T;
  NewNode_Ptr->Element = NewRec;

  if (Q_Empty(Seq)) {
    Seq->Current = NewNode_Ptr;
    Seq->Head = NewNode_Ptr;
    Seq->Current->Next_Ptr = NULL;
  }
```

```
  else {
    NewNode_Ptr->Next_Ptr = Seq->Current->Next_Ptr;
    Seq->Current->Next_Ptr = NewNode_Ptr;
  }
}
```

So we have now implemented Create_Sequence, Q_Empty, Go_To_Next, Append_After_Current, a fairly representative set of operations on Sequence_T. See Exercise (2) for the others.

Exercises

1 (a) The only fixed reference we have in the linked list of Figure 4.1 is through the head and then down the list. Try changing pointer values in Figures 4.2–4.4 in the reverse order. Why would this cause a problem?

   (b) Draw the diagrams for putting in a new node at the head of the list.

   (c) Draw the diagrams for putting in a new node at the end of the list.

   (d) Draw the diagrams for removing a node from somewhere in the middle of the list.

   (e) Draw the diagrams for removing a node from the head of the list.

   (f) Draw the diagrams for removing a node from the end of the list.

2 From compiling and running stud_db, in ch4\exercise, you know that Q_At_End, Go_To_Head, Get_Current, Insert_Before_Current and Delete_Current all need fixing in sequence..h/.cpp. In the exercises at the end of Chapter 3 you have already worked out a sensible order of implementation, so that you can test as you go along, and you have a test plan. For each function or procedure to be implemented use the specification to develop a design. Refer to the design of Append_After_Current. Use diagrams. Then implement and test the functions and procedures.

3 Sequence_T offers the facility to move in one direction only. For some applications it may be useful to be able to move backwards. We extend the specification of Sequence_T to get a new ADT called TwoWay_T, with the following two operations:

```
// PRE  NOT Q_Empty(TWSeq)
// POST IF current element first in TWSeq THEN
//         RETURNS TRUE
//      ELSE RETURNS FALSE
BOOLEAN
Q_At_Start(TwoWay_T TWSeq);
```

```
// PRE   NOT Q_Empty(TWSeq) AND
//       NOT Q_At_Start(TWSeq)
// POST current element in TWSeq' is the one before
//       current element in TWSeq
void
Go_To_Prev(TwoWay_T TWSeq);
```

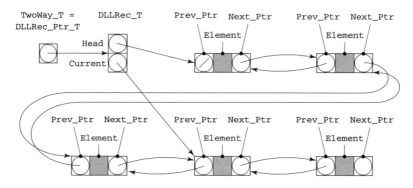

Figure 4.26 The `Two_Way_T` structure, a doubly linked list.

Figure 4.26 shows one data structure that can be used for this ADT.
`ch4\exercise` contains a skeleton in `two_way.h/.cpp`. `Q_At_Start`,
`Go_To_Prev`, `Insert_Before_Current` and `Delete_Current` all need
fixing. `tw_st_db.cpp` is the main module of the program using `TwoWay_T`.
The code for the structure is in `two_way.h`

```
typedef void *TwoWay_T;
```

and `two_way.cpp`

```
typedef struct Node_Tag {
  struct Node_Tag  *Prev_Ptr,
                   *Next_Ptr;
  Element_T Element;
} Node_T, *Node_Ptr_T;
typedef struct {
  Node_Ptr_T Head,
             Current;
} DLLRec_T, *DLLRec_Ptr_T;
```

`DLLRec` stands for *doubly linked list*. Figure 4.26 shows what the whole
structure looks like.

(a) From the code for `Append_After_Current` draw the pointer
     diagrams to show how this was designed. (This is called *reverse
     engineering*, designing from the implementation. You must not do
     this except as here, where it is meant to help you understand
     something!)

(b)   For the other functions and procedures to be implemented, work out a sensible order of implementation, so that you can test as you go along.

(c)   For each function to be implemented use the specification to draw up a test plan and a design. Use diagrams where helpful. Then implement and test them.

4.5 Summary

Now that you have read this chapter, you should have learned that:

- A linked list is a linear structure of nodes, each with a pointer to reference the next node, if there is one. This can be dynamically manipulated at run time. Each node contains real-world data as well as the pointer.
- Diagrams are practically indispensable when designing and implementing dynamic data structures such as linked lists.
- Switching pointers in the right order is also rather important.
- Sequence_T can be implemented as a linked list. In this chapter we have looked at one such implementation.
- Other, more complex, dynamic linear structures such as the doubly linked list can be implemented using the same principles.

CHAPTER 5

The stack: a linear ADT based on the sequence

5.1 Introduction

We have considered the container ADT Sequence_T and seen two implementations of it, using two different data structures, the array and the linked list. In turn the Sequence_T is a data structure for use by a programmer, who may wish to implement another ADT using Sequence_T. In this chapter we are going to see how such another ADT, the Stack_T, can be specified and implemented using Sequence_T. Then we shall look at a simple example of an important use of Stack_T, which makes it an essential data structure at all levels of computing. Figure 5.1 summarises the relationship between the four ADTs/data structures. The idea is that an ADT at one level is a data structure for the next level above. In the last half of the chapter the process of lexical analysis, together with the postfix representation system, will be introduced, providing a more advanced example of the use of Stack_T.

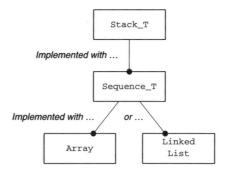

Figure 5.1 The relationships between the ADTs/data structures Stack_T, Sequence_T, array and linked list.

5.2 Why do we need a stack?

The application problems motivating this example are those where we read in a stream of characters from the keyboard into a store. We want to be able to correct this stream, as we type, by deleting any mistyped characters.

Suppose that a # is to indicate that the most recently entered character is to be deleted and that this is done before the next character is read, so that

```
John####James and Mary saw the dog
```

would be read as

```
James and Mary saw the dog
```

not

```
JohnJames and Mary saw the dog
```

which is what would happen if we allowed the #s to 'cancel'. If there are no characters to be deleted then #s are ignored.

Here is an example where the user tried to type in Dear Jones but made two mistakes, which he has corrected. The whole of his input string is Dee#ar Jonne##es. Note that the most recent element is on the left in this printout. This program is read_in in ch5\examples\read_in. We shall discuss the construction of the source later.

```
Stack is                         NextChar is D
Stack is D                       NextChar is e
Stack is e D                     NextChar is e
Stack is e e D                   NextChar is #
Stack is e D                     NextChar is a
Stack is a e D                   NextChar is r
Stack is r a e D                 NextChar is
Stack is   r a e D               NextChar is J
Stack is J   r a e D             NextChar is o
Stack is o J   r a e D           NextChar is n
Stack is n o J   r a e D         NextChar is n
Stack is n n o J   r a e D       NextChar is e
Stack is e n n o J   r a e D NextChar is #
Stack is n n o J   r a e D       NextChar is #
Stack is n o J   r a e D         NextChar is e
Stack is e n o J   r a e D       NextChar is s
        Final stack is s e n o J   r a e D
```

Our first task, as application programmer, is to be able to read in the line, correct it and write it out in *reverse* order. (This somewhat perverse operation is motivated by the desire to use a simple example for the development of the stack ADT! We shall do something more sensible when we have got Stack_T fully specified and implemented.)

Assume that the end of the stream is marked by an *end of line* character EOL, which is not erasable and is not to be stored.

The store that we read the characters into is called Stack. We now consider the operations that we would like to be able to perform on Stack. First, consider the problem of reading into Stack. Here is the pseudo-code.

```
READ new character INTO NextChar
FOR NextChar <> EOL DO
  IF NextChar <> '#'
    Put NextChar onto Stack
  ELSE
    IF Stack is not empty
      Remove last entered character
  READ new character INTO NextChar
```

Here we see at least three operations that we would like to perform on Stack:

- putting NextChar onto Stack – call this Push(NextChar, Stack);
- seeing if Stack is empty – call this Q_EmptyStack(Stack);
- removing the last entered character from Stack – call this Pop(Stack).

Note that if we regard Pop and Push as producing new versions of Stack then we can write the fact that Popping after Pushing produces the original as

```
Pop(Push(NextChar, Stack)) = Stack
```

This is an *axiom* about the behaviour of Stack. Axioms are statements that are always true. They are not program code. They provide the basis for reasoning about the use of the ADTs to which they apply.

In order to read the line out in reverse order we want to, repeatedly, get the value of the last entered character from Stack, print it and then remove this character from Stack.

```
FOR (NOT Q_EmptyStack(Stack))
  NextChar := last entered character
  Print NextChar
  Pop(Stack)
```

So a new operation is required which gets the value of the last entered character but does not remove it from Stack. Call this Top(Stack). (We are specifying the stack ADT here, and some hold that Pop should combine the two operations of removing and returning the top element. I prefer the approach above since it conforms to the maxim of 'One procedure – one purpose'. The argument that you often want to do both at once is also countered by the fact that often you do not, which means you end up having to do two things just to read but not remove the top element.)

With the Top operation, something that must now be true – that is an axiom – is

```
IF NOT Q_Empty(Stack)
   PUSH(Top(Stack), Pop(Stack)) = Stack
```

Our high-level operations are called by a main operation, which will presumably need to initialise Stack in some way. Call this initialisation Create_Stack(Stack) and that gives the axiom

```
Q_EmptyStack(Create_Stack(Stack))
```

We now have a set of operations on Stack. The reason for the name becomes clear, since the operations of Pushing and Popping mean that only the most recently stored element can be accessed, rather like a stack of trays in a restaurant dispenser. This is called the *last in, first out* property (*LIFO*).

This example is very simple but, as we shall see, indicative of the usefulness of the stack.

Figure 5.2 shows how the Stack_T is normally pictured.

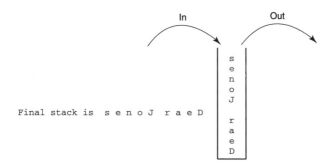

Figure 5.2 Picturing the Stack_T.

5.3 Completing the specification of Stack_T

Through the problem posed in the example we were able to identify and informally specify five desirable operations on Stack. In this section we shall complete the specification to give an ADT Stack_T.

5.3.1 Completing the set of operations on `Stack_T`

Before tightening up the specification, two further operations are needed, which do not apply to the completely abstract concept of a stack.

The first is the operation to check if `Stack` is full, which we call `Q_FullStack`.

The second is the operation to free up any memory used by `Stack`, if we do not require it any more and it is empty, which we call `Free_Stack`.

Both operations are required because our implementations are necessarily finite.

5.3.2 The complete specification of `Stack_T`

Here is the final specification of the ADT `Stack_T` in the form of a C++ header file.

```
// PRE   TRUE
// POST RETURNS an initialised Stack_T
Stack_T
Create_Stack();

// PRE   NOT Q_Full(Stack)
// POST elements of Stack' = elements of Stack union
//    {Element}
void
Push(Element_T NewElement, Stack_T Stack);

// PRE   TRUE
// POST IF Stack is empty
//         RETURNS TRUE
//      ELSE
//         RETURNS FALSE
BOOLEAN
Q_EmptyStack(Stack_T Stack);

// PRE   TRUE
// POST IF Stack is full
//         RETURNS TRUE
//      ELSE
//         RETURNS FALSE
BOOLEAN
Q_FullStack(Stack_T Stack);

// PRE   NOT Q_EmptyStack(Stack)
// POST Stack' is Stack with the most recently entered
//      element removed
void
Pop(Stack_T Stack);
```

```
// PRE   NOT Q_EmptyStack(Stack)
// POST RETURNS the value of the most recently
//        entered element of Stack *)
Element_T
Top(Stack_T Stack);

// PRE   Q_EmptyStack(Stack)
// POST all memory allocated to Stack is freed up
// NOTES Stack will need to be re-initialised
//        with Create_Stack() before being used again
void
Free_Stack(Stack_T Stack);
```

5.4 Implementing Stack_T using Sequence_T

From the example of reading in characters, particularly from the printout, the Stack_T is a linear *structure*, which is to say that it has the same structural properties as the Sequence_T. The difference is in the operations. Stack_T is a restricted Sequence_T, because all of its operations can be expressed in terms of the operations on Sequence_T. This leads directly to the design and implementation of Stack_T. We simply use Sequence_T as the underlying data structure. Since the first element of Stack_T is so important we ensure that the first element of the underlying Sequence_T is always the current element after the execution of any Stack_T operation, except where the empty stack is a result of the operation, of course.

Create_Stack, Q_EmptyStack and Q_FullStack are effectively just other names for the obvious Sequence_T operations.

```
Stack_T
Create_Stack() {
  return(Create_Sequence());
}

BOOLEAN
Q_EmptyStack(Stack_T Stack) {
  return(Q_Empty(Stack));
}

BOOLEAN
Q_FullStack(Stack_T Stack) {
  return(Q_Full(Stack));
}
```

For Push, either Stack is empty so we use Append_After_Current, or it is not empty, so we use Insert_Before_Current and then Go_To_Head. If the current element was first before Push on a non-empty Stack, then the new element will become the current element and also the first.

```
void
Push(Element_T NewElement, Stack_T Stack) {
  if (Q_Empty(Stack)) {
    Append_After_Current(NewElement, Stack);
  }
  else {
    Insert_Before_Current(NewElement, Stack);
    Go_To_Head(Stack);
  }
}
```

As long as the current element is first then `Delete_Current` will delete the first element. Since the post-condition of `Delete_Current` is that the current element is the first element, if the `Stack'` is not empty, we are guaranteed that the current element in a non-empty `Stack'` is indeed the first.

```
void
Pop(Stack_T Stack) {
  Delete_Current(Stack);
}
```

Because the current element is always the first, the implementation of `Top` will always return the current element as specified.

```
Element_T
Top(Stack_T Stack) {
  return(Get_Current(Stack));
}
```

`Free_Stack` is effectively just another name for the obvious `Sequence_T` operation.

```
void
Free_Stack(Stack_T Stack) {
  Free_Sequence(Stack);
}
```

In order to use `Sequence_T` in this way we need to add the following line to `stack.h`.

```
#include "sequence.h"

typedef Sequence_T Stack_T;
```

The source code for this implementation of `Stack_T` is given in `ch5\examples\read_in`. Which implementation of `Sequence_T` do we use? Either will do but the one used in this chapter is the linked-list-based one. See the

Exercises below. Note that the Element_T, as defined in data.h, is the char. In Chapters 3 and 4 it was the KAPRec_T. In this case the data are just characters and are not keyed. However, this does not affect the code for Sequence_T in any way. It is just that what Element_T 'hooks into' is the primitive type char rather than KAPRec_T or int as used in previous applications.

Exercises

1   Compile, link and run read_in. Now try switching the array-based implementation of Sequence_T to check that it works. Make sure you set MaxElements in sequence.cpp to be big enough.

```
#define MaxElements 200
```

2   How can we get to print out the stack in read_in in the right order? Figure 5.3 gives a clue. Reimplement read_in.cpp with a new option, plus supporting operations to do this.

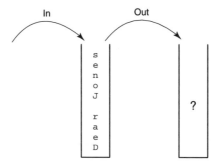

Figure 5.3 What's the other Stack_T for?.

3   Look at ch5\examples\stdb_stk for Stack_T using a KAPRec_T.
4   Reimplement Stack_T using a direct pointer-based structure. This means that you no longer use Sequence_T.

5.5 Lexical analysis

This section introduces some concepts and ideas necessary to demonstrate a simple example of an important application of stacks. There are many other applications, two of which we shall see in Chapter 6 on recursion and Chapter 9 on extending the binary search tree. The point about all such applications is that they exploit the properties of the stack.

5.5.1 Characters, lexical analysis and tokens

A source computer program can be viewed as a sequence of characters. In fact
that is just how you create your source program, by typing in the characters one
at a time on your keyboard! Part of the process of compilation is to group
together those characters that form significant items, called *tokens*, in the
language. For example, the piece of code

```
if (Count > 20) {
```

contains 11 such items. The first is the keyword `if` introducing the conditional
statement, the second is a space. The third is a left round bracket, the fourth is
the identifier `Count`, the fifth is a space, the sixth is the relational operator >, the
seventh is a space, the eighth is the integer `20`, the ninth is the right round bracket,
the tenth is a space and the eleventh is the opening curly bracket. Most of these
are represented by single characters but `if`, `Count` and `20` have two or more
characters each.

The process of *chunking* a stream of characters into a stream of tokens is called
lexical analysis. The rules for how to do this are part of the programming
language's *syntax*. Lexical analysis is part of the process of compilation.

We are not going to write a compiler! However, we shall look at an evaluator
for a much simpler but still non-trivial language. In integer arithmetic we have
left round brackets (, right round brackets), operators, +, −, * and /, and
integers. An integer is one or more digits.

5.5.2 A simple lexical analyser

`lex.cpp` is my implementation of a simple lexical analyser. It recognises the
token types indicated by the enumerated type `TokenType_TT`, declared in `lex.h`.

```
typedef enum {LRB_TT, RRB_TT, INT_TT, SemiCol_TT,
    Separator_TT, Operator_TT, EndOfLine_TT,
    Identifier_TT, NULL_TT} TokenType_T;
```

The ones of interest to us are `LRB_TT` (left round brackets), `RRB_TT` (right round
brackets), `INT_TT` (integers), `SemiCol_TT` (semicolons), `Separator_TT` (separat-
ors – here spaces and tabs), `Operator_TT` (operators +, −, * and /), and
`EndOfLine_TT` (end of line and carriage return). These are the *types* of *simple
arithmetic expressions* with non-negative integers. They are not the types of C++.
They are *values* of the user-defined type `TokenType_T`.

Here are the prototypes of the lexical operations.

`Start_Lex()` initialises the lexical analysis process and should be called
whenever lexical analysis is started after any high-level input operations using
`cin`.

```
// PRE   TRUE
// POST CurrChar the next character from stdin
void
Start_Lex();
```

Once lexical analysis has been started, GoTo_NewLine() 'throws away' the input until a new line is reached.

```
// PRE   TRUE
// POST CurrChar is the next newline
void
GoTo_NewLine() {
```

A new line having been reached, Start_NewLine() 'throws away' new lines until it finds a character input that is not a new line.

```
// PRE  GoTo_New_Line executed immediately before
// POST CurrChar contains the first character on the
//      next proper - i.e. non-empty - new line
//      and this was the last character from standard input
void
Start_New_Line();
```

In applications where we want to start lexical analysis on a new line then we call

```
Start_Lex();
GoTo_NewLine();
Start_New_Line();
```

Lex_Token() is the main input operator. If there is a valid token to be read then it is read in and Q_LexOK() will return TRUE until the next Lex_Token(). If not then Q_LexOK() will return FALSE until the next Lex_Token. In the second case, the programmer needs to recover the situation by doing something like going to the next non-empty new line and restarting the lexical analysis.

```
// PRE  - TRUE
// POST - IF there is a valid token on input THEN
//          token is read in
//            AND Get_TokenType returns its type
//            AND Q_LexOK() will return TRUE
//          ELSE Q_LexOK() will return FALSE
void
Lex_Token();
```

Get_TokenType() returns the type of the last token read in assuming that Q_LexOK() is TRUE.

```
// PRE  - Q_LexOK()
// POST - RETURNS type of last token
TokenType_T
Get_TokenType();
```

If the last token was read in OK and it was a character type with several values, such as the operator type, which has four values, then the particular value read in is returned by Get_CharVal().

```
// PRE  - Q_LexOK() AND type of last token is character
//         e.g. Operator_TT
// POST - RETURNS value of last token
char
Get_CharVal();
```

If the last token was read in OK and it was an integer type then the particular value read in is returned by Get_IntVal().

```
// PRE  - Q_LexOK() AND type of last token is integer
// POST - RETURNS value of last token
int
Get_IntVal();
```

Q_LexOK() returns TRUE if the last attempt to read in a token was successful, but FALSE otherwise.

```
// PRE  - Lex_Token() has been called
// POST - IF a valid token was read THEN
//           RETURNS TRUE
//         ELSE
//           RETURNS FALSE
BOOLEAN
Q_LexOK();
```

So far we have not connected up this lexing business with the use of stacks. Before we can do that we must look at postfix representation.

Exercise

1   demo_lex.exe, made up of demo_lex.cpp, lex.cpp, lex.h and
    my_const.h in ch5\examples\lex\lex_demo demonstrates the use of
    the lexical analyser. Run the program and type in a line containing
    integers, operators and round brackets. These are the tokens that
    demo_lex recognises. Each should be recognised. Repeat the process but

throw in a few other items like alphabetical characters. This should report a lexical error each time it comes to a non-token.

5.6 Infix, postfix and prefix expressions

In an arithmetic expression like `(32 - (7 + 5)) * (22 + 3*4)`, we are using *infix notation*, which is to say that the *operators* come in between the *operands*. In our example we have the breakdown for the five operators and their operands shown in Figure 5.4.

Operand	Operator	Operand
(32 - (7 + 5)	*	(22 + 3*4)
32	-	(7 + 5)
7	+	5
22	+	3 * 4
3	*	4

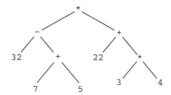

Figure 5.4 Table and tree diagram to show the structure of `(32 - (7 + 5)) * (22 + 3*4)`.

In order to evaluate the expression we have to use brackets, precedence and working from left to right. The rule you probably learned at school was 'Do the brackets first, then do multiplication and division before addition and subtraction, working from right to left each time'. The idea is that doing a bracket first means you have to treat that as a separate sub-expression all of its own and reapply the same rule, and so on. At some stage you will be able to do some actual arithmetic and the regress stops. (This is an example of recursion, to be covered in the next chapter.) This means that our expression gets evaluated as follows:

```
(32 - (7 + 5)) * (22 + 3*4) ==> (32 - 12) * (22 + 12) ==>
20 * 34 ==> 680
```

Infix notation is not the only notation, nor is it the most natural of notations. For example, how do you express an operator that takes three arguments in an infix expression? One alternative is *postfix*, or *reverse Polish notation* (*RPN*). In this notation the operators come after their operands. As a result no brackets or precedence rules are necessary for evaluation. In postfix our expression above would be

```
32  7  5  +  -  22  3  4  *  +  *
```

Of course, being used to 'talking infix' all our lives this is not intuitive! There are three operators at the end and it is not clear just what they are operating on. In order to see this we can put in brackets but this is just to show the implicit structure of what is there. As we shall see, the brackets are not necessary.

```
((32  (7  5  +)  -)  (22  (3  4  *)  +)  *)
```

In order to evaluate this we go through repeatedly evaluating any simple bracketed expression we can – e.g. (3 4 *) ==> 12 until there is nothing left to do.

```
((32  (7  5  +)  -)  (22  (3  4  *)  +)  *)  ==>
((32  12  -)  (22  12  +)  *)  ==>
(20  34  *)  ==>  680
```

There is another form called *prefix*, or *Polish notation* (*PN*), where the operators precede their operands. In prefix the expression becomes

```
*  -  32  +  7  5  +  22  *  3  4
```

or, with the unnecessary but helpful brackets

```
(*  (-  32  (+  7  5))  (+  22  (*  3  4)))
```

which evaluates as follows

```
(*  (-  32  (+  7  5))  (+  22  (*  3  4)))  ==>
(*  (-  32  12)  (+  22  12))  ==>
(*  20  34)  ==>  680
```

Both postfix and prefix notations are used extensively in computer science because they are a natural form for the computer. Operators with three or more operands can be defined because all the operands come before (postfix) or after (prefix) the operator.

5.7 Stacks and arithmetic

So far we have specified and implemented the `Stack_T` ADT, and then gone on to see what lexical analysis is about, and lastly discussed infix, postfix and prefix notation. We are now going to bring these three topics together to show an application of stacks, namely the evaluation of arithmetic expressions read from a command line. Cynics might feel that finding out how to convert expensive workstations into pocket calculators is not why they bought this book. The motivation is that arithmetic has a simple but non-trivial syntax. Once you understand these examples you will be in a position to understand how parsers work generally and be able to design and construct web browsers that parse HTML, for example.

The plan is that `lex.cpp/.h` is used to read in the tokens of a valid infix expression off the command line. `data.cpp/.h` calls the necessary `lex` operations and then packages the tokens up as records. `eval.cpp`, in turn, calls the `data` for its own operations to read in the infix expression to a stack to be converted to postfix and then evaluated.

5.7.1 Specifying and implementing `Element_T` as `ArithToken_T`

As with our earlier stack example, `Read_In.cpp`, we are dealing with unkeyed records so we do not use `KAPRec_T`. These unkeyed records are of course the tokens which result from lexical analysis. The structure in which they are to be stored is to be called an `ArithToken_T`, which will become the `Element_T` for `Sequence_T` and then `Stack_T`. This is declared as a void pointer in `data.h`.

```
typedef void *ArithToken_T;
```

One extension we shall make is that we want to check that the result of reading a record is a valid token. `Read_Rec` takes an extra `BOOLEAN` parameter to show the result of the operation. So the specification for `Read_Rec` becomes

```
// PRE  Flush_For_Read() has been executed since last regular
//   cin operation
// POST IF next token read from standard input is a valid
//   arithmetic token
//        ArithToken has that value
//        AND Q_ReadOK is TRUE
//        ELSE
//        Q_ReadOK is FALSE
void
Read_Rec(ArithToken_T &ArithToken, BOOLEAN &Q_ReadOK);
```

`ArithToken_T` may need to contain a character or an integer, as well as indicating the actual token type held. This is the reason for using a *variant record*, which is implemented using the union structure in C++. Essentially this allows us to say that a particular field of a record may be one of several types – here char or int – depending on what we need it for. We have to keep track of what type it is, but since we need to do this anyway there is no further overhead.

```
typedef  union {
         char CharVal;
         int  IntVal;
} TokVal_T;

typedef  struct {
         TokenType_T  TokenType;
         TokVal_T TokVal;
} ArithTokenRec_T, *ArithTokenRecPtr_T;
```

ArithTokenRecPtr_T is the 'real' record, or rather the pointer to it. To show how we use the union structure, how the lexical analysis ties in, and, once more, how the void pointer works, here are the implementations for Write_Rec and Read_Rec. Note how the switch is used with the union structure to work out what is to be done.

```
void
Read_Rec(ArithToken_T &ArithToken, BOOLEAN &Q_ReadOK){
  ArithTokenRecPtr_T NewArithToken;
  TokenType_T TT;

  Lex_Token();
  Skip_Separators();

  Q_ReadOK = Q_ValidAT();
  if (Q_ReadOK) {
    NewArithToken = new ArithTokenRec_T;
    TT = Get_TokenType();

    NewArithToken->TokenType = TT;
    switch(TT) {
      case Operator_TT:
        NewArithToken->TokVal.CharVal =
          Get_CharVal();
      break;
      case INT_TT:
        NewArithToken->TokVal.IntVal = Get_IntVal();
      break;
      default:
      break;
    }
    ArithToken = (ArithToken_T) NewArithToken;
  }
}
```

```
void
Write_Rec(ArithToken_T ArithToken) {
  ArithTokenRecPtr_T Tok;

  Tok = (ArithTokenRecPtr_T) ArithToken;
  switch(Tok->TokenType) {
    case LRB_TT:
      cout  <<  '(';
    break;
    case RRB_TT:
      cout  <<  ')';
    break;
    case Operator_TT:
      cout  << Tok->TokVal.CharVal;
    break;
    case INT_TT:
      cout  << Tok->TokVal.IntVal;
    break;
    default:
    break;
  }
}
```

There are a number of other operations specified in data.h, but we need only concern ourselves with two more at present.

```
// PRE   TRUE
// POST Read_Rec can be used
// NOTES This flushes any left over from standard cin
//       operations
//       any number of Read_Recs can be performed until the
//       next regular cin operation
void
Flush_For_Read();
```

Flush_To_Read is involved in the pre-condition for Read_Rec and is implemented using operations from lex.cpp.

```
// PRE   Q_Int(AT1) AND Q_Op(AT2) AND Q_Int(AT3)
// POST RETURNS result of (infix) AT1 AT2 AT3
ArithToken_T
Evaluate(ArithToken_T AT1, ArithToken_T AT2,
    ArithToken_T AT3);
```

Note the pre-conditions. Evaluate takes the three arithmetical tokens out of the ArithToken_Ts, works out their value as an expression, and puts that into an ArithToken_T and returns it. For example, if AT1 contained 23, AT2 contained +, AT3 contained 12, then it would work out 23 + 12 = 35, put 35 in a new ArithToken_T and return it.

This is demonstrated in `ch5\examples\lexstack` with the files `token_st.cpp` as the main file, and `data.h/.cpp`, `lex.h/.cpp`, `sequence.h/.cpp` and `my_const.h`. In order to use the `w` option you need to get an integer, an operator and an integer as the first three items on the stack. Entering

```
a
*
a
34
i
2
```

to the prompt gives the sequence 2 * 34 (why?) and `w` will evaluate this to 68, which can be seen using the `p` option.

Exercise

1 `read_in.cpp` had a procedure `Print_Stack(Stack_T Stack)`. Copy this into `token_st.cpp`, but you need to make some changes before compiling and running. `Print_Stack` in `read_in.cpp` expects `Stack_Ts` of `chars` not `ArithToken_Ts`. Add a new option and supporting wrapper operation to demonstrate your new addition.

5.7.2 Converting infix to postfix

Supposing we want to convert 7 - 5 to postfix. That's easy! 7 5 - = 2. What about 7 - 5 + 3? A little thought shows that this is 7 5 - 3 + because we want 7 5 - = 2 done first and then use 2 in 2 3 + = 5. Now consider 7 - 5 * 3. * has greater precedence than - so it has to be done first. We want the result of 5 3 * to be subtracted from 7. So we want 7 5 3 * - recall this brackets (unnecessarily but usefully) as 7 (5 3 *) -. How about 7 - 5 * 3 + 4? This turns out to be 7 5 3 * - 4 +. In contrast 7 - 5 * 3 / 4 has the postfix form 7 5 3 * 4 / -.

Two things to notice are that the operands are always in the same order as in the original infix expression, and that if operator P comes after operand X in the infix expression then it will also do so in the postfix expression.

Now the idea is that we read in the expression, token by token, and, if the next token is an integer, just push it straight to the output, which is a stack called Out. The trick is to get the operators in the right order. Suppose that I have 7 - 5 * 3 + 4. Then I push 7 to output, a stack called Out, and then read a -. I don't know what to do with this yet so I push it onto a stack called Siding. I now read 5 and push it to Out, then I read *. This has greater precedence than - but I don't know if there is going to be an operator of greater precedence coming after. (There will not be in this system but if I included exponentiation there would be – see the Exercise at the end of this section.) So I push * to Siding. 3 is read and pushed to Out. Then I find +. Since this has lower precedence than *, on the Siding, then I need to pop * and push it to Out because * must be done before + and be attached to the arguments that have preceded. I also now need to pop – and push it to Out because left to right evaluation means that – must take the preceding arguments and not +. I push + onto Siding. Finally I read and push 4 to Out. Then I empty Siding by popping and pushing the remaining operator + to Out. The following output from the infix to postfix program eval.exe, whose source can be found in ch5\exercise\lex\guard\, shows this process. Use option c and put in an extra newline at the end.

```
7 - 5 * 3 + 4

Token is 7    Out is 7               Siding is Stack is empty
Token is -    Out is 7               Siding is -
Token is 5    Out is 5 7             Siding is -
Token is *    Out is 5 7             Siding is * -
Token is 3    Out is 3 5 7           Siding is * -
Token is +    Out is - * 3 5 7       Siding is +
Token is 4    Out is 4 - * 3 5 7     Siding is +

              Out is + 4 - * 3 5 7
```

Note that Out contains the postfix expression in *reverse* order but this is not prefix.

You are recommended to try some conversions, without brackets, on paper and then check your results using eval.exe. By doing this you should be able to work out why the following algorithm works. As in the discussion, it uses the Siding stack to take account of left to right evaluation and precedence of operators.

```
FOR NOT EOS
   Read Token
   IF Token is an operand
     Push(Token, Out)
   IF Token is an operator
     IF Q_EmptyStack(Siding)
       Push(Token, Siding)
     ELSE
       FOR
         Q_EmptyStack(Siding)
         AND precedence of Token >= precedence of
Top(Siding)NOT

         Push(Top(Siding), Out)
         Pop(Siding)
```

```
     Push(Token, Siding)

FOR NOT Q_EmptyStack(Siding)
  Push(Top(Siding), Out)
  Pop(Siding)
```

But what about the brackets? This algorithm can deal with things like 9 - 3 *
8 + 4 but not (9 - 3) * (8 + 4).

If part of the expression is bracketed, like (9 - 3) in (9 - 3) * (8 + 4)
then it is a sub-expression to be converted in turn. Indeed it may contain further
bracketed sub-expressions and so on.

What we do is to mark the beginning of a sub-expression by pushing the left
round bracket onto Siding. Then we carry on processing as before until we reach
the matching right round bracket. This means that all the operators still on
Siding down to the marker left bracket need to be popped off Siding and
onto Out.

```
(6 * (7 - 3 * 2) - 7) * 2

Token is (      Out is Stack is empty      Siding is (
Token is 6      Out is 6                   Siding is (
Token is *      Out is 6                   Siding is * (
Token is (      Out is 6                   Siding is ( * (
Token is 7      Out is 7 6                 Siding is ( * (
Token is -      Out is 7 6                 Siding is - ( * (
Token is 3      Out is 3 7 6               Siding is - ( * (
Token is *      Out is 3 7 6               Siding is * - ( * (
Token is 2      Out is 2 3 7 6             Siding is * - ( * (
Token is )      Out is - * 2 3 7 6         Siding is * (
Token is -      Out is * - * 2 3 7 6       Siding is - (
Token is 7      Out is 7 * - * 2 3 7 6     Siding is - (
Token is )      Out is - 7 * - * 2 3 7 6   Siding is empty
Token is *      Out is - 7 * - * 2 3 7 6   Siding is *
Token is 2      Out is 2 - 7 * - * 2 3 7 6 Siding is *

          Out is * 2 - 7 * - * 2 3 7 6
```

We amend our pseudo-code as follows.

```
FOR NOT EOS
  Read Token
  IF Token is an operand
    Push(Token, Out)

  IF Token is a left round bracket
    Push(Token, Siding)

  IF Token is a right round bracket
```

```
   FOR Top(Siding) <> left round bracket
     Push(Top(Siding), Out);
     Pop(Siding);
   Pop(Siding)

 IF Token is an operator
   FOR
     NOT Q_EmptyStack(Siding)
     AND precedence of Token >=
       precedence of Top(Siding)
     AND Top(Siding) <> left round bracket

     Push(Top(Siding), Out)
     Pop(Siding)
   Push(Token, Siding)

FOR NOT Q_EmptyStack(Siding)
  Push(Top(Siding), Out)
  Pop(Siding)
```

There are two things to deal with before coding. First, look at the compound BOOLEAN in the FOR loop dealing with the operator.

```
NOT Q_EmptyStack(Siding)
AND precedence of Token >= precedence of Top(Siding)
AND Top(Siding) <> left round bracket
```

It is possible that Q_EmptyStack(Siding) will be TRUE but we still have to get the value of Top(Siding). Unfortunately the pre-condition of Top(Siding) is NOT Q_EmptyStack(Siding). This is OK in the design since the BOOLEAN will be FALSE if any one of its constituents is FALSE, and if Q_EmptyStack(Siding) is TRUE then NOT Q_EmptyStack(Siding) will be FALSE. However, if we implemented directly from this, we may find that the undefined result of Top causes problems.[1] Here is an alternative design for that section.

```
IF Token is an operator
  IF Q_EmptyStack(Siding)
    Set Q_Stop to TRUE
  ELSE
    Set Q_Stop to FALSE
  FOR NOT Q_Stop
    Set SidingToken to Top(Siding)
    IF Get_Precedence(Token) >
      Get_Precedence(SidingToken)
      Set Q_Stop to TRUE
```

---

[1] This depends on the implementation. It is possible that it does *lazy evaluation* – e.g. if it is working out P && Q, and P is FALSE, it doesn't bother with Q, but if we don't know then we must assume that it does not.

```
IF Q_LRB(SidingToken)
   Set Q_Stop to TRUE
   Push(SidingToken, Out)
   Pop(Siding)
   IF Q_EmptyStack(Siding)
      Set Q_Stop to TRUE
Push(Token, Siding)
```

The first design was not a waste of time. It got us onto the right track and it clarified the issues sufficiently to spot where the BOOLEAN problem might arise. The implementation can be found in ch5\examples\noguard\eval.cpp.

The second issue is what happens if the expression read in is not a syntactically correct infix expression. How to spot this and deal with it is shown in ch5\examples\guard\eval.cpp.

Exercise

1   Design and implement a function Power as follows:

```
// PRE   x >= 0 AND y >= 0
// POST RETURNS x raised to the power y
// e.g. Power(3, 5) = 3*3*3*3*3 = 243
int
Power(int x, int y);
```

Power is the integer exponential function. We do exponential before multiplication and division in arithmetic. So

```
7 * 4^5 = 7 * 1024 = 7168
```

where we use ^ to indicate exponentiation.

In lex.h/.cpp add ^ as a new operator, so that lex.h/.cpp can recognise it. Test this using demo_lex.

Now amend eval so that it can deal with ^.

5.7.3 Evaluating a postfix expression

Assuming that we have converted a valid infix expression to postfix, how do we evaluate it? From the above algorithm we have to pop all the elements off the Out stack and push them onto another stack to get it the right way round. So if Out was * 2 - 7 * - * 2 3 7 6, as above, what we want is 6 7 3 2 * - * 7 - 2 *, but this is fairly straightforward.

What we notice is that we can only evaluate where we find two integers followed by an operator. Now if the expression is in valid postfix form then we can work through popping and pushing integers to a stack called Temp. When we come to an operator, we pop off the last two integers from Temp, work out the result and push it onto Temp. In this way there will always be guaranteed two integers for every operator that we come across. eval.exe has an evaluation option and this gives the output for the expression 6 7 3 2 * - * 7 - 2 *. (Type in the original infix expression, choose the convert option then the evaluate option.)

```
Stack is 6 7 3 2 * - * 7 - 2 *
Stack is 7 3 2 * - * 7 - 2 *      Temp is 6
Stack is 3 2 * - * 7 - 2 *        Temp is 7 6
Stack is 2 * - * 7 - 2 *          Temp is 3 7 6
Stack is * - * 7 - 2 *            Temp is 2 3 7 6
Stack is - * 7 - 2 *              Temp is 6 7 6
Stack is * 7 - 2 *                Temp is 1 6
Stack is 7 - 2 *                  Temp is 6
Stack is - 2 *                    Temp is 7 6
Stack is 2 *                      Temp is -1
Stack is *                        Temp is 2 -1
Stack is Stack is empty           Temp is -2
```

Just as with the conversion process, you are strongly recommended to try paper examples and then check them against eval.exe.

Once you are happy with a few examples, then you should be able to follow this evaluation algorithm quite easily.

```
FOR NOT Q_EmptyStack(Stack)
   ArithToken = Top(Stack)
   Pop(Stack)
   IF ArithToken is an integer
     Push(ArithToken, Temp)
   ELSE
     Operand2 = Top(Temp)
     Pop(Temp)
     Operand1 = Top(Temp)
     Pop(Temp)
     Result = apply ArithToken (operator) to
              Operand1 and Operand2)
     Push(Result, Temp)
```

Note that Operand2 comes off the stack first because of the LIFO property.

Having specified and implemented Stack_T, we have used it on a more advanced application. I want to stress how the idea of ADTs as mechanisms is illustrated here. A stack is very much a dynamic thing, a piece of working machinery. We shall see later how the Stack_T and other component mechanisms are put together to make a larger machine.

5.8 The ADT Queue_T

Stack_T is LIFO – last in, first out. A more usual linear structure is the queue which is FIFO – first in, first out, or there will be trouble at the supermarket checkouts! This structure is also used extensively in computing as well as the grocery trade. Here is its specification.

```
// PRE   TRUE
// POST RETURNS an initialised Queue_T
Queue_T
Create_Queue();

// PRE   NOT Q_FullQueue(Queue)
// POST elements of Queue' = elements of Queue union
//    {Element}
void
EnQueue(QueueElement NewElement, Queue_T Queue);

// PRE   TRUE
// POST IF Queue is empty
//         RETURNS TRUE
//      ELSE
//         RETURNS FALSE
BOOLEAN
Q_EmptyQueue(Queue_T Queue);

// PRE   NOT Q_EmptyQueue(Queue)
// POST Queue' is Queue with the most recently entered
//      element removed
void
DeQueue(Queue_T Queue);

// PRE   NOT Q_EmptyQueue(Queue)
// POST RETURNS the value of the least recently
//      entered element of Queue *)
QueueElement
Front(Queue_T Queue);

// PRE   Q_EmptyQueue(Queue)
// POST all memory allocated to Queue is freed up
// NOTES Queue will need to be re-initialised
//       with Create_Queue() before being used again
void
Free_Queue(Queue_T Queue);
```

Here is the code for the implementation of its data structure. Note that, unlike the code for the pointer-based version of Stack_T, we need to know where the last element is, so we have a separate field Last for that alongside Head. New items will be added to the end, via Last, and taken from the front, via Head.

```
typedef struct Node_Tag {
  struct Node_Tag  *Next_Ptr;
  QueueElement  Element;
} Node_T, *Node_Ptr_T;

typedef struct {
  Node_Ptr_T Head,
             Last;
} QueueRec_T, *QueueRec_Ptr_T;
```

Exercises

1 Draw the pointer diagram for the data structure for `Queue_T` with four elements in.
2 Draw pointer diagrams to show insertion into an empty `Queue_T`.
3 Draw pointer diagrams to show insertion into a `Queue_T` with three elements.
4 Draw pointer diagrams to show deletion from a `Queue_T` with just one element.
5 Draw pointer diagrams to show deletion from a `Queue_T` with three elements.
6 Implement the `Queue_T`. Use `Qu_demo.cpp` and `queue.h` in `ch5\exercise\queue` as a framework.

5.9 Summary

In this chapter we have covered the following:

- The LIFO linear ADT `Stack_T` has been introduced using a simple example.
- The idea of a stack arose from the requirements of a simple problem.
- A more rigorous specification led to the ADT `Stack_T`.
- The ADT `Stack_T` was implemented using `Sequence_T` as an underlying data structure.
- The pointer-based implementation of `Stack_T` was left as an exercise.
- The technique of lexical analysis as the process of converting a stream of characters into a stream of symbols was described.
- Postfix and prefix notations for arithmetic were introduced.
- The processes of converting infix to postfix and evaluating postfix expressions were discussed.

- The automation of these processes, using the `Stack_T`, was shown using pseudo-code.
- The specification of the FIFO linear ADT `Queue_T` was given and the implementation left as an exercise.

CHAPTER 6

Recursion

6.1 Introduction

You should know what is said in the rest of this paragraph already from your first programming course, but if not go back to your notes and ensure that you do! A computer program is an *algorithm* to solve a problem written in a standard form suitable for the appropriate compiler. An algorithm is a specification of a sequence of primitive steps to solve a problem. It is almost always the case that certain sub-sequences of primitive steps need to be repeated until a condition becomes true. This is done through *iteration*, which needs a *control structure*. In the C++ programming language this is provided by the for statement, or the while, or the do ... while statement.

One other control structure to accomplish repetition is *recursion*. To start with, recursion appears to be completely counter-intuitive. I remember in the early days of cheap personal computers, my first sight of a recursive program in a computer magazine. I didn't bother to copy it out, as I had with others, because it was clearly a misprint! Or so I thought. I tried it some time later and it worked!

Not only does recursion work, in the sense that all high-level computer languages support it, it is an indispensable tool in developing computer solutions to real-world problems. For example, problems encountered in very different areas of computer applications, such as database system implementation, network algorithms, time tabling, compiler implementation and natural language processing, can be solved by the recursive approach.

Critics of recursive techniques usually claim that recursive techniques are less efficient than non-recursive ones. But, as we shall see, although this can be an issue, the criticism misses the main point, that of a problem-solving approach first and foremost.

We shall start by getting an idea of recursion from an easy example. Then we shall look at recursive processes and their implementation. Recursive ADTs and data structures follow. Finally we look at some heavy-duty problem solving with recursion. This last section prepares the way for algorithms to be used on the graph data structure.

6.2 Recursion: an example and a definition

I have just said that recursion seems counter-intuitive at first. This is not to put you off but rather to give you the indication that it is like riding a bike, with some hard going in parts, to begin with. Later you may wonder how you ever thought it tricky! Try and forget how to ride a bike.

To give you some confidence let us turn to a recursive procedure that almost certainly you have been using for a number of years. Suppose that a new friend says to give her a ring and that she 'is in the book'. The telephone book for an area runs to several hundred pages, say 500 for argument's sake. Do you start at the beginning and work through page after page until you find her name? This would involve looking at 250 pages, on average. It is rather more likely that you employ something like the following algorithm.

```
Search Telephone Directory for Name

Choose Page of Telephone Directory in middle¹
IF Name on Page THEN
   // simplest case found
   Look Through Page for it
ELSE
   IF Name on a previous page THEN
      Search First half of Telephone Directory for Name
   ELSE
      Search Second half of Telephone Directory for Name
   END
END
END Search
```

Note that I have put the name of the procedure, *Search*, in italics. This is to emphasise the fact that the procedure calls itself! The words 'vicious' and 'circle' come to mind! However, you have used essentially this algorithm many times to find phone numbers and it works. What happens is that each time *Search* calls itself, it does so with a 'simpler' argument. In this case that means that the segment of directory is smaller than it was in the calling instance of *Search*. At some stage it comes to a simplest case. This is where the name is on the page chosen.

Search is a recursive procedure. That means it calls itself. It is finite, since it terminates eventually. That means that each call is a 'simpler' instance of search, ending up with a simplest case. Other things besides procedures can be recursive. Here is a definition of recursion:

---

¹ In fact you probably use something more sophisticated. If the name is Smith, you start near the end, for example. But the underlying idea is the same.

> R is a *recursive function, procedure, solution, definition* etc.
> if R can be *evaluated, executed, found, made* etc.
> in terms of a
> *similar but simpler*
> function, procedure, solution, definition
> and there is a *simplest case* at which the
> evaluation, procedure, solution, definition etc.
> eventually arrives.

6.3 Another example and implementation in C++

If you had eight different objects how many ways could you arrange them? If you number the places `'a'`, `'b'`, `'c'`, `'d'`, `'e'`, `'f'`, `'g'` and `'h'`, then you have to choose one from eight objects to put in position `'a'`. Then you are left with seven to choose from to put in position `'b'`. This leaves six to choose from for position `'c'`, and so on until you have only one object left to place in position `'h'`. This means that there are $8*7*6...*1 = 40320$ arrangements. Note the dots. We could have written $8*7*6*5*4*3*2*1$. The same reasoning applies to arranging 20, 100 or 1000 objects. The dots become of practical importance now, especially when we write $1000*999*998...*1$.

The above are instances of the function $n*(n-1)*(n-2)...1$ with $n = 8$, then 20, then 100 then 1000. This function is called n *factorial* and written $n!$. It is an important function in statistics and probability. You can use it to work out just how dismal your prospects of winning the National Lottery are. You can also use it to work out the average complexity of sorting algorithms and use it in many other computing applications.

Since $(n-1)! = (n-1)*(n-2)...1$, then $n! = n*(n-1)*(n-2)...1 = n*(n-1)!$. That is to say that the factorial function is recursive. It gets simpler because the next thing to work out is the factorial of the last argument minus one. When does it stop? Well, to be quite right we take $0! = 1$ as the simplest case. The reasons for this are to do with the gamma function, from which the factorial comes, and we need not worry about them, but $0!$ often appears in practical statistical calculations, so it is best to include it. This gives us the following recursive definition of the factorial function:

```
n! =   1,        if n = 0
       n*(n-1)!, otherwise
```

The definition is sufficient to lead to the following C++ code. Note the pre-condition that $n >= 0$. Obviously we have to write something like Factorial_R(n) rather than $n!$ in C++. That aside, it should be clear how the function reflects the definition of $n!$.

```
// PRE   n >= 0
// POST RETURNS n!
int
Factorial_R(int n) {
  if (n == 0) {
    return(1);
  }
  else {
    return(n*Factorial_R(n-1));
  }
}
```

Convention

All my recursive procedures and functions have identifiers ending in _R.

This function is demonstrated in ch6\examples\fact.cpp, a single file program, using option r. Two other functions are demonstrated. Option s runs the recursive function but with extra output to show the progress. Option i runs I_Factorial in the iterative form – that is there is no recursion.

```
// PRE   n >= 0
// POST RETURNS n!
int
I_Factorial(int n) {
int   Index,
      Result;

  Result = 1;
  for(Index = 1; Index <= n; Index++) {
    Result = Result*Index;
  }
  return(Result);
}
```

This is not much longer that Factorial_R. So why bother with Factorial_R? The answer is that at the outset of a new topic we often use examples so simple that it is not difficult to see how they could be done otherwise with existing knowledge. The idea is to 'get a feel' for the topic. In fact these easy examples of recursion implementations are often impractical in terms of efficiency.

6.4 How recursion is implemented

Figure 6.1 shows how recursion is implemented on the computer. Each time a function or procedure is called, a copy is made of the function or procedure code – object code of course – and put in an *activation record*, together with any

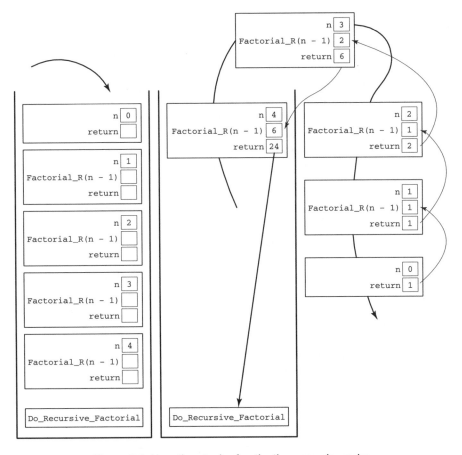

Figure 6.1 How the stack of activation records works.

parameters. This record is put in a stack. The stacking will go on until one record contains code that can run to completion with no further calls. In this case it is Factorial_R(0). When this is worked out, the record is popped, there being no further use for it, and the result returned to the appropriate slot in the activation record at the top of the stack. This must be the one that called the activation record just popped.

The point is that recursion is really no more mysterious or difficult to implement than functions and procedures are generally. In implementation we are calling copies of the code blocks for each function or procedure. This is also a good example of the use of stacks. It is probably worth stressing at this point that the compiler takes care of all these details for you. Although the stack is just the sort of stack we looked at in the last chapter, you do not have to program it yourself!

In fact modern compilers often optimise by *in-line coding*. Essentially they replace procedure and function calls by the actual code bodies of those procedures and functions to give one big program with no procedures or functions. This saves the activation stack for other purposes. However, they cannot always do this with recursive procedures. Sometimes *tail recursion optimisation* can help. This is where the recursive call is the last statement in the recursive operation, and so a stack record can be replaced with another stack record. But if the recursive call is not the last statement then the stack must be used. If the recursion is too 'deep' then we get stack overflow, since only so much room is allocated for the stack. If you are prepared to reboot your computer try `ch6\examples\reclimit\ reclimit`, which just recurses and prints out how far it has got until... This is a warning, not a reason not to use recursion. Many recursive solutions do not recurse deeply but do a lot of 'shallow' chains of calls. More importantly, as the next sections show, recursion is a problem-solving technique.

6.5 Problem solving using recursion

We often use recursion to solve a problem, design and implement a recursively based program to test our solution, and then maybe re-engineer the solution to find an iterative solution. It is often difficult to see through to the iterative solution without having first solved the problem recursively. In this section we shall look at two problems. Both are simple, in the sense that they are fairly easy to state, and seem abstract. Despite this apparent abstraction, they clearly show the recursive approach to problem solving which is used in such applications as scheduling, planning, dynamic modelling and compiling.

6.5.1 The Towers of Hanoi

There are those who find this example something of an old chestnut. That it may be but I believe that it is a rather useful old chestnut for two reasons. First, it is a problem which can be stated simply, but its solution demonstrates the power and application of recursion. With a 'real-world problem' a lot of excavation is often required before finding the bones of the problem, to which the same techniques can then be applied. Second, the towers problem is intimately related to the binary Gray code, much used in communication technology.

The problem

The (legendary) Towers of Hanoi problem concerns three pegs and a set of 64 discs, all of different sizes. Each disc has a hole in the centre and could be placed on any peg. At the beginning all the discs are on one peg, say 1, and if disc X is above disc Y then disc X has to be smaller than disc Y. The object is to get all the discs, in the same order, onto another peg, say C, using peg B as an intermediary. But each move must observe the restriction that no disc may be put on a smaller. Figures 6.2 and 6.3 illustrate the problem with just five discs.

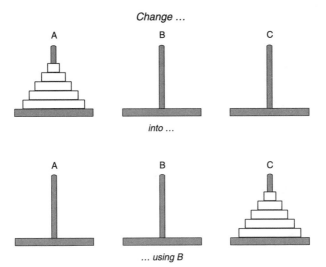

Figure 6.2 The Towers of Hanoi problem.

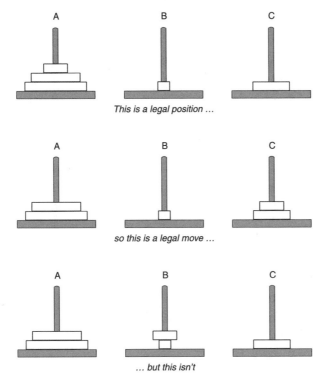

Figure 6.3 Legal and illegal moves.

The recursive solution

The solution is an algorithm that will achieve this. If we could move 63 discs from A to B, then move the biggest disc from A to C, then move the 63 discs again from B to C we will have done it.

Suppose that Move_Tower(n, Source, Via, Destination) moves the top n discs from peg Source to peg Destination, using peg Via as an intermediary, following the rules. Move_Disc(Source, Destination) moves the top disc from Source onto Destination. Then we can solve the problem, for our more modest five discs, as shown in Figure 6.4. Of course then we have to solve the problem of Move_Tower(4, A, C, B), etc. but that can be similarly, but more simply, solved, until we get to a simplest case. Here is the pseudo-code for Move_Tower.

```
Move_Tower(n, Source, Via, Destination)
   IF n > 0
     Move_Tower(n - 1, Source, Destination, Via)
     Move_Disc(Source, Destination)
     Move_Tower(n - 1, Via, Source, Destination)
```

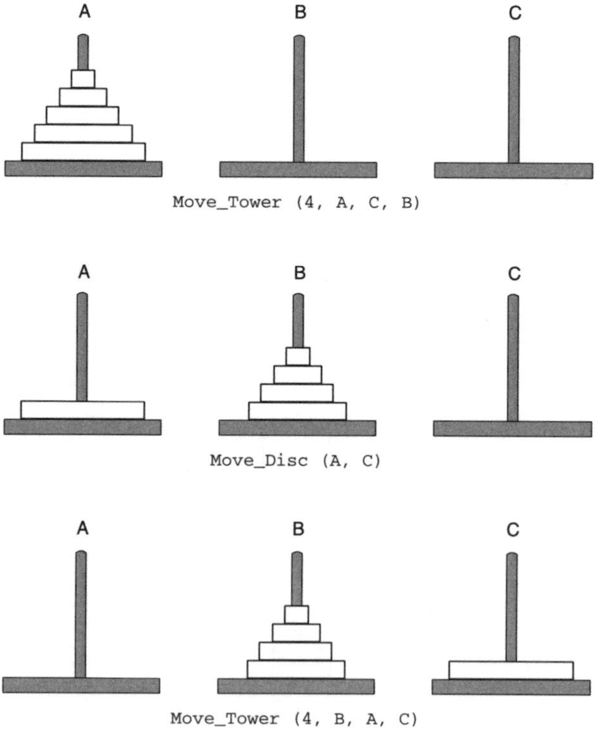

Move_Tower (4, A, C, B)

Move_Disc (A, C)

Move_Tower (4, B, A, C)

Figure 6.4 Solving the Towers of Hanoi.

Move_Tower is clearly a recursive algorithm. When n > 0, there is a call to the 'simpler' case, with n - 1 discs. When n = 0 we have the simplest case. In this case we do nothing.

Move_Tower can be implemented directly as the following C++ procedure, where

```
// PRE   TRUE
// POST Solution to Hanoi problem shown on screen with moves
//    and peg states
void
Move_Tower_R(int NumDiscs, Peg_T From, Peg_T Via, Peg_T To) {
  if (NumDiscs > 0) {
    Move_Tower_R(NumDiscs - 1, From, To, Via);
    Move_Disc(NumDiscs, From, To);
    Move_Tower_R(NumDiscs - 1, Via, From, To);
  }
}
```

Note that we have included the parameter NumDiscs in the call to Move_Disc. At any call to Move_Tower_R(r, _, _, _), we are moving the top r - 1 discs, to get at the one underneath. Since these will always be the first r discs in ascending order of size, the one moved in Move_Disc is the rth in ascending order of size.

Move_Tower_R is implemented in ch6\examples\hanoi\s_hanoi.cpp under the option (s)olve Hanoi. Running this, where we have set up the system with four discs, gives the following result. I have added the indentation afterwards to show the structure.

```
Moving disc 1 from peg A to peg B
  Moving disc 2 from peg A to peg C
Moving disc 1 from peg B to peg C
    Moving disc 3 from peg A to peg B
Moving disc 1 from peg C to peg A
  Moving disc 2 from peg C to peg B
Moving disc 1 from peg A to peg B
      Moving disc 4 from peg A to peg C
Moving disc 1 from peg B to peg C
  Moving disc 2 from peg B to peg A
Moving disc 1 from peg C to peg A
    Moving disc 3 from peg B to peg C
Moving disc 1 from peg A to peg B
  Moving disc 2 from peg A to peg C
Moving disc 1 from peg B to peg C
```

You might find it useful to follow this with a stack of four coins of different sizes to get a feel for the problem and its solution. Is there any danger of the recursion overflowing the stack? A lot of recursive calls are made – $2^{NumDiscs - 1}$ to be exact. But the recursion never goes deeper than NumDiscs, then comes up and goes back down again.

Exercise

1   Draw a diagram showing the recursion. Here is the start.

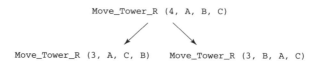

Move_Tower_R (4, A, B, C)

Move_Tower_R (3, A, C, B)   Move_Tower_R (3, B, A, C)

The iterative solution

Now we have the recursive solution coded up and can look at some sample runs, we can begin to think about the iterative solution. We see that the smallest disc, number 1, is chosen for alternate moves, 2 is chosen every 4 moves, 3 every 8 moves and so on. The total number of moves is 1 for 1 disc, 3 for 2 discs, 7 for 3 discs, 15 for 4 discs and, in general, $2^n - 1$ for n discs. We can prove this formula by *induction*, which is a method of proof intimately connected to recursion. We can also use induction to prove that 1 is chosen for alternate moves. Neither proof is given here.

So, having derived a solution by recursion, we have been able to see patterns in the step-by-step solution. Induction then shows that these patterns are real and not a coincidence. From this we can derive an iterative solution.

If 1 moves on alternate moves, what happens on the moves in between? Well, if we have just moved 1, then we do not want to move it for the next move. That means that one of the top discs on the other two pegs must be moved. Since we cannot move either onto disc 1, the smallest, then the move must be from one to the other. Clearly the move is to find the smaller of the top discs on the other two pegs and move it to the other. There is a small variation, which is that one of the other pegs may be empty, in which case we just choose the disk on top of the non-empty other peg to move. What happens if both other pegs are empty? This means that we have finished, so we need to stop. In order to do this we can use the $2^n - 1$ formula. Or we can test for the first two stacks being empty.

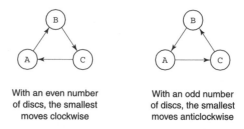

With an even number   With an odd number
of discs, the smallest   of discs, the smallest
moves clockwise   moves anticlockwise

Figure 6.5 The direction of the smallest disc.

One final point is that the direction taken by 1 is clockwise if n is even and anticlockwise when n is odd, as shown in Figure 6.5.

Here is the pseudo-code for an iterative solution. Hanoi is an, as yet, undefined structure representing the state of the pegs.

```
It_Hanoi(NumDiscs, Hanoi)
1   Initialise NumMoves, Direction
2   FOR Index = 1 TO NumMoves
3   IF Index is odd
4     Move disk 1 in Direction
5   ELSE
6     Move next smallest disk

1.1   SET NumMoves TO 2^NumDiscs - 1
1.2   IF NumDiscs is even
1.3     SET Direction TO ClockWise
1.4   ELSE
1.5     SET Direction TO AntiClockWise
1.6   SET CurrPeg TO A

4.1   SET From TO CurrPeg
4.2   SET To TO next peg from CurrPeg in Direction
4.3   Move(From, To, Hanoi)
4.4   SET CurrPeg TO To

6.1   SET Peg1 TO next peg from CurrPeg in Direction
6.2   SET Peg2 TO next peg from Peg1 in Direction
6.3   IF Peg1 is empty
6.4     SET From = Peg2
6.5     SET To TO Peg1
6.6   ELSE
6.7     IF Peg2 is empty
6.8       SET From TO Peg1
6.9       SET To TO Peg2
6.10   ELSE
6.11     IF top disc of Peg1 > top disc of Peg2
6.12       SET From TO Peg2
6.13       SET To TO Peg1
6.14     ELSE
6.15       SET From TO Peg1
6.16       SET To TO Peg2
6.17   Move(From, To, Hanoi)
```

Note that there are two operations to perform on the structure Hanoi. In line with practice so far we shall now define an ADT Hanoi_T. Informally the purpose of a variable of Hanoi_T is to keep tabs on the moves and states of the pegs. Lines 4.3, 6.3, 6.7, 6.11 and 6.17 indicate some operations that will be required. We shall also need to be able to set it up with n discs on peg A. This gives us the following operation specifications:

```
// PRE   Peg1 and Peg2 of Hanoi not empty
// POST IF disc on Peg1 bigger than that on Peg2
//         RETURNS TRUE
//         ELSE
//         RETURNS FALSE
BOOLEAN
Q_BiggerDisc(Peg_T Peg1, Peg_T Peg2, Hanoi_T Hanoi);

// PRE   TRUE
// POST IF Peg of Hanoi is empty
//         RETURNS TRUE
//         ELSE
//         RETURNS FALSE
BOOLEAN
Q_EmptyPeg(Peg_T Peg, Hanoi_T Hanoi);

// PRE   TRUE
// POST Top disc moved from FromPeg to ToPeg
//       AND message written to screen
//       0 ==> A, 1 ==> B, 2 ==> C for pegs
void
Move_Disc(Peg_T FromPeg, Peg_T ToPeg, Hanoi_T Hanoi);
```

To start off we need to set the start state.

```
// PRE   TRUE
// POST Hanoi with NumDiscs set up as problem
void
Reset_Hanoi(Hanoi_T Hanoi, int NumDiscs);
```

In a program run we need to print out the current state. The left is top comment just shows that the pegs are printed left to right, rather than top to bottom.

```
// PRE   TRUE
// POST Towers of Hanoi printed to screen (left is top)
void
Print_Hanoi(Hanoi_T Hanoi);
```

The pegs are of a type Peg_T. A number of operations may be required internally, usually by Hanoi_T, as well as the Hanoi_T operations that involve Peg_T. In addition we want to move pegs in lines 4.2, 6.1 and 6.2. Direction_T is a very limited ADT. We only need to set or get the value of a variable of this type, which we do using the C++ assignment statement.

```
// PRE   TRUE
// POST RETURNS next peg after peg in direction Direction
Peg_T
Next_Peg(Peg_T Peg, Direction_T Direction);
```

Given these specifications we can now turn our pseudo-code into a C++ procedure.

```
// PRE   Reset(Hanoi, NumDiscs) has been called since
//       last call to Do_Hanoi_R(Hanoi...) or
//       It_Hanoi(Hanoi...)
// POST Solution to Hanoi problem shown on screen
void
It_Hanoi(Hanoi_T Hanoi, int NumDiscs);
```

This can be found in ch6\examples\han_demo, with some extra code to allow you to step through the execution with a 'stop and display' option. Note that this is a rather long procedure and it is not at all clear how it does its stuff unless we have worked through from the tips we got from looking at the printout produced by the recursive solution.

We now consider the actual implementation of Hanoi_T. We can only put discs on top of other discs on a peg, and only remove the top disc. This suggests a stack! Hanoi_T is just three stacks. This time we shall not use opaque types, so all the declarations are in hanoi.h. We could easily have used an opaque Hanoi_T but this would perhaps have obscured the main point.

```
typedef Stack_T Hanoi_T[3];
typedef enum Peg_T {A, B, C};
typedef enum Direction_T {ClockWise, AntiClockWise};
typedef Element_T Disc_T;
```

Because Peg_T is enumerated, it is 'really' an int, and can thus be used for indexing the Hanoi_T array as shown in the Print_Hanoi procedure in hanoi.cpp.

Print_Stack_R will be discussed in Section 6.6.

Char_For_Peg uses casting and the ASCII code to return a character corresponding to a value of an enumerated type. Nothing to do with recursion!

Recursion to iteration: a summary

It is perhaps useful to summarise this long section. The Towers of Hanoi, though an abstract problem, has relevance both because it shows how to use recursion as a problem-solving device and because it is linked to other topics in computer science. Taking the first issue we see that a recursive solution can be derived in a straightforward manner. This solution only takes a few lines of pseudo-code and C++ code. By running it to get the step-by-step trace of the algorithm we notice patterns. The rules suggested by these patterns can be proved by induction. This gives the basis for an iterative solution, which has advantages as a practical piece of code. However, it would have been very much more difficult to find it without the insight offered by the recursive solution. This will often be the case.

6.5.2 Blob breeding

Time for some biology. Consider the following grossly simplified model for the reproduction of a simple asexual being called a *blob*.

(1) Blobs never die.
(2) A reproductively mature blob buds off an offspring every hour.
(3) A blob reaches reproductive maturity exactly two hours after budding off from its parent blob.

A newly budded off blob is placed in an otherwise uninhabited tank of nutrient. How many blobs will there be at the end of the

- first hour,
- second hour,
  :
- nth hour?

A solution by recursive problem solving

Suppose the number of blobs at the end of the nth hour is B(n). Of these there are B(n-1) which were alive at the end of hour n - 1 and live on. As well as that there are those who budded off at the end of hour n. How many of these are there? These must be the offspring of all the blobs alive at the end of hour n - 2. This is because a blob alive at the end of hour n - 2 is two or more hours old and thus reproductively mature, *or* is an hour old and will be reproductively mature after just one more hour – that is at the end of hour n - 1, *or* is newly budded off and will thus become reproductively mature after two hours at the end of the nth hour, producing its first offspring at this point. The first six hours are shown in Table 6.1. The end of hour 0 is just the start of the whole process. Note that each column, except for the start, shows the same sequence displaced by one place which makes sense when you think about it.

Table 6.1 Number of blobs alive for the first six hours.

End of hour	Reproductive	Non-reproductive	Total
0	0	1	1
1	0	1	1
2	1	1	2
3	1	2	3
4	2	3	5
5	3	5	8
6	5	8	13

Hence $B(n) = B(n-1) + B(n-2)$. Also we know $B(0) = 1$ and $B(1) = 1$. This recursively defined sequence of integers is known as the *Fibonacci series* after the thirteenth-century Italian mathematician. He apparently developed it as a model for rabbit numbers. I have used blobs to save problems about litter sizes and rabbit lifetimes. It is an example of biological modelling using *recurrence relations*, where some simple assumptions can lead to a mathematical model. Although a gross oversimplification for rabbits, and probably even blobs, nevertheless such approaches, with more realistic assumptions, can be very successful for modelling quite complex ecologies.

Note that each recursion involves *two* simpler calls, $B(n-1)$ and $B(n-2)$. It is difficult to see how to arrive at an iterative solution without first going through this recursive problem-solving stage. We could go on to code the Fibonacci function fairly straightforwardly. This is in the single-file program ch6\examples\fibo\fibo.cpp. The option is r.

```
// PRE   n >= 0
// POST RETURNS the nth Fibonacci number, n>= 0
int
Fibo_R(int n) {
  if ((n == 0) || (n == 1)) {
    return(1);
  }
  else {
    return(Fibo_R(n - 1) + Fibo_R(n - 2));
  }
}
```

Suppose we want to see just how much work is done in a recursive call. An obvious way is to put in a variable parameter which can return the number of calls made. The following amended version is given by the option c.

```
// PRE   n >= 0
// POST RETURNS the nth Fibonacci number
//       outputs the details of the call being made
//       Count is the number of times that Fibo_R is called
int
FiboCount_R(int n, int &Count) {
  cout << "Calling FiboCount_R("
       << n
       << ", "
       << Count
       << ")\n";
  Count++;
  if ((n == 0) || (n == 1)) {
    return(1);
  }
```

```
    else {
       return(FiboCount_R(n-1, Count)+FiboCount_R(n-2, Count));
    }
}
```

This produces the following interaction, where the user has asked for the fifth Fibonacci number.

```
Please type in a non-negative integer
==> 5
Calling FiboCount_R(5, 0)
Calling FiboCount_R(4, 1)
Calling FiboCount_R(3, 2)
Calling FiboCount_R(2, 3)
Calling FiboCount_R(1, 4)
Calling FiboCount_R(0, 5)
Calling FiboCount_R(1, 6)
Calling FiboCount_R(2, 7)
Calling FiboCount_R(1, 8)
Calling FiboCount_R(0, 9)
Calling FiboCount_R(3, 10)
Calling FiboCount_R(2, 11)
Calling FiboCount_R(1, 12)
Calling FiboCount_R(0, 13)
Calling FiboCount_R(1, 14)
```

```
To evaluate Fibonacci (5) recursively we need to make 15 calls
```

```
Fibonacci(5) is 8
```

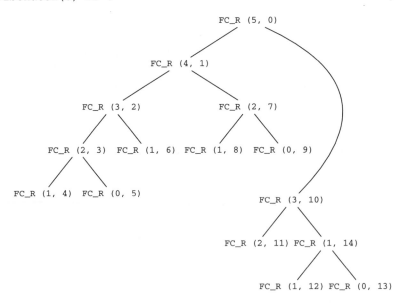

Figure 6.6 The tree of recursive calls in Fibonacci.

This is an example of *tree recursion*, where the process generates an *exponential* number of calls. This is shown in Figure 6.6. Compare this with the diagram for Hanoi you drew in the recursive solution exercise. Once again this is an example of where a recursive program is not the best solution but the process of recursive problem solving can lead us to an iterative solution.

An iterative solution

Suppose you were asked to find the sixth Fibonacci number. Now you know the relationship you would probably write out 1, 1, 2, 3, 5, 8, 13, because once we have the first two numbers each number in the series is just the sum of the two previous ones. This can be coded as follows.

```
// PRE   n >= 0
// POST RETURNS n!
int
I_Fibo(int n) {
  int  Index;
  int  FibMinus2,
       FibMinus1,
       Fib,

  if ((n == 0) || (n == 1)) {
    Fib = 1;
  }
  else {
    FibMinus2 = 1;
    FibMinus1 = 1;
    for(Index = 2; Index <= n; Index++) {
      Fib = FibMinus1 + FibMinus2;
      // Set up previous two values for next time
      FibMinus2 = FibMinus1;
      FibMinus1 = Fib;
    }
  }
  return(Fib);
}
```

6.6 Recursive operations on stacks

In this section we shall see how we can define recursive operations on stacks. The point of this exercise is to develop understanding of recursion used with structures. The operations will be used in the final section.

6.6.1 Recursively printing a Stack_T

In ch5\examples\read_in\read_in.cpp we used a local stack called Temp. Using recursion we do not need this local stack.

The reasoning goes like this. To print an empty stack do nothing. To print a non-empty stack, get the value of the top element, print it, pop the stack, print the popped stack, and then push the top element back on it again because we need to have the original stack restored at the end of execution. Each time the stack gets 'simpler' – because it is popped – and must end up with the simplest case – the empty stack. Here is the code for Print_Stack_R.

```
// PRE   TRUE
// POST Stack printed out in order of recentness
void
Print_Stack_R(Stack_T Stack) {
  Element_T NextEl;

  if (!Q_EmptyStack(Stack)) {
    NextEl = Top(Stack);
    Write_Rec(NextEl);
    cout  << " ";
    Pop(Stack);
    Print_Stack_R(Stack);
    Push(NextEl, Stack);
  }
}
```

You may still be finding recursion a little challenging but I can assure you that once you begin to 'think recursively', this is easier to follow that the iterative version. However, there is a price! Instead of having a local stack we are making the stack holding the activation records do all the work, since it effectively stores the values of successive tops of the stack. Nevertheless, this is a good exercise in getting to think recursively. We shall look at one more example. You are urged to try the exercise that follows that.

6.6.2 Recursively checking for membership of a Stack_T

How can we test if a particular element is in a stack? If the top element is the element we are checking for, then clearly it is a member. If the stack is empty, then clearly it is *not* a member. If neither of these cases holds, then the element is a member of the stack if and only if it is a member of the stack resulting from popping the original stack. Since we popped the original stack, we need to restore it prior to end of execution. Here is the code for Q_Member_R.

```
// PRE   TRUE
// POST IF Element is in Stack
//         RETURNS TRUE
//      ELSE
//         RETURNS FALSE
BOOLEAN
Q_Member_R(Element_T Element, Stack_T Stack) {
  Element_T TopEl;
```

```
    if (Q_EmptyStack(Stack)) {
      return(FALSE);
    }
    else {
      TopEl = Top(Stack);
      if (Element == TopEl) {
        return(TRUE);
      }
      else {
        Pop(Stack);
        if (Q_Member_R(Element, Stack)) {
          Push(TopEl, Stack);
          return(TRUE);
        }
        else {
          Push(TopEl, Stack);
          return(FALSE);
        }
      }
    }
}
```

Exercise

1   In ch6\exercises\recutils, there is a multi-file program
utildemo.cpp which is to demonstrate the recursive utilities already given
above and some you are to correct. The program works with an array of
stacks, since you may need to work with more than one. So each stack is
identified by a number in the range 0 to MaxStacks-1. If you run the
program you will get the usual silly messages. Examination of the code, in
rec_util.cpp, will show some hints. The pre- and post-conditions of each
function and procedure can be found in rec_util.h. Your task is to fix
the bodies in rec_utils.cpp. The solution will be found in
ch6\solutions\recutils.

6.7 The simplified knapsack problem

To conclude this chapter we shall look at a problem that is more related to real-
world problems of resource allocation. Although a simplified version of a more
complex problem, the intent is that you can see how recursive techniques can be
brought to bear. If you look in books on operations research and graph theory,
you will find many algorithms designed to solve real-world problems which are
based on recursion in the same general way as this problem. Study of the

development of the solution to this problem will help you understand those algorithms and how to code them.

6.7.1 The knapsack problem stated

The *knapsack problem* is a classical optimisation problem in operations research and mechanical reasoning. The one below is actually a simplification of the classical problem.

A hiker can carry exactly `Target` kilograms in her knapsack. She has a choice of a number of items of various `Weights`. Is it possible to select exactly `Target` kilograms in weight of items from those available? For example P1, P2, P3 and P4 are four instances of this problem.

```
      Target      Weights of Items
P1    20          {2, 4, 7, 8, 10, 17}
P2    30          {3, 7, 10, 15, 16, 22}
P3    15          {2, 3, 5}
P4    12          {4, 6, 3, 5, 3, 10}
```

With small problems like this, we can see fairly quickly that P1 has a solution with {2, 8, 10}, P2 has no solution and neither does P3. In the case of P3 the total of `Weights` does not even add to `Target`, so clearly no sub-set will do so. P4 has several solutions. Since the items are distinct the two solutions {4, 3, 5} and {4, 5, 3} are different because what we really want is a set of items. For the same reason {6, 3, 3} is a solution because the repeated 3s are for two distinct items. However, that is not a complication we need worry about. All we want to do is find one solution. How can we program a solution to the general problem?

6.7.2 Solving the simplified knapsack problem

The first example has `Target` = 20 and `Weights` = {2, 4, 7, 8, 10, 17}. Call this problem A. Either the 2 at the front is part of a solution or it is not. If we can solve problem B with `Target` = 20 - 2 = 18 and `Weights` = {4, 7, 8, 10, 17} then we have solved problem A and 2 is part of that solution. But if not, then if we can solve problem C with `Target` = 20 and `Weights` = {4, 7, 8, 10, 17} then we have solved problem A, but 2 is *not* part of the solution. If neither B nor C can be solved then neither can A.

This is the recursive step of a recursive solution. Each sub-problem will be a new knapsack problem with a (possibly new) value of `Target` and a new value of `Weights`. This is illustrated in Figure 6.7.

What are the simplest cases? If a call is made with `Target` equal to 0, then the problem is solved. If a call is made with `Target` less than 0 then this is a failure. If a call is made with `Target` > 0 but no weights in the list, then this is a failure.

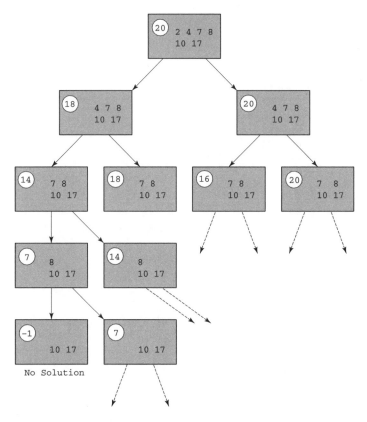

Figure 6.7 A recursive approach to solving the simplified knapsack problem.

Although we have not yet looked at the design of the code, here is the output from the finished program to give a 'feel' for the search for a solution.

```
Input Target ==> 21
Target is 21 Weights are 8 1 6 7 8 9
Target is 13 Weights are 1 6 7 8 9
Target is 12 Weights are 6 7 8 9
Target is 6 Weights are 7 8 9
Target is -1 Weights are 8 9
Target is 6 Weights are 8 9
Target is -2 Weights are 9
Target is 6 Weights are 9
Target is -3 Weights are
Target is 6 Weights are
Target is 12 Weights are 7 8 9
Target is 5 Weights are 8 9
Target is -3 Weights are 9
Target is 5 Weights are 9
```

```
Target is -4 Weights are
Target is 5 Weights are
Target is 12 Weights are 8 9
Target is 4 Weights are 9
Target is -5 Weights are
Target is 4 Weights are
Target is 12 Weights are 9
Target is 3 Weights are
Target is 12 Weights are
Target is 13 Weights are 6 7 8 9
Target is 7 Weights are 7 8 9
Target is 0 Weights are 8 9
Success with weights
8 6 7
leaving weights
1 8 9
```

This leads us to the following pseudo-code.

```
Do_Knap(Target, Weights)
1   IF Target == 0
2     RETURN Success and an empty set of weights
3   IF Target < 0
4     RETURN Failure
5   IF Weights is an empty set
6     RETURN Failure
7   SET NextWeight TO Next member of Weights
         which is removed from Weights
8   SET NextTarget TO Target - NextWeight;
9   SET SolWith TO Do_Knap_R(NextTarget, Weights)
10  IF SolWith = Success and a set of weights SWWeights
11    RETURN Success and
              SWWeights together with NextWeight
12  SET SolWithout TO Do_Knap_R(Target, Weights);
13  IF SolWithout = Success and
              a set of weights SWOWeights
14    RETURN Success and SWOWeights
15          put NextWeight back onto front of Weights
16    RETURN Failure
```

This is coded as Do_Knap in ch6\examples\knapsack\knapdemo.cpp. Here are the type definitions and pre- and post-conditions.

```
typedef Element_T Weight_T;
typedef Stack_T Weights_T;
typedef struct {
  BOOLEAN Q_Success;
  Weights_T Weights;
} KnapResult_T;
```

```
// PRE   TRUE
// POST IF elements of Weights add to Target
//        RETURNS those elements in Weights field
//               with Q_Success field set to TRUE
//        ELSE
//        RETURNS with Q_Success field set to FALSE
KnapResult_T
Do_Knap_R(Weight_T Target, Weights_T Weights);
```

If you look at the body of the code, you will see how once again the `Stack_T`, synonymed as `Weights_T`, has shown itself to be a useful data structure.

Exercises

1   What is the iterative solution to the simplified knapsack problem? If you consider what the tree recursion involves, see Figure 6.7, then you will see that at level n, counting the top node as being at level 1, if we go left, as we look at it, then the first of the remaining weights is included, but if we go right then it is not. So left-left-right-left-right on {3, 6, 2, 7, 8} gives the sub-set {3, 6, 7}. If we assign 1 to left and 0 to right then we get the binary representation 11010 of an integer, here 26. So 26 represents the sub-set {3, 6, 7}. In fact we could generate all possible sub-sets for n weights by going through the numbers from 0 to 2^n-1, work out their binary representation and then pick out the elements of the set corresponding to 1s in the binary representation.

Design and implement an iterative procedure for the simplified knapsack problem that takes a set of weights and works out the weight of every sub-set until it has done so for all of them or finds one that equals the target. In the latter case it should print out the result. Add this procedure to knapdemo.cpp.

2   `Do_Knap_R` has the advantage that it stops searching when a call is made with `Target` less than 0 or a call is made with `Target` > 0 but no weights in the list. This *prunes* the search. Can you amend your solution in (1) to do this?

6.8 Summary

In this chapter we have covered the following:

*   The concept of recursion has been introduced by example and definition.
*   Recursion is implemented using the activation stack, which means that overflow problems may occur with deep recursions.

- Recursion is primarily a problem-solving tool and often shows the way to a recursive solution. The Towers of Hanoi and the Fibonacci series problems both illustrate this.
- Recursion can be used to process data structures, such as the Stack_T, which can be seen as a recursive structure.
- The simplified knapsack problem is an example of recursive problem solving for a simple but non-trivial task.

CHAPTER 7

The binary search tree:
a recursively defined ADT

7.1 Introduction

So far we have looked at three container types, each of which holds a set of elements of another type. They are the array, the Sequence_T and the Stack_T. In the last chapter, we saw how to define recursive functions on the Stack_T. In this chapter we shall look at the idea of a recursive type and then specify an important recursive ADT, the binary tree, or BT_T, and its specialisation, the binary search tree, or BST_T. We shall then see how the BST_T can be straightforwardly implemented by recursive problem solving, in terms of the BT_T.

7.2 Recursive structures

Think again about the Stack_T. It was introduced in the context of the text-editing problem. We could get back the most recently entered Element_T, and we could Pop an Element_T to get another Stack_T. In fact we could say that a Stack_T is

- either the empty Stack_T,
- or an Element_T, the last entered one, and a Stack_T, the Stack_T we get by removing the last entered Element_T.

This is a recursive definition because we either have the simplest case – the empty Stack_T – or we redefine it in terms of an Element_T and a simpler Stack_T – the one we get from Popping the original Stack_T.

In fact our recursive processing of the stack was really based on this idea. Now we can do recursive processing of arrays and Sequence_Ts but they are more iteratively inclined. We are going to move on to *non-linear* structures and types, which are most easily defined recursively, and whose operations are most easily designed and implemented using recursion – in the first instance. As with recursive problem solving generally, we shall see how we can step from a recursive implementation to an iterative implementation.

7.3 The tree family of structures

The simplest non-linear structure is the *tree*. We shall look at reasons for using trees, then give some general definitions concerning trees.

7.3.1 Uses of trees

There are two main types of application for tree ADTs. The first type involves using trees as a natural hierarchical structure. In the second type using tree structures improves efficiency of data retrieval.

Natural hierarchical structures

Many applications involve data having a natural *hierarchical* structure, or *nested* representation, or *one to many* relationship. Here are some examples:

- components of a manufactured product;
- management structure of an organisation;
- planning by decomposing (recursively) tasks into sub-tasks;
- evaluating arithmetic expressions by (recursively) evaluating sub-expressions.

An instance of the last example is as follows.

```
(4 - 2) * 6 - (7 - (3 + 1))
```

This can be represented and then *reduced*, in the process of evaluation, as shown in Figures 7.1 to 7.6.

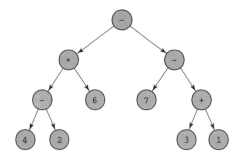

Figure 7.1 An expression tree.

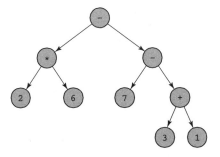

Figure 7.2 First reduction of the tree.

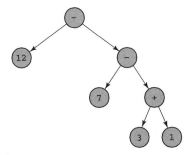

Figure 7.3 Second reduction of the tree.

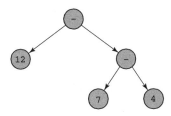

Figure 7.4 Third reduction of the tree.

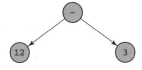

Figure 7.5 Fourth reduction of the tree.

Figure 7.6 Final reduction of the tree.

Improved efficiency of data retrieval in a tree structure

The properties of a tree structure can be used to increase the efficiency of insertion and retrieval of data items, although the relationship between the items may not suggest a tree structure at all. For example, we could put the names of people into a tree structure as shown in Figure 7.7. Some nodes contain two names, others just one. If you study the relationship between names with respect to the nodes they occupy, you should notice that there is a way to find a name, starting from the top. For a large tree the time taken to retrieve a name is very significantly shorter, on average, than if the names were in an unordered linear structure. We shall look at a simpler tree for efficient data retrieval later in this chapter.

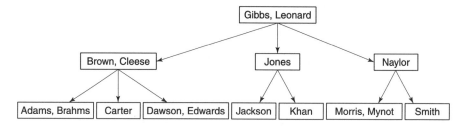

Figure 7.7 A tree of names.

Note that, apart from the ordering, the real relationship between the people with the names is not likely to be modelled using this hierarchical structure. Gibbs may be the telephone receptionist, Khan the managing director, Brown the tea boy and so on. This structure is purely for ease of retrieval of a name.

7.3.2 The general tree: definitions

A *tree* of nodes of type `Element_T` is either

- the *empty tree*;
- or an `Element_T`, the *root*, and a finite set of disjoint non-empty trees of type `Element_T`, which are the *sub-trees*.

The trees in a set are *disjoint* if they do not share any elements. The set could be empty, in which case there are no sub-trees. Figure 7.8 shows an intuitive diagram

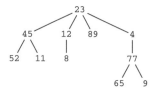

Figure 7.8 A tree 'growing down'.

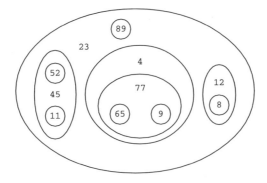

Figure 7.9 A tree as a set of sets of sets...

of a tree, but growing downwards, while Figure 7.9 shows a diagram that fits in more closely with the definition. The Element_T here is just int. In practice, of course, the Element_T will be a student record, an invoice record, or the URL of a page on the World Wide Web.

Each diagram could be constructed from the other. At this point we are working with the most general definition of a tree so the ordering of sub-trees is not important.

(23, (45, (52), (11)), (12, (8)), (89), (4, (77, (65), (9)))) is a further representation of the same tree. Note how the brackets are used to show the structure, doing the work of the lines in Figure 7.8 and the circles making up the set diagrams in Figure 7.9.

If we use the common diagram for a tree as shown in Figure 7.7 – note the *root* is at the top – and Figure 7.8, then any Element_T E2 which is directly connected to and below an Element_T E1 is a *child* of E1, and E1 is the *parent* of E2. If E2 and E3 are children of E1, then E2 and E3 are *siblings*. Each Element_T, except the root, has one and only one parent. If an Element_T has no children it is a *leaf*. If an Element_T is not a leaf then it is *internal*. In Figures 7.8 and 7.9, 23 is the root; 52, 11, 8, 89, 65 and 9 are all leaves; 23, 45, 12, 4 and 77 are internal.

The places in a tree where paths diverge are called nodes. The definition mentioned 'disjoint sub-trees'. As we shall see we can have trees where the same values for Element_Ts appear in more than one place. The important thing is that it is the sets of nodes that are disjoint and if a value appears at more than one node then we consider that there are several Element_Ts, each of the same value and each with its own distinct node. Sometimes the terms 'node' and 'element' may be used interchangeably, where there is no possibility of confusion.

Exercises

1   Draw a tree, in the manner of Figure 7.8, and then draw a corresponding diagram in the manner of Figure 7.9.

2   Draw a tree, in the manner of Figure 7.9, and then draw a corresponding diagram in the manner of Figure 7.8.

3   Write down the bracketed expressions corresponding to the trees you have used in (1) and (2).

7.3.3 The binary tree

The simplest tree[1] is the *binary tree*.

Defining the binary tree

A *binary tree* of nodes of type `Element_T` is either

- the *empty tree*;
- or an `Element_T`, the *root*, and two sub-trees, the *left sub-tree* and the *right sub-tree*.

Although this is not quite a specialisation of the definition of a general tree, the binary tree is a specialisation of the general tree, but it is clearest to make the definition of the binary tree as given. There are always sub-trees but they may be empty. The arithmetic tree in Section 7.3.1 is a binary tree.

Specifying the binary tree ADT: BT_T

What we have defined so far is a structure. We need some operations on it. By analogy with the `Stack_T`, we need an operation to give us a newly created empty tree. The ADT shall be called the `BT_T` (Binary Tree Type).

```
// PRE   TRUE
// POST RETURNS the empty tree
BT_T
Create_Tree();
```

We shall also need an operation to check if a tree is empty.

```
// PRE   TRUE
// POST IF Tree is empty
//          RETURNS TRUE
//       ELSE
//          RETURNS FALSE
BOOLEAN
Q_EmptyTree(BT_T Tree);
```

---

[1] Strictly the simplest non-trivial tree. A sequence of elements would technically be a tree, under the definition of a general tree, but each parent has only one child.

Following this there are several different ways to complete a specification of operations on a BT_T. I am taking what could be called a *functional* approach. Since the definition is about the structure and its components we shall define several functions which return individual components or put components together to return the whole structure. This gives a set of natural primitives which facilitate the definition of higher-level operations on the BT_T. Later we shall see how the practical implementation issues can be brought to bear to transform these higher-level operations into efficient higher-level operations.

An operation to retrieve the root of the tree is required.

```
// PRE   Tree is not empty
// POST RETURNS the record in the root
Element_T
Get_Root(BT_T Tree);
```

We then require operations to give us the left and right sub-trees. Note that the empty tree can be returned.

```
// PRE   TRUE
// POST IF Tree is not empty
//         RETURNS the left sub-tree of Tree
//      ELSE
//         RETURNS the empty tree
BT_T
Get_Left(BT_T Tree);

// PRE   TRUE
// POST IF Tree is not empty
//         RETURNS the right sub-tree of Tree
//      ELSE
//         RETURNS the empty tree
BT_T
Get_Right(BT_T Tree);
```

Finally we need an operation which takes a new root, a new left tree and a new right tree and gives the tree formed from these components.

```
// PRE    TRUE
// POST RETURNS the tree whose head is Root and tail is Tree
BT_T
Make_Tree(BT_T Left, Element_T Element, BT_T Right);
```

In Figure 7.8, the node containing 11 is the root of a tree given by the expression

```
Make_Tree(Create_Tree(), 11, Create_Tree())
```

and the tree, whose root is 12, is given by the expression

```
Make_Tree(Make_Tree(Create_Tree(), 8, Create_Tree()), 12,
Create_Tree())
```

In fact we are not going to have to worry about constructing such expressions explicitly, but it is important to see how they are constructed. Compare them with the corresponding diagrams for trees in both the style of Figure 7.8 and that of Figure 7.9, as well as the bracketed expression. All four representation styles look very different but all represent the same underlying structure.

Note that Make_Tree is a sort of inverse to Get_Root, Get_Left and Get_Right combined. In fact we can write down some axioms, which include this point.

```
Q_EmptyTree(Create_Tree())
NOT Q_EmptyTree(Make_Tree(_, _, _))
Get_Left(Make_Tree(Left, _, _) = Left
Get_Root(Make_Tree(_, Root, _) = Root
Get_Right(Make_Tree(_, _, Right) = Right
```

So we now have primitive operations which allow us to build and manipulate BT_Ts. The issue is what is our policy for building such trees and this will be discussed next. The implementation of BT_Ts is left until the next chapter.

Exercise

1   Figure 7.8 contains a number of trees. Each element shown is the root of a tree. We have already seen the Make_Tree type expression for trees with roots 11 and 12. For each other tree construct
     (a)   the diagram in the style of Figure 7.8
     (b)   the diagram in the style of Figure 7.9
     (c)   the bracketed expression
     (d)   the expression, using Make_Tree etc.

7.4 The binary search tree

Here we are going to look at a specialisation of the binary tree, in the form of the binary search tree.

7.4.1 Defining the binary search tree

Recall that an entity of type BT_T, consisting of elements of type Element_T, was either the empty tree or a single Element_T, the root, with two BT_Ts, the left

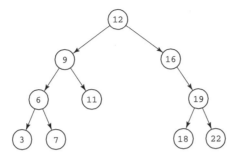

Figure 7.10 A binary tree with the binary search tree property.

sub-tree and the right sub-tree. From this we specified six basic operations on the BT_T.

A *Binary Search Tree*, BST_T, such as that in Figure 7.10, is a BT_T with the following additional features.

(1)   Every Element_T has a key of ordinal type Key_T.
(2)   Get_Left(BST) and Get_Right(BST) are both BST_Ts.
(3)   If BST is a non-empty BST_T, then the keys of all the Element_Ts in Get_Left(BST) are less than that of Get_Root(BST), and all the keys of all the Element_Ts in Get_Right(BST) are greater than that of Get_Root(BST).

Property (1) means that we have some way of ordering the Element_Ts.

Property (2) is recursive because it involves BST_Ts.

Property (3) is the *binary search tree property* (BST property). Note that property (3) implies that there are no duplicate keys. In fact we can easily discuss a variant BST_T which does allow for duplicate keys, and we shall do so later, but it is best to consider this simplest case first.

For now, we will not bother with the details of the Element_T, other than the keys. Furthermore, I shall refer to the nodes by the key they contain, as long as no confusion can ensue. I shall also say things like 'the left sub-tree of the node 9', which is short for 'the left sub-tree of the tree whose root has key 9'.

Exercises

1   Check that the BST property holds for each sub-tree in Figure 7.10.
2   ch7\exercise contains a multi-file implementation of a BST_T demonstrator with main() in treedemo. Compile, link and run it. The program allows you to build up a BST_T and examine it. The elements of the tree, implemented in data.h/.cpp, each contains an integer and a

name string. a will add a single element from the keyboard, while 1 will load a file of elements. d draws a diagram on screen of the current state of the BST_T, showing the key values. This diagram is sideways, with 'left' up and 'right' down. At this stage do not concern yourself with the code or the other options. The object of this exercise is to get a 'feel' for the BST_T.

Using a and d, build up a BST_T of a few elements and view them.

Use the 1 option to load test1.dat. View it, adding more elements with the a option.

7.4.2 Checking to see if an element is present

The BST_T is a specialisation of the BT_T, so it must be possible to implement it using the operations specified in Section 7.3.3 on the BT_T. In order to introduce one of the simplest operations first, let us assume that we have a BST_T already set up. Imagine, for example, that it was the BST_T in Figure 7.10. We want an operation to see if an Element_T with a given Key_T is present or not in the tree.

```
// PRE   TRUE
// POST IF Rec is in BST
//         RETURNS TRUE
//       ELSE
//         RETURNS FALSE
BOOLEAN
Q_BST_Present(Key_T Key, BST_T BST);
```

We can *refine the specification* given the BST property and the following reasoning.

(i)   If BST is empty then clearly Key is not the key of any member of BST, and we want to return FALSE.

(ii) If the root of BST has a key equal to Key, then clearly we want to return TRUE.

(iii) If Key is less than the key value of the root of BST, then, *if* there is an Element_T, with key value Key in BST, this can be so *if and only if* that Element_T is in the left sub-tree of BST, which we check by using Q_BST_Present on Get_Left(BST).

(iv) If Key is more than the key value of the root of BST, then, *if* there is an Element_T, with key value Key in BST, this can be so *if and only if* that Element_T is in the right sub-tree of BST, which we check by using Q_BST_Present on Get_Right(BST).

(i) and (ii) are obvious. (iii) and (iv) follow from the BST property. It is essential that you see how we reason from the definition of a BST_T to the conclusions in

(iii) and (iv). Now imagine that Figure 7.10 is a map of a system of branching paths, and the Key_Ts are numbers prominently displayed at each branch. We use 'branch' to cover the cases where there is only one path and a dead end (e.g. node 16) or two dead ends (e.g. node 7). Further imagine that you do not have this map but are standing at the very first branch with the number 12 in front of you. You want to see if there is a branch with the number 18. How can this be done? You could exhaustively search the system using backtracking but there is a much simpler way of doing it. If 18 is in the system then it must be along the corridor to your left. (Unfortunately your left in the system of paths is my right as we look at the map – this is because our trees are upside down!) You go left and find 16. 18 must be to the left of this (and there is only one path), so you go left and find 19. 18 must be along the right path from this and you go that way and there it is.

Suppose that you had tried to find 13. Then you would have arrived at 16 and found that where the path to 13 would be was just a dead end.

In both cases above, all you had to do was to remember the simple rule about which branch to take, (iii) and (iv) above, and when to stop, (i) and (ii) above. Taking account of the fact mentioned that left and right going through the paths are the other way round from how we view the tree on the page this gives us the refined specification for the post-condition of Q_BST_Present.

```
IF (Q_EmptyTree(BST))
  RETURN(FALSE)
ELSE
  IF (Rec < Get_Root(BST))
    RETURN(Q_BST_Present(Key, Get_Left(BST)))
  ELSE
    IF (Rec > Get_Root(BST))
      RETURN(Q_BST_Present(Key, Get_Right(BST)))
    ELSE
      RETURN(TRUE)
```

where we have the following operation defined in data.h.

```
// PRE   TRUE
// POST RETURNS key value of Rec
Key_T
Get_Key(DataRec_T DataRec);
```

Assuming that we had implemented the operations for BT_T then this operation for BST_T is just one step from code. Here is the code. Note that following my convention I have renamed it Q_BST_Present_R because it is recursive.

```
// PRE   TRUE
// POST IF record with key Key is in BST
//        RETURNS TRUE
//      ELSE
//        RETURNS FALSE
```

```
BOOLEAN
Q_BST_Present_R(Key_T Key, BST_T BST) {
  if (Q_EmptyTree(BST)) {
    return(FALSE);
  }
  else {
    if (Key < Get_Key(Get_Root(BST))) {
      return(Q_BST_Present_R(Key, Get_Left(BST)));
    }
    else {
      if (Key > Get_Key(Get_Root(BST))) {
        return(Q_BST_Present_R(Key, Get_Right(BST)));
      }
      else {
        return(TRUE);
      }
    }
  }
}
```

Q_BST_Present_R is demonstrated with option c. Make sure you have a tree by using l or a.

Exercise

1   Compile and run the executable treedemo from ch7\exercise. Another option g is specified to prompt the user for a key value and get the whole record associated with that key value. It uses function BST_Retrieve_R, specified in BST_Tree.h, which has not been fully implemented in BST_Tree.h. If you try the g option you will get silly messages. Using the same approach as above, consider cases, refine the specification to get a design for BST_Retrieve_R, and then implement and test it.

7.4.3 Inserting an element

Of course, it's not good enough just to assume that we have a BST_T! We need some way of building one, from an empty tree as given by Create_Tree(). For this we need the insertion operation. As a first pass we might have the following specification for an insertion operation.

```
(* PRE NOT Q_BST_Present_R(Rec, BST) *)
(* POST RETURNS BST with Rec inserted *)
PROCEDURE BST_Insert_R(Rec : Element_T; BST : BST_T) : BST_T;
```

Given this, we are at liberty to define BST_Insert in any way we like as long as the pre- and post-conditions are satisfied. Note that we require that the result is a

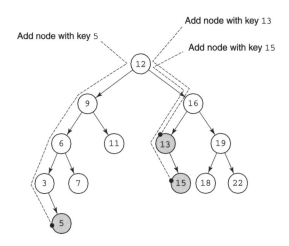

Figure 7.11 Inserting nodes with keys 5, 13 and 15 into a BST.

BST_T – that is, has the BST property. We could define a very complicated process of taking the existing BST_T apart, then putting it back together with the new Element_T to make a new BST_T. However, a little thought indicates a very straightforward way of doing this, as shown in Figure 7.11. A minimal amount of fuss will occur if we attach new nodes to leaves. This being so, where will a new node with key 13 go? Just as with checking for the presence of an Element_T, there is a clear path through to where it should be and we just attach it there. If we now add 5, this too has a clear place to go. When we add 15, this gets attached to the right of 13. See Figure 7.11. What happens is we find the first sub-tree on the path, where the new Element_T should go, and make this into a new BST_T with the new Element_T as the root and only member. Make sure you understand what is going on here. Once you do then we can think about refining the specification towards design.

In terms of our definition of a BST_T, we can reason as follows:

(i)   If BST is empty, then we create the BST_T with both sub-trees empty and whose root is Rec.
(ii) If Rec is less than the root of BST, then we create the BST_T whose
      • left sub-tree is the result of inserting Rec into the left sub-tree of BST;
      • root is the root of BST;
      • right sub-tree is the right sub-tree of BST.
(iii) If Rec is greater than the root of BST, then we create the BST_T whose
      • left sub-tree is the left sub-tree of BST;
      • root is the root of BST;
      • right sub-tree is the result of inserting Rec into the right sub-tree of BST.

The refined specification for the post-condition of BST_Insert is

```
IF Q_EmptyTree(BST)
  RETURN(Make_Tree( Create_Tree(),
                    Rec,
                    Create_Tree()))
ELSE
  IF Get_Key(Rec) < Get_Key(Get_Root(BST))
    RETURN(Make_Tree(
      BST_Insert(Rec, Get_Left(BST)),
      Get_Root(BST),
      Get_Right(BST)))
  ELSE
    RETURN(Make_Tree(
      Get_Left(BST),
      Get_Root(BST),
      BST_Insert(Rec, Get_Right(BST))));
```

Here is the code. As you can see it is but a step from the refined specification. Because the refinement has given us a recursive algorithm, I have renamed it as BST_Insert_R.

```
// PRE   NOT Q_BST_Present_R(Rec, BST)
// POST RETURNS BST with Rec inserted
BST_T
BST_Insert_R(Element_T Rec, BST_T BST) {
  if (Q_EmptyTree(BST)) {
    return(Make_Tree(
            Create_Tree(),
            Rec,
            Create_Tree()));
  }
  else {
    if (Get_Key(Rec) < Get_Key(Get_Root(BST))) {
      return(Make_Tree(
              BST_Insert_R(Rec, Get_Left(BST)),
              Get_Root(BST),
              Get_Right(BST)));
    }
    else {
      return(Make_Tree(
              Get_Left(BST),
              Get_Root(BST),
              BST_Insert_R(Rec, Get_Right(BST))));
    }
  }
}
```

Exercise

1   Write down a sequence of key and name values. The actual values of the
names are not important but you will need something to put in. Draw the
tree of keys that results from inserting these values. Check your answer by
using the a and d options in treedemo.

7.4.4 Deleting an element

If the BST_T is to be used as a practical data structure in, for example, database
systems, then presumably it will be necessary to have a deletion operation. In this
section we shall once again use the method of refinement of a specification to get
the design and implementation of an operation BST_Delete. Here is the basic
specification.

```
// PRE   TRUE
// POST IF (Q_BST_Present(Rec, BST)
//        RETURNS BST with Rec deleted
//      ELSE
//        RETURNS BST
BST_T
BST_Delete(Key_T Key, BST_T BST);
```

We have made the decision that if there is no Element_T with key value Key,
then the original value BST is returned. An alternative approach would have been
that we would not use BST_Delete unless an Element_T with value Key was
present – that is the pre-condition would be Q_BST_Present(Key, BST), and
the post-condition would be simply RETURNS BST with Element_T with key Key
deleted. However, we are taking the first approach and so shall stick to it. Note
also that the pre-conditions of BST_Insert_R mean that there are no duplicate
keys.

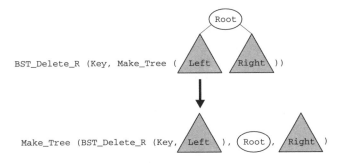

Figure 7.12 Key less than that of root of BST.

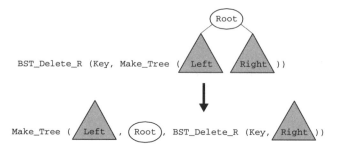

Figure 7.13 Key greater than that of root of BST.

We can reason about what is to be done in seven cases as follows. In the diagrams the triangles are the sub-trees.

(1) If `Key` is less than the key value of the root of `BST` then the node to be deleted, if it is present, must be in the left sub-tree. So the operation returns the tree whose left sub-tree is the result of `BST_Delete(Key, Get_Left(BST))`, whose root is `Get_Root(BST)` and whose right sub-tree is `Get_Right(BST)`. This is shown in Figure 7.12 by the transformation from one tree, the input, into another tree, the output.

(2) If `Key` is greater than the key value of the root of `BST` then the node to be deleted, if it is present, must be in the right sub-tree. So the operation returns the tree whose left sub-tree is `Get_Left(BST)`, whose root is `Get_Root(BST)` and whose right sub-tree is the result of `BST_Delete(-Key, Get_Right(BST). )`. This is shown in Figure 7.13.

We have considered the recursive cases first because they ought, by now, to be easier to consider. It's the 'simplest' case in recursion that is often more challenging to work out! Sooner or later we end up with one of the following four cases:

(3) If `BST` is empty – i.e. `BST = Create_Tree()` – then there is no more to be done so just return `BST` – i.e. `Create_Tree()` – as shown in Figure 7.14.

(4) If `BST` contains just one `Element_T` and that has key value `Key`, then just return the empty tree, since that is the result of deleting the single `Element_T` – as shown in Figure 7.15.

(5) If the root of `BST` has key value `Key`, and the left sub-tree is empty, then return the right sub-tree – as shown in Figure 7.16.

(6) If the root of `BST` has key value `Key`, and the right sub-tree is empty, then return the left sub-tree – as shown in Figure 7.17.

(7) If the root of `BST` has key value `Key`, and neither sub-tree is empty then we have a problem tree – as shown in Figure 7.18. If we just delete the root then we end up with two unconnected trees, as shown in Figure 7.19.

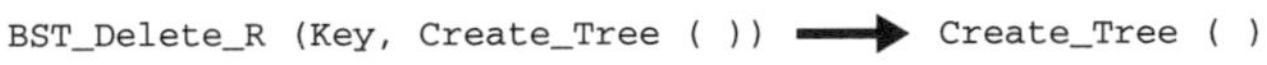

BST_Delete_R (Key, Create_Tree ( ))
Create_Tree ( )

Figure 7.14 `BST` is empty.

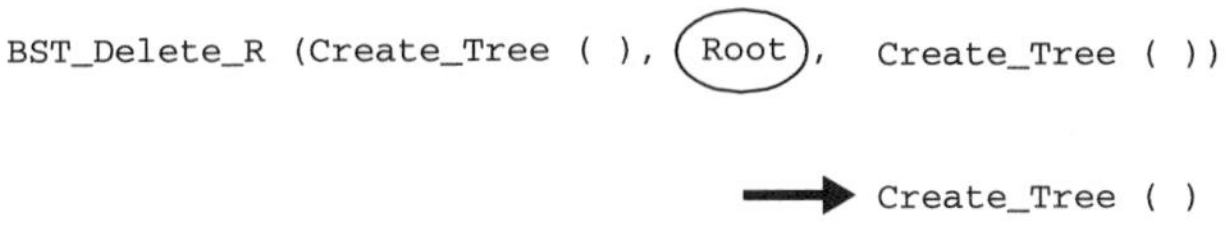

BST_Delete_R (Create_Tree ( ), Root, Create_Tree ( ))
Create_Tree ( )

Figure 7.15 `BST` contains just one `Element_T` with key value `Key`.

BST_Delete_R (Create_Tree ( ), Root, Right)
Right

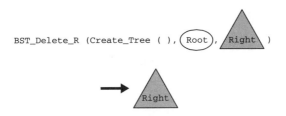

Figure 7.16 Root `Element_T` of `BST` has key value `Key` and left sub-tree is empty.

BST_Delete_R (Left , Root, Create_Tree ( ))
Left

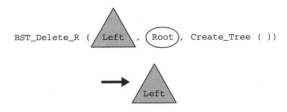

Figure 7.17 Root `Element_T` of `BST` has key value `Key` and right sub-tree is empty.

Root
BST_Delete_R (Key, Make_Tree (Left Right))
?

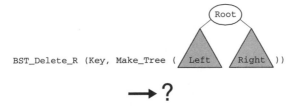

Figure 7.18 Root `Element_T` of `BST` has key value `Key` and neither sub-tree is empty.

!
Left
Right

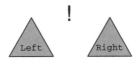

Figure 7.19 A bad solution to the case where the root `Element_T` of `BST` has key value `Key` and neither sub-tree is empty.

Think carefully what we want to achieve. We want all the Element_Ts of the BST_T, except the root, in the returned value, and, because a BST_T is returned, then we want the binary search tree to hold. So we have to restructure the remaining Element_Ts into a BST_T. There are many ways of doing this, but it makes sense to go for one which has minimal restructuring. What we need is an Element_T that can replace the root to 'hold' the two sub-trees together. This must be an Element_T

(a) whose key value is greater than all those in the left sub-tree of the returned BST_T
(b) whose key value is less than all those in the right sub-tree of the returned BST_T
(c) which is one of the Element_Ts in the left sub-tree or the right sub-tree of the original BST_T, since we cannot introduce new Element_Ts.

Suppose such an Element_T were to be *removed* from the left sub-tree to be *used as the new root*, satisfying condition (c). Which, if any, could it be? For clarity we shall use an example as shown in Figure 7.20. Condition (a), above, can only be satisfied if we use 21, which is the biggest key in the left sub-tree. It is also the *rightmost* key in the left sub-tree; that is, if we start with the root of the left sub-tree and keep going right that is where we end. Note that condition (b) must also be satisfied by taking 21, since all keys in the left sub-tree are less than those in the right sub-tree. So how can we reconstruct the tree without the Element_T of key value 24, the root, and 21 as the new root? Note that if we wanted to delete the Element_T with key value 21 from the left sub-tree, then this is necessarily one of the simpler cases above. The rightmost has no right

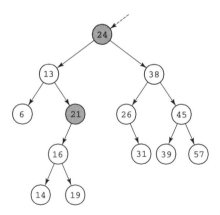

Figure 7.20 The node to be deleted has key 24 and is the root of a sub-tree with non-empty left and right sub-trees. The biggest node in the left sub-tree is the rightmost, that with key 21.

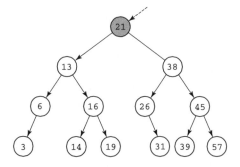

Figure 7.21 The node with key 21 replaces the node with key 24, maintaining the BST property, but it must also be deleted from the left sub-tree, which is easy because it has only a left sub-tree itself.

sub-tree. It may or may not have a left sub-tree. Here it does. The algorithm is as follows.

Set NewRoot to the rightmost Element_T of Get_Left(BST). Return the tree whose left sub-tree is the result of BST_Delete(Get_Key(NewRoot), Left(BST)), whose root is NewRoot and whose right sub-tree is Get_Right(BST).

This is shown in Figures 7.20 and 7.21. This gives the following refinement for BST_Delete. Note that condition (4), above, is just a special case of both conditions (5) and (6).

```
IF Q_EmptyTree(BST) THEN
   RETURN(BST)
IF Key < Get_Key(Get_Root(BST)) THEN
   RETURN(Make_Tree(
           BST_Delete_R(Key, Get_Left(BST)),
           Get_Root(BST),
           Get_Right(BST)))
IF Key > Get_Key(Get_Root(BST)) THEN
   RETURN(Make_Tree(
           Get_Left(BST),
           Get_Root(BST),
           BST_Delete_R(Key, Get_Right(BST))))
IF Q_Leaf(BST) THEN
   RETURN(Create_Tree())
IF Q_EmptyTree(Get_Left(BST)) THEN
   RETURN(Get_Right(BST))
IF Q_EmptyTree(Get_Right(BST)) THEN
   RETURN(Get_Left(BST))
SET NewRoot TO Get_RightMost(Get_Left(BST))
RETURN(Make_Tree( BST_Delete_R( Get_Key(NewRoot),
                   Get_Left(BST)),
                   NewRoot,
                   Get_Right(BST)))
```

Exercises

1   From ch7\solution compile and run treedemo.exe. (Do not look at the source code! This is a further exercise!) Build a small tree with about six or seven elements so that the d option can show them all. Copy the tree to paper, remembering that 'top' is 'left'. Now draw a sequence of diagrams to show what would happen if the root were deleted. Check your answer with the d option.

2   Some of BST_Delete_R, the recursive implementation from our recursive refinement, has been implemented. However, some of it, as well as almost all of Get_RightMost has not been implemented.
    (a)   Design and implement Get_RightMost using any of the six primitive operations on BT_T required.
    (b)   Finish off the implementation of BST_Delete_R.

7.5 Search time benefits of a BST_T

We now examine in more detail why a BST_T is a useful data structure. The point is that due to the BST property you can go directly to where a number is, if it is in the system, or go directly to a dead end that tells you it is not in the system. To see why this is useful, consider the series of fully balanced binary trees in Figure 7.22.

If a fully balanced binary tree has n levels, then it contains 2^n-1 nodes, of which 2^{n-1} are leaves. Table 7.1 summarises the figures for the first 10 binary trees.

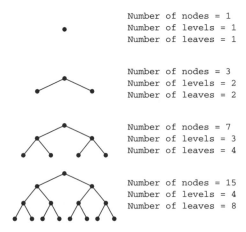

Figure 7.22 The start of the sequence of fully balanced binary trees.

Table 7.1 Summary of figures for the first 10 binary trees.

Number of levels	Number of nodes	Number of leaves	Depth of leaves
1	1	1	0
2	3	2	1
3	7	4	2
4	15	8	3
5	31	16	4
6	63	32	5
7	127	64	6
8	255	128	7
9	511	256	8
10	1023	512	9

Each time a new level is added, the number of nodes is just over doubled, but the depth of the leaves only increases by 1. So, to find a leaf node in a tree of 9 levels will take twice as long as finding a node in a tree of 5 levels, because the depth in the first is 8 and in the second the depth is 4. But the tree of 9 levels has over 16 times as many nodes. If the binary tree is a BST_T, then the search method described before will find the node in time proportional to the depth of the leaves. The point is that although the number of nodes goes up very quickly (exponentially), the search time only increases slowly (linearly).

As we shall see, this is something of an idealisation. BST_Ts in general tend to be 'ragged' at the bottom, rather than fully balanced, but if they are not too straggly, we find that there is a reasonable benefit in this organisation.

One problem that can arise is where the records are entered in key order. In that case we get a linear structure, as shown in Figure 7.23, where the keys 12, 23, 56, 78 and 94 are entered in that order. This is not as unlikely as it may seem. The file that records are loaded from may have already been sorted into order, or the process of allocating keys may just assign them in ascending order. These are not fatal problems as long as the designers and programmers are aware of them. An illustration of how such a problem might arise is given in the next chapter.

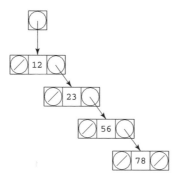

Figure 7.23 A linear tree!

7.6 Summary

Now that you have read this chapter, you should have learned that:

- Non-linear structures, such as trees, are often best defined recursively.
- Tree structures may be useful either because (part of) the real world problem has a naturally occurring tree structure within it or because tree structures can lead to more efficient storage and retrieval of data.
- The binary tree is the simplest non-linear structure, with the ADT BT_T having six primitive operations defined on it.
- Given the BST property, the operations for the binary search tree ADT, BST_T, can be specified, and the BST_T implemented in terms of the BT_T primitives.
- A well-balanced BST_T can provide retrieval time proportional to the logarithm of the number of nodes in the BST_T.
- A 'badly constructed' BST_T can degenerate towards one or more large lists, losing the benefits of tree storage.

CHAPTER 8

Implementing the BT_T *and refining the* BST_T

8.1 Introduction

In the last chapter we looked at a specialised binary tree, the binary search tree. This was implemented in terms of the ADT BT_T, which was specified but not implemented, although the code for the BT_T was present in the sample and exercise programs that you used. In this chapter we shall look at the implementation of BT_T, other higher-level operations, including traversals, that use BT_T, a procedural reimplementation of BST_T and a non-recursive reimplementation of the operations on BST_T. In the next chapter we shall see a means of moving through a BST_T, one node at a time in key order.

8.2 Implementing BT_T

The implementation of the BST_T has assumed that of the BT_T. If the specification of the BT_T had been carried through into design and implementation, then we would be able to implement BST_T. In fact, of course, it has been implemented else none of the examples would work! Nothing has been said about it, in order to emphasis the point that we can design and implement code for an ADT that depends on other ADTs over whose design and implementation we may have no control, though we do know and rely upon the specification. Here then is the implementation of the BT_T.

8.2.1 The data structure

In rec_tree.h we find

```
typedef void  *BT_T;
```

The data structure is implemented as follows. Figure 8.1 is a representation of the physical structure.

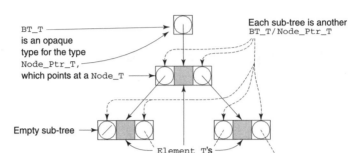

Figure 8.1 The `BT_T` data structure.

```
typedef struct TN_T {
  struct TN_T *Left_Ptr,
              *Right_Ptr;
  Element_T DataRec;
} Node_T, *Node_Ptr_T;
```

Compare this with the code for the `Sequence_T`.

```
TYPE
  Node_Ptr_T = POINTER TO Node_T;

  Node_T = RECORD
    Next_Ptr : Node_Ptr_T;
    Element : Element_T;
  END;

  SeqRec_T = RECORD
    Head,
    Current,
    BeforeCurrent : Node_Ptr_T;
  END;

  SeqRec_Ptr_T = POINTER TO SeqRec_T;

  Sequence_T = SeqRec_Ptr_T;
```

The similarity is that both have nodes and pointers to those nodes, essential to dynamic structures. But `BT_T` has two pointers in each node as opposed to `Sequence_T`'s single pointer. If we think of `Sequence_T` having a head, and a *tail*, which is the rest of the `Sequence_T` after you remove the head, then `BT_T` has a head, or root as we should call it, and two tails, the left and right sub-trees. Also `Sequence_T` has the trio of `Head`, `Current` and `BeforeCurrent`. In this specification of `BT_T` we have no notion of a `Current` element. When we use `BT_T` for the `BST_T` all the operations of insertion, retrieval and deletion are by key value, because the BST_T is a *value*-oriented structure, specifically the values of Key_T. Sequence_T, in contrast, is a *position*-oriented structure, whose operations are dependent on Current.

8.2.2 The implementation of the operations

The six primitive operations on BT_T are implemented on the data structure as follows:

```
// PRE   TRUE
// POST RETURNS the empty tree
BT_T
Create_Tree() {
  return(NULL);
}
```

Create_Tree simply returns a NULL value, as shown in Figure 8.2. This initialises the BT_T on the left-hand side of the calling assignment statement in, for example,

```
NewTree = Create_Tree();
```

```
NewTree = Create_Tree ( );

Create_Tree ( )    ➡    ⊘
```

Figure 8.2 Create_Tree.

```
// PRE   TRUE
// POST IF Tree is empty RETURNS TRUE ELSE RETURNS FALSE
BOOLEAN
Q_EmptyTree(BT_T Tree) {
  return(Tree == NULL);
}
```

Q_EmptyTree just checks to see if Tree has a NULL value, as shown in Figure 8.3.

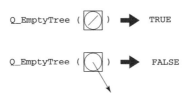

Figure 8.3 Q_EmptyTree.

```
// PRE  Tree is not empty
// POST RETURNS the root record
Element_T
Get_Root(BT_T Tree) {
  Node_Ptr_T Node_Ptr;

  Node_Ptr = (Node_Ptr_T) Tree;
  return(Node_Ptr->Element);
}
```

Get_Root returns a copy of the Element_T in the node, as shown in Figure 8.4. Because BT_T is an opaque type declared with a void pointer, the cast is the first statement. This also applies to the next two operations, Get_Left and Get_Right.

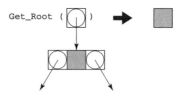

Figure 8.4 Get_Root.

```
// PRE  TRUE
// POST IF Tree is not empty
//        RETURNS the left sub-tree of Tree
//      ELSE
//        RETURNS the empty tree
BT_T
Get_Left(BT_T Tree) {
  Node_Ptr_T Node_Ptr;

  Node_Ptr = (Node_Ptr_T) Tree;
  if (Node_Ptr == NULL) {
    return(NULL);
  }
  else {
    return((void *) Node_Ptr->Left_Ptr);
  }
}
```

Get_Left returns the left pointer in the node referenced by Tree, as shown in Figure 8.5.

```
// PRE  TRUE
// POST IF Tree is not empty
//        RETURNS the right sub-tree of Tree
//      ELSE
//        RETURNS the empty tree
```

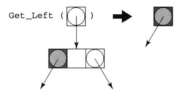

Figure 8.5 Get_Left.

```
BT_T
Get_Right(BT_T Tree) {
  Node_Ptr_T Node_Ptr;

  Node_Ptr = (Node_Ptr_T) Tree;

  if (Node_Ptr == NULL) {
    return(NULL);
  }
  else {
    return((void *) Node_Ptr->Right_Ptr);
  }
}
```

Correspondingly, Get_Right returns the right pointer in the node referenced by Tree, as shown in Figure 8.6.

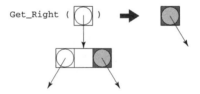

Figure 8.6 Get_Right.

```
// PRE   TRUE
// POST  RETURNS the tree whose root is Root,
//       left sub-tree is Left,
//       right sub-tree is Right
BT_T
Make_Tree(BT_T Left, Element_T Element, BT_T Right) {

  Node_Ptr_T NewTree;

  NewTree = new Node_T;
  NumberAllocated++;
  NewTree->Element = Element;
  NewTree->Left_Ptr = (Node_Ptr_T) Left;
  NewTree->Right_Ptr = (Node_Ptr_T) Right;
  return((void *) NewTree);
}
```

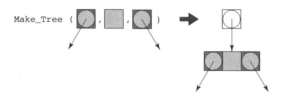

Figure 8.7 Make_Tree.

Make_Tree creates a new node, referenced by NewTree, with NEW. It then puts the argument left and right sub-trees, which are pointers since they are BT_Ts, into the new node by assigning the left and right pointers of the new node to the argument sub-trees. The Element_T to be the root of the new tree is put into the new node. Finally the pointer to the new node, NewTree, is returned as the resultant BT_T. See Figure 8.7.

BT_T has been thought of in an essentially recursive way, though none of the primitives is implemented recursively. It is the operations that use them that can be recursive, as we shall see.

8.3 Higher-level functions and procedures

The primitives of BT_T are used by the operations of BST_T. Usually, but not always, these are recursive. Because they use BT_T operations as primitives, they are called *high-level operations* on the BT_T. BST_Insert_R, Q_Present_R and so on are examples of these. Note, however, that they are primitive operations on the BST_T. There are other operations we can design and implement in terms of the primitives of BT_T. These utility operations are all in ch8\examples\ tree1\BST_util.h/.cpp. The main program is treedemo.cpp. There is a sub-menu, option t, for traversal procedures, described next.

8.3.1 In-order traversal

Suppose we want to print out, in key order, all the records in the tree. Since this is a way of describing the *traversal* of the tree, we use the word *in-order*.

```
// PRE   TRUE
// POST Elements of BST are printed in-order
void
InOrder_R(BST_T BST);
```

How can this be done? We have no current element so we cannot traverse the BST_T as we did the Sequence_T, nor is it easy to see just how we would do that. Once again, as with the operations on BST_T, we return to the definition of the BST_T and use some reasoning with recursion.

If I can print out, in key order, all the elements of the left sub-tree, then print out the root, then print out, in key order, all the elements of the right sub-tree, then I have printed out all the elements of the whole tree in key order. Check back to the definition of the BST_T property to convince yourself that this is true. I must also take account of the case where the tree to be printed is empty, in which case nothing is to be done. So we can refine the post-condition part of the specification of InOrder as follows.

```
IF NOT Q_EmptyTree(BST)
   InOrder(Get_Left(BST))
   Write_Rec(Get_Root(BST))
   InOrder(Get_Right(BST))
```

and this just about corresponds to the actual code, renaming InOrder as InOrder_R to show that it is recursive, according to our convention.

```
// PRE   TRUE
// POST Elements of BST are printed in-order
void
InOrder_R(BST_T BST) {
   if (!Q_EmptyTree(BST)) {
     InOrder_R(Get_Left(BST));
     Write_Rec(Get_Root(BST));
     cout << "\n";
     InOrder_R(Get_Right(BST));
   }
}
```

treedemo shows this under the traversal sub-menu. Figure 8.8 shows an in-order traversal. The dotted lines surround the tree and sub-trees at the different

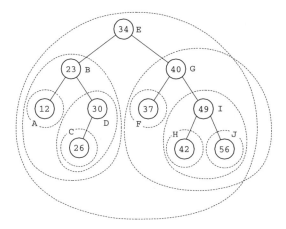

Figure 8.8 In-order traversal of a BST_T. The keys are printed in the order shown by the alphabetical labels, so each label is a print event.

levels. If a node has one or two empty sub-trees – e.g. 30 and 37 – then the traversal of those sub-trees just involves ignoring them, as shown by the one branch if statement.

If we apply in-order traversal to print the BST_T, with root 34, shown in Figure 8.8, first we have to traverse the left sub-tree, whose root is 23. To do that we have to traverse that one's left sub-tree, whose root is 12. To traverse that one we traverse its left sub-tree but this is empty, so the recursion stops in this direction. Now we can print the root, 12, the event A. As the right sub-tree is empty, the recursion stops here. We can now print out the root, 23, of the sub-tree one level up, the event for B. We now have to traverse the right sub-tree, whose root is 30. This involves traversing that one's left sub-tree, whose root is 26. This has an empty left sub-tree, so we can print the root 26, giving event C. The right sub-tree is empty, so we can go up one level and print the root 30 of the sub-tree at that level, giving event D. Having now traversed the whole left sub-tree of the original BST_T, we can go on to print its root 34, event E. Then...

Phew! As you can see, talking through a recursive process is a lot more tedious and tricky than just stating the recursion. It is useful to unravel recursion 'by hand' a few times to convince yourself it works, but in practice you must learn to think recursively.

The traversal involves an operation at each node. Here it has been printing out the record, but traversal can involve any sort of processing at the node. We shall stick with the printing example for now but introduce others later.

Exercises

1   Complete the account of the in-order traversal above in your own words.
2   On paper, construct a small BST_T with between six and 10 members and apply in-order traversal. Use the a and then t/i option in treedemo to check your results. There is a more obvious check of course!

8.3.2 Post-order traversal

What in-order traversal does is

(1) Traverse the left sub-tree.
(2) Process the root – e.g. print it out.
(3) Traverse the right sub-tree.

Although we have been traversing a BST_T, with InOrder_R, traversal is a general operation on a BT_T. We can define other traversals. *Post-order* traversal

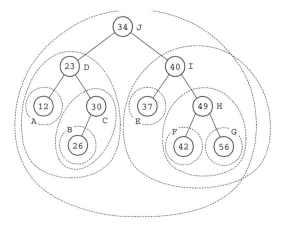

Figure 8.9 Post-order traversal of a BST_T.

(1) Traverses the left sub-tree.
(2) Traverses the right sub-tree.
(3) Processes the root – e.g. prints it out.

Figure 8.9 shows the order of processing events on a post-order traversal. Here is the code for post-order traversal, with printing as the process (Write_Rec) again:

```
void
PostOrder_R(BST_T BST) {
  if (!Q_EmptyTree(BST)) {
    PostOrder_R(Get_Left(BST));
    PostOrder_R(Get_Right(BST));
    Write_Rec(Get_Root(BST));
    cout << "\n";
  }
}
```

Post-order traversal does not immediately seem to produce any useful result. However, it has its application, as Exercise (5) at the end of Section 8.3 shows.

Exercises

1   Write the account of the post-order traversal above in your own words.
2   On paper, construct a small BST_T with between six and 10 members and apply post-order traversal. Use the a and then t/o option in treedemo to check your results.

8.3.3 Pre-order traversal

Not surprisingly, pre-order traversal has the following form:

(1) Processes the root – e.g. prints it out.
(2) Traverses the left sub-tree.
(3) Traverses the right sub-tree.

Here is the code.

```
void
PreOrder_R(BST_T BST) {
  if (!Q_EmptyTree(BST)) {
    Write_Rec(Get_Root(BST));
    cout << "\n";
    PreOrder_R(Get_Left(BST));
    PreOrder_R(Get_Right(BST));
  }
}
```

Exercises

1   Apply pre-order traversal to the tree used in Figures 8.8 and 8.9. Write the account of the pre-order traversal in your own words.
2   On paper, construct a small BST_T with between six and 10 members and apply pre-order traversal. Use the a and then t/e option in treedemo to check your results.

8.3.4 Selective traversal

We often want to deal selectively with records in a file. If a particular condition is true of a record, or perhaps just its key, only then do we want to apply some procedure, such as printing, to it. For example, suppose that we wanted to print out the records of all the people whose names lie within a certain range, say between Dennett and Kant. This involves a minor modification to the InOrder design, as shown below.

```
// PRE   TRUE
// POST Elements of BST with Name values
//       between Name1 and Name2 are printed in-order
Print_NameRange(BST, Name1, Name2) {
  IF  NOT Q_EmptyTree(BST)
    Print_NameRange(Get_Left(BST), Name1, Name2);
    IF Name1 <= Get_Name(Get_Root(BST)) <= Name2
      Write_Rec(Get_Root(BST));
    Print_NameRange(Get_Right(BST), Name1, Name2);
```

The C++ code is in `bst_util.cpp` under

```
Print_NameRange_R(BST_T BST, char *Name1, char *Name2)
```

Option `t/s` in `treedemo` demonstrates this procedure.

In general, if we want to apply some operations `Op`, to every record that meets a condition `Cond`, then we have the following design:

```
Apply_Operation_Upon_Condition_R(BT_T BT, ...)

  IF NOT Q_Empty(BT)
    Apply_Operation_Upon_Condition_R(Get_Left(BT), ...)
    IF Cond is TRUE for Get_Root(BST)
      Apply Op to Get_Root(BST)
    Apply_Operation_Upon_Condition_R(Get_Right(BT), ...)
```

The dots in the parameter list indicate that there may be parameters used to determine the condition.

8.3.5 Counting the nodes in the tree

A useful operation is that which tells us how many `Element_Ts` are in the `BST_T`.

```
// PRE   TRUE
// POST RETURNS size of BST
int
Size_R(BST_T BST);
```

By now you should be getting used to the idea of applying reasoning to refining the specification, and, since this a `BST_T`, you will need to apply recursive reasoning. If we know how many elements are in the left sub-tree and in the right sub-tree of `BST`, then all we do is add together those two figures and an extra 1, for the root of `BST`, and that's the answer. Again we must take account of the special case where `BST` is empty. The size of an empty `BST` is 0. Here is the refinement of the post-condition.

```
IF Q_EmptyTree(BST)
  RETURN(0)
ELSE
  RETURN(Size(Get_Left(BST)) +
     1 +
     Size(Get_Right(BST)));
```

The C++ code, renamed as `Size_R`, is in `bst_util.cpp`. Option `s` of the main menu of `treedemo` demonstrates this function.

8.3.6 Creating a new tree of selected records

In Section 8.3.4 we saw how to print out records selected by a particular condition. How could we retain the selection in the program for subsequent processing? One way is to store them in another BST_T. Suppose that we have the following specification.

```
// PRE  TRUE
// POST RETURNS tree of elements of BST
//      with Name values between Name1 and Name2
BST_T
Make_NameRangeBST_R(BST, Name1, Name2)
```

We can reason as follows. If BST is empty then just return BST. Otherwise suppose we use Make_NameRangeBST_R to extract all the required records from the left sub-tree of BST and put them in a new BST_T called LeftTree. Similarly all the selected records from the right sub-tree are put in a BST_T called RightTree. What about the root? Either it is one of the selected records or it is not. If it is then we just create a new tree, with left and right sub-trees LeftTree and RightTree respectively and root that of BST. If it is not then we have a problem. However, we have seen this problem before in deleting from the BST_T. If either LeftTree or RightTree is empty then the answer is simple – return the other. Otherwise we get the rightmost element of LeftTree as the new root, and delete its occurrence in LeftTree, before making a new tree. Here is the code for the function.

```
BST_T
Make_NameRangeBST(BST, Name1, Name2)

  IF  NOT Q_EmptyTree(BST)
    LeftTree =
      Make_NameRangeBST(Get_Left(BST),Name1,Name2);
    RightTree =
      Make_NameRangeBST(Get_Right(BST),Name1,Name2);
    IF Name1 <= Get_Name(Get_Root(BST)) <= Name2
      RETURN(Make_Tree(LeftTree, Get_Root(BST), RightTree));
    ELSE
      IF Q_EmptyTree(LeftTree)
        RETURN(RightTree)
    ELSE
      IF Q_EmptyTree(RightTree)
        RETURN(LeftTree);
      ELSE
        Root = Get_RightMost(LeftTree);
        RETURN(Make_Tree(
          BST_Delete_R(Get_Key(Root), LeftTree), Root,
              RightTree));
    ELSE
      // Q_EmptyTree(BST)
      RETURN(BST);
```

Note that we have to make `Get_RightMost` available outside of `BST_Tree.cpp` so its prototype is added to `BST_Tree.h`.

Exercises

1   The following keys are entered into an empty binary search tree:

   34, 12, 5, 45, 39, 7, 46, 8

   (a)   Draw the resulting BST.
   (b)   Show the results of an in-order traversal of the BST.
   (c)   Show the results of a pre-order traversal of the BST.
   (d)   Show the results of a post-order traversal of the BST.

2   If you run `ch8\tree1\examples\treedemo` you will find option u for the sum of keys does not work as it should. In fact the whole of the `Sum_R` function in `bst_util.cpp` needs replacing but no other code must be altered. Design and implement a `Sum_R` function that meets the specification. Be careful of the pre-condition!

3   You will also find that the f option, on the traversal menu (t option from main menu) for reflecting a binary tree does not work. Compile and run the solution code from `ch8\tree1\solution` to see just how this should work. `Reflect_BT_R(BT_T BT)` in `bst_util.cpp` is the function whose code is to be rewritten.

```
// PRE    TRUE
// POST RETURNS tree of elements of BT
//       reflected left for right
BT_T
Reflect_BT_R(BT_T BT)
```

Here is a hint. To reflect a tree we need to swap its left and right sub-trees. But each of these needs to be reflected.

4   (a)   Represent the following expression in binary tree form.

   ((7+12) * 8 - (23 - 4 *5))

   (b)   Show the results of a post-order traversal of the binary tree.
   (c)   Use `eval.exe` from `ch5\examples\lex\guard` to convert the expression to postfix. Comment on your results.

5   `treedemo.exe` allows us to load from file with the l option and save to file with the v option. Run `treedemo.exe` and load `test2.dat`. Use d to see the structure and s to find the size. Now save the database to a new file, say `test3.dat`. Use i to reinitialise the database to empty. Then load `test3.dat`. Use d again to look at the structure. Can you see a problem? Here is part of the code for saving, a procedure called by `Save_Tree_To_File`, in `bst_util.cpp`.

```
// PRE   TRUE
// POST Records in Tree written to OutFile
void
Save_Aux_R(BST_T Tree, ofstream &OutFile) {
  if (!Q_EmptyTree(Tree)) {
    Write_DataRec_To_File(Get_Root(Tree), OutFile);
    Save_Aux_R(Get_Left(Tree), OutFile);
    Save_Aux_R(Get_Right(Tree), OutFile);
  }
}
```

Can you see why the problem arises? What solution can you suggest that will ensure that a reloaded database has exactly the same structure as when it was saved?

6 The option h calls `Find_Depth_R`, in `bst_util.cpp`, which produces a whole load of nonsense. To find how deep a binary tree is, we find the depth of the left and right sub-trees, take the larger of these depths, and add 1 to it. How deep is an empty tree? Design and implement `Find_Depth_R`.

7 More twaddle is produced with option y, which should print out the key with the nth node by key order. The implementation of `Get_NthKey_R`, in `bst_util.cpp`, is the problem. Suppose we are trying to find the 14th node. If there are 27 nodes in the left sub-tree, then clearly it will be the 14th in that tree. If there are only 8 nodes in the left sub-tree, then it must be the $(14 - 8 - 1)$th of the right sub-tree (why?). If there are 13 nodes in the left sub-tree then it must be the root node of the whole tree. Design and implement `Get_NthKey_R`.

8.4 Functional to procedural implementation

Recall the definition of `BST_Insert_R`.

```
BST_T
BST_Insert_R(Element_T Rec, BST_T BST) {
  if (Q_EmptyTree(BST)) {
    return(Make_Tree( Create_Tree(), Rec,
                      Create_Tree()));
  }
  else {
    if (Get_Key(Rec) < Get_Key(Get_Root(BST))) {
      return(Make_Tree(
        BST_Insert_R(Rec, Get_Left(BST)),
                     Get_Root(BST),
                     Get_Right(BST)));
    }
```

```
    else {
      return(Make_Tree( Get_Left(BST),
                        Get_Root(BST),
                        BST_Insert_R(Rec, Get_Right(BST)))));
    }
  }
}
```

The implementation of `Make_Tree` in `ch8\tree1\examples\` is as follows:

```
BT_T
Make_Tree(BT_T Left, Element_T Element, BT_T Right) {
  Node_Ptr_T NewTree;

  NewTree = new Node_T;
  NumberAllocated++;
  NewTree->Element = Element;
  NewTree->Left_Ptr = (Node_Ptr_T) Left;
  NewTree->Right_Ptr = (Node_Ptr_T) Right;
  return((void *) NewTree);
}
```

Note the line `NumberAllocated++;`. This has been put in to keep a tally of the number of nodes allocated.

In `Add_New_Record` in `treedemo.mod` we have the following line:

```
DBase = BST_Insert_R(DataRec, DBase)
```

If you follow the code through you will see that something like that shown in Figures 8.10 and 8.11 is going on. A new tree is created which reuses existing nodes, keyed 12 and 5, but making duplicates of nodes, keyed 8 and 4, and then losing all reference to the original nodes. *Semantically* there are no problems but the implementation wastes memory because every time it recurses down n levels, it creates n new nodes, duplicating existing ones, which then become 'lost' to the system. This is because of the assignment of `DBase` to a function of itself – perfectly legitimately – and the way that `Make_Tree` works. But if this were used for a very updated intensive application, it would soon run out of memory.

We have taken a *functional approach* because we can learn much about how to design and implement a `BST_T` from doing so. Functional languages, such as Haskell or LISP, are based on transforming tree structures in a rather more general manner than above. However, functional languages have an *automatic garbage collector* which can keep tabs on memory allocations no longer required and return them to the system for further use. Java has the same facility. We have no such luxury. A new option n, in `ch8\tree1\examples\treedemo`, shows us what is happening. The following run, with inessential details omitted, shows that

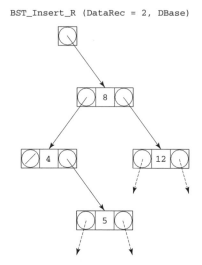

Figure 8.10 The situation prior to inserting 2 into the BST.

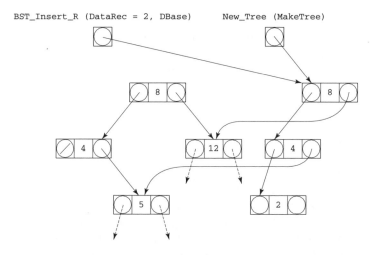

Figure 8.11 The situation after inserting 2 into the BST.

the number of nodes allocated gets to be vastly more than the number needed! It even increases on deletions!

```
Next request [0] ==> n
Number of nodes allocated is 0

Next request [1] ==> l
Please type name of file to load from ==> test1.dat
```

```
. . . . . . . . . . . . . . . . . . . . . . . . . . . . . . . . . . . . . . . .
Next request [2] ==> n
Number of nodes allocated is 68

Next request [3] ==> s
Size is 17

Next request [4] ==> a
Type record in
Number ==> 95
Name ==> kellog

Next request [5] ==> n
Number of nodes allocated is 75

Next request [6] ==> e
Type key of record to be erased ==> 76

Next request [7] ==> n
Number of nodes allocated is 80
```

Instead of implementing a garbage collector, we shall reimplement the code procedurally rather than functionally. What this amounts to is working with the same object each time rather than constructing a new one. Or rather, working though the same object – that is the whole BST_T – until we find the component – that is the BST_T sub-tree – of that object to change.

Figure 8.12 illustrates this. Starting with the root, here DBase, BST_Insert_R calls itself recursively on the left or right sub-tree, as appropriate, until it finds an empty one and then makes this the root of the new single-node sub-tree to contain

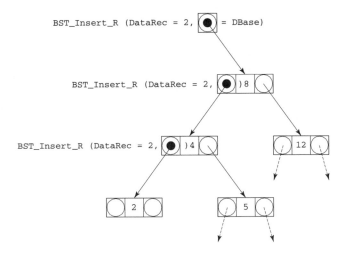

Figure 8.12 Procedurally inserting 2 into the BST.

the new Element_T, here 2. So only one new node gets produced. Here is the code for the new BST_Insert.

```
// PRE   NOT Q_BST_Present_R(Rec, BST)
// POST BST' = BST with Rec inserted
void
BST_Insert_R(Element_T Rec, BST_T &BST) {
  Node_Ptr_T Node_Ptr;
  Node_Ptr_T NewNode_Ptr;

  Node_Ptr = (Node_Ptr_T) BST;
  if (Node_Ptr == NULL) {
    NewNode_Ptr = new Node_T;
    NumberAllocated++;
    NewNode_Ptr->Element = Rec;
    NewNode_Ptr->Left_Ptr = NULL;
    NewNode_Ptr->Right_Ptr = NULL;
    BST = NewNode_Ptr;
  }
  else {
    if (Get_Key(Rec)< Get_Key(Node_Ptr->Element)) {
      BST_Insert_R(Rec, (void*)(Node_Ptr->Left_Ptr));
    }
    else {
      BST_Insert_R(Rec, (void *) Node_Ptr->Right_Ptr);
    }
  }
}
```

In order for this to work BST has to be a variable parameter. In addition the procedure has to have direct access to the underlying data structure, so all the code for BT_T has to be moved up to the BST_Tree.cpp. BST_T is no longer implemented in terms of BT_T. They are now 'on the same level'. Because of this we have the NumberAllocated++; line in BST_Insert_R as well as in Make_Tree. This code is in ch8\tree2\examples with main program treedemo. The code for the primitive operations on BT_T is retained because the operations in bst_util.cpp require it.

Note that the specification, in terms of C++ prototypes, has changed slightly because the insertion and deletion operations have changed from functions to procedures. At a higher level of specification, where we talk about operations rather than functions and procedures, the specification remains constant because the issue of function or procedure can be seen as a question of implementation.

Exercises

1   Reimplement Q_BST_Present_R in the same way, removing all use of the BT_T primitive operations.

2   Reimplement `BST_Retrieve_R` in the same way, removing all use of the
     `BT_T` primitive operations.

3   To reimplement `BST_Delete_R` we need to turn it into a procedure – i.e.
     with a void returned type – as we did with `BST_Insert_R`. If a node is
     actually deleted, then something corresponding to `NumberAllocated++`
     needs to be included somewhere. The work will also entail a small change
     in `Erase_Record` in `treedemo.cpp`. Design and implement the necessary
     changes to `BST_Delete_R` and `Erase_Record`.

8.5 Eliminating recursion

Although the overheads associated with making recursive calls are not as big an
issue as formerly in many applications, we must recognise that this may still be a
factor at times, particularly where many-level recursion is involved. In this
section we are going to look at a non-recursive procedural implementation of the
`BST_T` to show how this can be remedied. In doing so we shall see more advanced
examples of pointer manipulation, including pointers to pointers, which illustrate
some more general issues.

8.5.1 Non-recursive insertion

The `BT_T` is a recursive structure but we can search through it iteratively to find
where a new record must go. We could start with the top level as follows:

```
Set up new node containing data record
Find where new node is to go
Insert new node
```

We might try to locate the place for insertion as follows. As before, the pre-
conditions are `Q_BST_Present_R(Key, BST)`, where `Key` is the key value of the
record to be inserted.

```
SET Node_Ptr TO BST
FOR Node_Ptr NOT NULL
   IF Key of record in node referenced by Node_Ptr > Key
      SET Node_Ptr TO value of Left_Ptr in node referenced
   ELSE
      SET Node_Ptr TO value of Right_Ptr in node referenced
```

However, although the various values that `Node_Ptr` takes do trace the required
path through the tree, the drawback is that as soon as the trace stops `Node_Ptr`
has the value `NULL`. This is the same value as the pointer which we wish to redirect
to point at a new node containing the record to be inserted. But it is a different

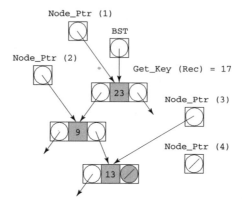

Figure 8.13 A first attempt at non-recursive insertion fails!

pointer! Figure 8.13 shows what happens when we try to find where to put a new record with key 17. There are only four steps for brevity. Node_Ptr (n) shows what Node_Ptr is doing at step n, so there is only one field called Node_Ptr. We can see that the problem is that *finding the value* of the pointer to be redirected is not the same as *being able to redirect it*. It is very much like the difference between a value parameter and a variable parameter in a procedure.

The problem is that we want to stop just before making the final switch of value of Node_Ptr. If we do this we have the reference to the node, one of whose pointers has to be replaced. Using tree language, we have to refer to the prospective *parent* of the node to be inserted. This being so we shall use a pointer called Parent_Ptr, a pointer to the prospective parent.

The usual case, where BST is not empty, is illustrated by Figure 8.14. We have a record with key 17. Whatever else happens we have to create a node for this

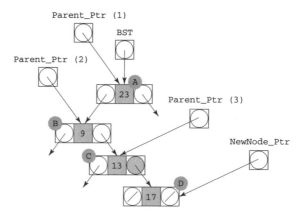

Figure 8.14 Successful non-recursive insertion into a BST_T.

record and set the fields. This is node D, referenced by NewNode_Ptr. Once this is done, we compare key values to see which way to go. We start with Node_Ptr (1) equal to BST. Since 17 is less than 23, it is left that we go. But first we look ahead to see if A, the node referenced by Parent_Ptr, is just another node on the path, or the node where the insertion occurs, by setting the value of the left pointer to that of NewNode_Ptr. Since it has a non-empty left sub-tree, we set the value of Parent_Ptr (2) to reference B, the root node of this sub-tree. This time the comparison, 17 is greater than 9, makes us go right. Once again we look ahead. The right sub-tree of B is not empty. So we switch Parent_Ptr (3) to reference C. 17 is greater than 13, so we look to the right sub-tree of C. This is empty but, where before we rushed on to make Node_Ptr (4) reference a NULL value, here we use the fact that we are referencing the node in which we wish to change a value. Here are the two essential lines as C++ code.

```
if (Parent_Ptr->Right_Ptr == NULL) {
  Parent_Ptr->Right_Ptr = NewNode_Ptr;
```

Because we know the address of the Right_Ptr field of Parent_Ptr, via Parent_Ptr, we can reset it. There is a special case. If BST is empty then we need to set it to NewNode_Ptr. (Note that it is a variable parameter.) If not, then in a loop that moves down through the tree, we use Parent_Ptr to reference the node that *may* need changing and do not move on unless we know that no such change is required. Since we need to use some sort of pointer notation, and because C++ is a good enough notation for this, and also because Figure 8.14 shows better than any pseudo-code what we want our pointers to do, we shall mix pseudo-code and C++. Read this through, looking at Figure 8.14, then examine the actual C++ code in ch8\tree3\examples\BST_Tree.cpp.

```
// PRE  NOT Q_BST_Present(Rec, BST)
// POST BST' is BST with Rec inserted
BST_Insert(Rec, BST)

SET up new node referenced by NewNode_Ptr
IF BST = NULL
  BST = NewNode_Ptr;
ELSE
  SET Parent_Ptr TO BST
  SET Q_OKInsert TO FALSE
  SET Key TO Get_Key(Rec)
  FOR NOT Q_OKInsert
    IF Key < Get_Key(Parent_Ptr->Element)
      IF Parent_Ptr->Left_Ptr = NULL
        SET Parent_Ptr->Left_Ptr TO NewNode_Ptr
        SET Q_OKInsert TO TRUE
      ELSE
        SET Parent_Ptr TO Parent_Ptr->Left_Ptr
```

```
ELSE
  IF Parent_Ptr->Right_Ptr = NULL
     SET Parent_Ptr->Right_Ptr TO NewNode_Ptr
     SET Q_OKInsert TO TRUE
  ELSE
     SET Parent_Ptr TO Parent_Ptr->Right_Ptr
```

Exercises

1   Reimplement Q_BST_Present_R to a non-recursive Q_BST_Present_R.
2   Reimplement BST_Retrieve_R to a non-recursive BST_Retrieve_R.

8.5.2 Non-recursive deletion

We shall approach non-recursive deletion in two steps. First, in BST_Delete, we find the node to be deleted, if any, in such a way that the reference to it, from its parent, can be changed. Of course, with our specification of deletion it may be that there is no node to be deleted and there is nothing to be done. Then we pass the reference to the node to be deleted as a reference parameter to another procedure, BST_Delete_Root, which deletes the root of a BST_T.

Finding the node to be deleted is almost the same as finding where to insert it in the first place, so we can recycle Figure 8.14 as Figure 8.15, where we want to delete the node with key 17. The difference is that we have to check the key of the root of the left or right sub-tree of the node that Parent_Ptr is referencing. If it is what we want then we need to pass over the pointer from the node that

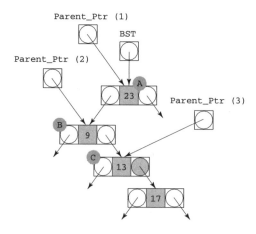

Figure 8.15 Finding the pointer to the node to be deleted.

`Parent_Ptr` is referencing. In this case it will be the greyed out right pointer of the node keyed 13. This will be changed by the second procedure `BST_Delete_Root`.

Below is the pseudo-code for finding the pointer to the node to be deleted, such that it can be referenced.

```
// PRE   TRUE
// POST IF (Q_BST_Present(Key, BST)
//           BST' is BST with record with Key deleted
BST_Delete(Key, BST) {

  IF BST <> NULL
    IF Key = Get_Key(BST->Element))
      BST_Delete_Root(BST)
    ELSE
      SET Q_FoundDelete TO FALSE
      SET Parent_Ptr TO BST
      FOR NOT Q_FoundDelete
        IF Key < Get_Key(Parent_Ptr->Element)
          IF Parent_Ptr->Left_Ptr = NULL)
            SET Q_FoundDelete TO TRUE
          ELSE
            IF Key= Get_Key(Parent_Ptr->Left_Ptr->Element)
              SET Q_FoundDelete TO TRUE;
              BST_Delete_Root(Parent_Ptr->Left_Ptr)
            ELSE
              SET Parent_Ptr TO Parent_Ptr->Left_Ptr;
        ELSE
          IF Parent_Ptr->Right_Ptr = NULL
            SET Q_FoundDelete TO TRUE
          ELSE
            IF Key =
                Get_Key(Parent_Ptr->Right_Ptr->Element)
              SET Q_FoundDelete TO TRUE
              BST_Delete_Root(Parent_Ptr->Right_Ptr)
            ELSE
              Parent_Ptr = Parent_Ptr->Right_Ptr;
```

Note that there are three places where the second procedure `BST_Delete_Root` is called. These are for the cases where

- the node to be deleted is the root of the original `BST_T`;
- the node to be deleted has been identified as that referenced by the left pointer of the node referenced by `Parent_Ptr`;
- the node to be deleted has been identified as that referenced by the right pointer of the node referenced by `Parent_Ptr`.

If the first case does not hold, then the loop is entered, and the usual moving to left and/or right occurs until the pointer referenced by `Parent_Ptr` either points

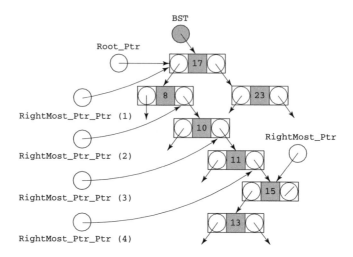

Figure 8.16 Getting a pointer to point at the pointer to the rightmost node.

at the node with the key being sought, or there is a NULL pointer in the next left or right pointer, as appropriate, in the node it points at, indicating that there is nothing to delete.

If BST_Delete calls BST_Delete_Root then it does so with a reference parameter, which is a pointer to the node to be deleted. Usually this will be the left or right pointer of one of the nodes in the original tree, but it could be the pointer to the root. Either way the problem resolves to that of deleting the root node. Recall that the cases are an empty left sub-tree, an empty right sub-tree and neither tree being empty. Leaving the first two cases as relatively straightforward, let us look at the third case. Remember that we find the rightmost record in the left sub-tree as the new root record. In fact we are going to use the rightmost node in the left sub-tree as the new root node. Figure 8.16 shows how we can do the first stage by using a *pointer to a pointer*, called RightMost_Ptr_Ptr. First, it starts out by pointing at the right-hand pointer in the root of the left sub-tree of the root.

Remember that *Some_Ptr means the thing Some_Ptr is pointing at and we can reassign the value of the thing Some_Ptr is pointing at as follows:

```
*Some_Ptr = NewValue;
```

Also recall that &Thing gives us the address of Thing and we can use the address of Thing to change it.

The first piece of pseudo-code derives from the two simple cases and Figure 8.16.

```
// PRE  NOT Q_EmptyTree(BST)
// POST BST' = BST without root node
BST_Delete_Root(BST)
```

```
SET Root_Ptr TO BST
IF BST->Left_Ptr = NULL
  SET BST TO BST->Right_Ptr;
ELSE
  IF BST->Right_Ptr = NULL
    SET BST TO BST->Left_Ptr;
  ELSE
    RightMost_Ptr_Ptr = &(BST->Left_Ptr);
    FOR (*RightMost_Ptr_Ptr)->Right_Ptr <> NULL
      SET RightMost_Ptr_Ptr TO
        &((*RightMost_Ptr_Ptr)->Right_Ptr);
```

Figure 8.17 deals with the next stage, which is rearranging the tree. Since we want the record with key 15 to be the new root record, we may as well make the whole node the new root node. This is done by pointer switching, in the order shown. BST now references the node with key 15.

From Figure 8.17 we can derive the pseudo-code for the second stage.

```
SET RightMost_Ptr TO *RightMost_Ptr_Ptr;
SET *RightMost_Ptr_Ptr TO
    (*RightMost_Ptr_Ptr)->Left_Ptr;
SET RightMost_Ptr->Left_Ptr TO BST->Left_Ptr;
SET RightMost_Ptr->Right_Ptr TO BST->Right_Ptr;
SET BST TO RightMost_Ptr;
delete(Root_Ptr);
```

The actual C++ code in ch8\tree3\examples\BST_Tree.cpp is commented, but it may be worth looking at this after you have had a go at

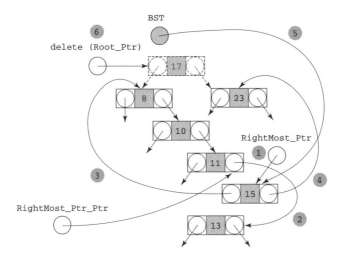

Figure 8.17 Rearranging the tree into a valid BST_T with the node to be deleted left out.

following the moves from the diagrams to the pseudo-code. Note that the diagrams do not consider the simpler cases in finding or deleting the required node.

8.6 Summary

In this chapter we have covered the following:

- The `BT_T`, the underlying structure for the `BST_T`, has been implemented.
- Higher-level operations on the `BT_T`, including traversals, have been implemented in terms of the `BT_T` primitives.
- BST_T has been reimplemented in a procedural rather than functional form.
- Recursion has been eliminated from the `BST_T` in favour of iteration.

CHAPTER 9

Extending the BST_T *and its use*

9.1 Introduction

In this chapter we shall look at a useful extension to the BST_T, and then see an example of how the same physical set of data records can have several different structures put on it.

9.2 Iterative traversal of a BST_T

One problem with the traversal operations as defined in Chapter 8 is that they go 'straight through'. Once the recursion starts, that's it! You cannot just move forward one at a time as we did with the Sequence_T. And at first sight it seems that there is no way that we can say what we mean by Go_To_Next in a non-linear structure like a BT_T or BST_T. A further implementation issue is that recursive traversal requires as many activation records as there are nodes in the tree. These are not all on the activation stack at once but it could be an expensive overhead. In this section we shall see how we can avoid both of these problems.

9.2.1 Iteration

There *is* an idea of the next item in a tree, in fact several ideas. The one I shall use here is the most natural and that is to take the next node to be that which we would encounter in an in-order traversal. Then the first would be the leftmost node of the tree. Let us use the tree in Figure 9.1 as an example.

The operation of moving to the next node we shall call Iterate, since this fits in with object-oriented speak. Clearly we want to go to 9 to start with. But we need to remember to return to 15 and 27 in that order. So if we Push the addresses of – that is pointers to – the nodes 27 and 15, in that order, on a stack, then that will do the trick. When we Iterate we just Top and Pop the pointer to 15 off the stack. But the next Iterate is different, because 15 has a right sub-tree. No problem – we just go to the root of the right sub-tree, which is 20. Then to Iterate again we Top and Pop the pointer to 27 off the stack. Of course there would be a problem if 20 had any sub-trees. In fact this problem will turn up

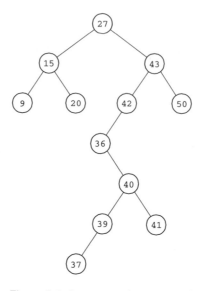

Figure 9.1 A BST_T to be traversed.

when we next Iterate, because just taking the right sub-tree of 27 gives us the tree with root 43 and this is not the next node in the iteration. That honour falls to 36. So we Push 43 and 42 on the stack, and then Iterate to 36, because it has no left sub-tree. The next Iterate takes us to 37, having pushed 40 and 39 on the stack. Figure 9.2 shows the complete iterated traversal. This gives an idea of what is involved but we shall delay looking at the complete algorithm until after specification of the ADT Iterator_T in the next section.

C	Stack	C	Stack	C	Stack
9	15 27	36	42 43	41	42 43
15	27	37	39 40 42 43	42	43
20	27	39	40 42 43	43	
27		40	42 43	50	

Figure 9.2 Iterated traversal in terms of the state of the current element C and the stack Stack, whose top is to the left.

Exercise

1   The iterator demonstration is in ch9\code\examples\iterate. The main program is treedemo. Use l to load itdemo.dat, and then i to get the iterator sub-menu. r starts off the iteration. Use i to iterate one place, p to

print the current record and s to view the keys of the records whose tree nodes have been stacked. Note that the s option is only a demonstration, since the stack is meant to be completely hidden from the iterator user under normal circumstances. Try other .dat files or make up your own. Write down what you think the states of the stack will be, using a similar layout to Figure 9.2. The important thing is to see what the iterator is doing using the stack.

9.2.2 Specifying Iterator_T

We are going to define a new ADT BST_Iterator_T that works with the BST_T. It is implemented as a separate structure but some of its operations necessarily involve a BST_T. Here is its specification.

These two operations deal with the birth and death of the BST_Iterator_T!

```
// PRE   TRUE
// POST Iterator is created
BST_Iterator_T
Create_Iterator();

// PRE Create_Iterator(Iterator) has been called
//    AND since last, if any, call to
//    Destroy_Iterator(Iterator)
// POST Iterator is destroyed
void
Destroy_Iterator(BST_Iterator_T Iterator);
```

This operation sets the iteration to start on a given BST_T. Iterator_T and BST_T work together, but they are separate ADTs and must be 'formally introduced'.

```
// PRE   NOT Q_EmptyTree(BST)
// POST Q_StartOfIteration(Iterator')
void
Start_Iteration(BST_Iterator_T &Iterator, BST_T BST);
```

These three BOOLEAN operations check the state of Iterator.

```
// PRE   TRUE
// POST IF Start_Iteration(Iterator, BST) has been executed
//           correctly for some value BST
//        RETURNS TRUE
//        ELSE
//           RETURNS FALSE
Q_Bound_To_BST(BST_Iterator_T Iterator);
```

```
// PRE   Q_Bound_To_BST(Iterator)
// POST IF iteration at ordinally keyed first node
//          RETURNS TRUE
//       ELSE
//          RETURNS FALSE
BOOLEAN
Q_StartOfIteration(BST_Iterator_T Iterator);

// PRE   Q_Bound_To_BST(Iterator)
// POST IF iteration is at ordinally keyed last node
//          RETURNS TRUE
//       ELSE
//          RETURNS FALSE
BOOLEAN
Q_EndOfIteration(BST_Iterator_T Iterator);
```

This is the basic iteration operation.

```
// PRE   Q_Bound_To_BST(Iterator, BST)
//          for some value BST
//          AND NOT Q_EndOfIteration(Iterator)
// POST NOT Q_Iteration_Reset(Iterator') AND
//          current is next node in iteration
void
Iterate(BST_Iterator_T &Iterator);
```

Here is the basic retrieval operation.

```
// PRE   Q_Bound_To_BST(Iterator, BST)
//       for some value BST
//          RETURNS current record in iteration
Element_T
Get_Current(BST_Iterator_T Iterator);
```

This operation shows how far through the iteration we are.

```
// PRE   Q_Iteration_Started(Iterator)
// POST RETURNS number of current record in iteration
int
Get_CurrentNumber(BST_Iterator_T Iterator);
```

9.2.3 Implementing Iterator_T

Iterator_T is implemented, as an opaque type, in iterator.h/.cpp. The data
structure is coded in iterator.cpp.

```
typedef struct {
  Stack_T Stack;
  SElement_T Current;
```

```
    int CurrentNumber;
    BOOLEAN Q_Bound;
} BST_ItRec_T, *BST_ItRec_Ptr_T;
```

SELement_T is a stack element. This is just a void pointer – see stack.h. In the example we stacked the keys of the nodes. In fact this will not be good enough. Knowing the key is not sufficient to find the left and right sub-trees of the node with that key. What we stack are pointers to nodes of the BST_T. Figure 9.3 shows the situation about halfway through a complete iteration.

The two major operations are Start_Iteration and Iterate. If you follow them then the others are straightforward.

For Start_Iteration, if you look again at the example in Figure 9.1, you will see that we want to go left as far as we can, until we meet 9, stacking the nodes we meet on the way. The node, whose key is 9, becomes the current node. Of course we stack pointers to the nodes. These pointers are, of course, of type BST_T. Here is the pseudo-code.

```
Start_Iteration(Iterator, BST)

    Empty Iterator->Stack
    SET NodeIndex TO BST
    FOR NOT Q_EmptyTree(Get_Left(NodeIndex))
        Push(NodeIndex, ItRec->Stack)
        SET NodeIndex TO Get_Left(NodeIndex)
    ItRec->Current = NodeIndex
    ItRec->CurrentNumber = 1
    ItRec->Q_Bound = TRUE
```

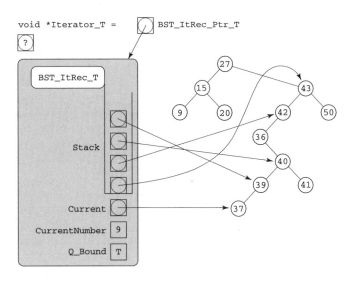

Figure 9.3 An example of an implementation of the ADT Iterator_T.

This is coded with some additions to do with type opacity and maintaining the current number.

How do we Iterate? If the current node has a right sub-tree then clearly the next node is in that direction. If the root node of that right sub-tree has no left sub-tree, as for 20 in Figure 9.1, then that node is the next current node. However, if that root node does have a left sub-tree, as when we are moving on from 36, then we must move left as far as we can down it, stacking nodes as we go. So that is why we move from 36 to 37, stacking 40 and 39, as shown in Figure 9.2.

If the current node has no right sub-tree, then the next current node must be one of those previously stacked. In fact it must be the last one. This is because every time we stack and move left, the stacked node must be greater, in key value, than any of the nodes in the left sub-tree. If we got to the current node by moving left, then the parent node is the last stacked and the next greatest in key value. If we got to the last node by moving right, then the parent node is less in key value and has already been current. If the parent was accessed by moving right, then its parent is less in key value and has already been current. And so on back to a node which was accessed by moving left. Then its parent is the next biggest in key value and the next current.

```
Iterate(Iterator)
  BST_ItRec_Ptr_T ItRec;

  IF Q_EmptyTree(Get_Right(ItRec->Current))
    ItRec->Current = Top(ItRec->Stack)
    Pop(ItRec->Stack)
  ELSE
    ItRec->Current = Get_Right(ItRec->Current)
    FOR NOT Q_EmptyTree(Get_Left(ItRec->Current))
      Push(ItRec->Current, ItRec->Stack)
      ItRec->Current = Get_Left(ItRec->Current)
```

As with Start_Iteration, this is coded with some additions to do with type opacity and maintaining the current number.

9.3 Overlaid structures on one set of data

The use of Stack_T to contain pointers to nodes in a BST_T highlights the fact that we can use one set of physical records – the node records for the BST_T – referenced by two different data structures. In the Iterator_T case this was for structural reasons of accessing the main data structure. This could be used for ordering the data records according to two or more attributes of interest.

9.3.1 The clubs syndicate example

Consider a syndicate of clubs. Applicants may join one or more of the five clubs known as Diogenes, Drones, Runagates, HellFire and Tufty. Records are kept as follows. On joining, the new member's record is stored in a central roll which is ordered by membership number. It is also stored by member name in another roll. On top of this there is a roll for each club listing, ordered by key. This is implemented in ch9\code\examples\overlay\clubs.cpp. Compile and run this. Use l to load clubs.dat. Use t to go into the traversal options. You can list members by number (i), or by name (n). Using option c you can list out members for each of the five clubs.

Here are six operations that we would like to perform on an ADT ClubsDB_T.

```
// PRE   TRUE
// POST user is prompted for record
//      IF record is not in ClubsDB
//         it is added to ClubsDB
//      ELSE
//         appropriate message
void
Add_New_Record(ClubsDB_T &ClubsDB);


// PRE   TRUE
// POST Prints out size of tree
void
Print_Size(BST_T DBase) ;


// PRE   TRUE
// POST User is prompted for filename
//      IF this is a file of Element_Ts
//      these are loaded into DBase
//      except for those already there
//      which are printed with appropriate message
void
Load_Clubs_From_File(ClubsDB_T &ClubsDB);


// PRE   TRUE
// POST Prints out membership of ClubsDB by number
void
Print_Members_ByNumber(ClubsDB_T ClubsDB);


// PRE   TRUE
// POST Prints out membership of ClubsDB by name
void
Print_Members_ByName(ClubsDB_T ClubsDB);


// PRE   TRUE
// POST Prompts user for club
```

```
//      IF club has members
//          Prints out members inorderwise
//      ELSE
//          Message
void
Print_ClubMembership(ClubsDB_T ClubsDB);
```

9.3.2 Multiple BST_Ts

There are other operations to add in the exercises. When it comes to implementation we could have one main data structure – based on the BST_T ADT perhaps – that stores records by number. So Add_New_Record, Print_Size, Load_Clubs_From_File and Print_Members_ByNumber are relatively straightforward. But what about Print_Members_ByName and Print_ClubMembership? For the latter, we could have five more BST_Ts, one for each club. If the nodes of the BST_T contained the actual DataRec_T, then we would duplicate, or worse (a member may belong to all five clubs), these records physically. But we can use the ADT KAPRec_T, thus only duplicating the KAPRec_Ts. So a member of all five clubs would have six little KAPRec_Ts, including the one for the main BST_T, one for each tree, all pointing at a big DataRec_T. Figure 9.4 illustrates this. There are six separate structures overlaying the one set of physical DataRec_Ts.

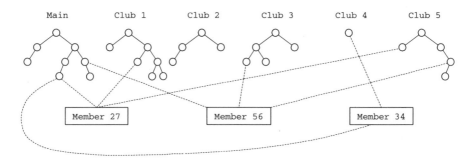

Figure 9.4 Main is the complete membership database and only one data record is held for each member, but several clubs – e.g. Club 3 and Club 5 – may reference the same physical member data record – e.g. 56.

9.3.3 Multiple keys

But this approach does not immediately solve the problem of Print_Members_ByName because we need to sort by name and not number. What we require is something illustrated by the example in Figure 9.5. Two different BST_Ts are sorted by different fields, yet both reference exactly the same set of physical data records.

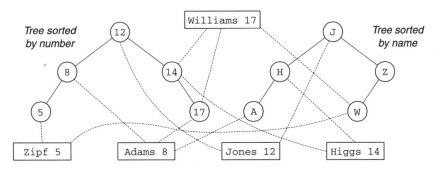

Figure 9.5 Two BST_Ts, the left sorted by number and the right sorted by name,
reference the same set of physical data records.

Somehow we want to sort one BST_T by number and the other by name. This is
not a problem without obvious solutions. The first is to have two BST_Ts, say
NumberBST_T and NameBST_T. Both store KAPRec_Ts as defined below.

```
typedef struct {
  Number_T Number;
  char *Name;
  DataRec_T *Address;
} KAPRec_T;
```

Previously KAPRec_T had only one key, of course, but we want the Number and
Name fields to be keys for the first and second trees respectively. The binary tree
data structures are exactly the same but we need to use different names for the
types as indicated above. The procedure and function *structures* are the same but
we need to give them different names, such as NumberBST_Insert_R. Or rather
this is the case with the sub-set of C++ we are using. The difference is in comparing
keys for insertion, retrieval etc. In the structure of NumberBST_Insert_R
we have

```
Get_KAPRecNumber(KAPRec1) < Get_KAPRecNumber(KAPRec2)
```

and for NameBST_Insert_R we have

```
strcmp( Get_KAPRecName(KAPRec1),
        Get_KAPRecName(KAPRec2)) < 0
```

because we need a different comparison function for strings from that for ints.
  This is not so bad but it involves copying and editing a substantial file.
Furthermore we may wish to use a number of different fields for keys. For
example, an invoice has an invoice number, a customer number, a customer
name, a date and an amount. (A customer may have more than one customer
number perhaps.) It might be handy to have a BST_T for each of these fields, so

that we could search for a particular invoice number, for all the invoices for a particular customer by number or by name, for the invoices between certain dates, or for all invoices over a certain amount. Five slightly different implementations of the BST_T are required.

9.3.4 Passing pointers to functions as parameters

The alternative is to be able somehow to pass across the desired comparison function between two records for the particular key of interest as a parameter. This involves passing a pointer to the function to the insertion procedure. In clubs.cpp, we define the comparison functions on number and name as follows:

```
// PRE   TRUE
// POST IF Rec1 precedes Rec2 by Number field
//        RETURNS TRUE
//        ELSE
//        RETURNS FALSE
BOOLEAN
Q_Number_Precedes(KAPRec_T KAPRec1, KAPRec_T KAPRec2) {
   return( Get_KAPRecNumber(KAPRec1) <
           Get_KAPRecNumber(KAPRec2));
}

// PRE   TRUE
// POST IF Rec1 precedes Rec2 by Name field
//        RETURNS TRUE
//        ELSE
//        RETURNS FALSE
BOOLEAN
Q_Name_Precedes(KAPRec_T KAPRec1, KAPRec_T KAPRec2) {
   return(strcmp( Get_KAPRecName(KAPRec1),
                  Get_KAPRecName(KAPRec2)) < 0);
}
```

We have a new definition for BST_Insert_R.

```
// PRE   NOT Q_BST_Present_R(Rec, BST)
// POST RETURNS BST with Rec inserted by Q_Precedes
void
BST_Insert_R(
     BOOLEAN (* Q_Precedes) (Element_T, Element_T),
     Element_T Rec, BST_T &BST) {
   ................
   if (Q_Precedes(Rec, Parent->Element)) {
     if (Parent->Left_Ptr == NULL) {
   ................
```

Q_Precedes is the formal parameter, and, just like a formal parameter for data, we have to give its type. In addition we have to say that it is a pointer. So the declaration

```
BOOLEAN (* Q_Precedes) (Element_T, Element_T)
```

says 'This parameter is called Q_Precedes and is a pointer to a function that takes two Element_Ts and returns a BOOLEAN'.

Before we look at how we call such a function as the new BST_Insert_R – that is one that takes another procedure or function as an argument, we had better look at the main data structure for the clubs database.

```
typedef  BST_T ClubRolls_T[NumClubs];
typedef  struct {
  BST_T  MainRoll,
         NameRoll;
  ClubRolls_T   ClubRolls;
} ClubsDB_T;
```

The structure is simply seven BST_Ts, one for each of number and name order, and one for each of the five clubs. The structure of the membership record is as given by the following declarations.

```
typedef int Number_T;

typedef struct {
  int Day,
      Month,
      Year;
} Date_T;

typedef enum {Diogenes, Drones, Runagates, HellFire, Tufty,
NoClub} Club_T;

typedef BOOLEAN Clubs_T[NumClubs];
typedef struct {
  Number_T Number;
  char *Name;
  Date_T Date;
  Clubs_T Clubs;
  BOOLEAN Q_OnWaitingList;
} DataRec_T;
```

Note that Clubs_T is just an array of BOOLEANs which will be set to TRUE or FALSE depending on whether the applicant wishes to be a member of that club or not. In data.h/.cpp are the operations on these structures, including

```
// PRE   TRUE
// POST prompts user for applicant record
//      which is read into Rec
void
Read_Rec(DataRec_T &Rec);
```

Here is the piece of code from `Add_New_Record`, in `clubs.cpp`, which sets up a new record in the database, called `ClubsDB` of type `ClubsDB_T`.

```
BST_Insert_R(Q_Number_Precedes, KAPRec,
             ClubsDB.MainRoll);
BST_Insert_R(Q_Name_Precedes, KAPRec,
             ClubsDB.NameRoll);
for (Club = FirstClub; Club <= LastClub; Club++) {
  if(Q_Member_Of_Club(Club, Get_DataRec(KAPRec))) {
      BST_Insert_R(Q_Number_Precedes, KAPRec,
                   ClubsDB.ClubRolls[Club]);
```

We see `Q_Number_Precedes` passed across as the actual parameter. But should it not be a pointer to a function? In C++, just as array names are pointers to the arrays themselves, function names are pointers to the actual function code, so there is no need to have any further level of referencing.

9.4 Some points about non-unique keys in a `BST_T`

If we look at the insertion operation for the standard `BST_T` of Chapter 8 in `ch8\examples\tree3\bst_tree.cpp`, then the line

```
if (Key < Get_Key(Parent->Element)) {
```

shows that elements which have keys that are duplicates of keys in one or more other elements in the tree will be inserted into the right sub-tree. This is shown in Figure 9.6, where the sequence of records with keys 12-9-5-17-7-5-3-5-6-6-5-6-5-5 is inserted. From this and the rule for insertion we can see that to find the first occurrence, if any, of a key we use the usual retrieval algorithm. To find the next one we just apply the algorithm to the right sub-tree, whose root contained the first occurrence of the key. Subsequent retrievals of records with the same key just apply the search algorithm on the right sub-tree, whose root contains the current occurrence of the key. Note that if a record with the ordinally next key k+1 is inserted after one or more occurrences of a key k, then this 'closes off' where subsequent records with key k can go. A list of records with key k develops. In this case, at step i, the insertion of record with key 6 means that, at step j, the next record with key 5 must go to its left and all subsequent records with key 5, and no others, will go that way, forming a list. This shows a

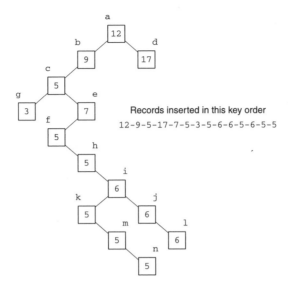

Figure 9.6 Inserting into a BST with non-unique keys and strict inequality to the left, with the letters a to n showing order of insertion.

weakness of using a non-unique key, which is a tendency to 'listiness'. (It also highlights a potential solution, which is to put the lists in their proper place. See Chapter 11 Exercises.)

Exercises

1   There is a Date_T field in DataRec_T. Extend ClubsDB_T so that it also has a BST_T holding records by date order. You will find some useful functions in data.h/.cpp. Add appropriate functionality to clubs.cpp to view the results.

2   The BOOLEAN field Q_OnWaitingList of the DataRec_T can be set to FALSE or TRUE, depending on whether the applicant can join up straight away or has to wait. Set up another BST_T, holding waiting applicants by number. Add appropriate functionality to clubs.cpp to view the results.

3   The operation of Q_BST_Present has been left to operate only on the Number_T field. Amend it to take an extra parameter, which is of course a pointer to a comparison function, and add extra functionality to demonstrate this acting on the names database component of ClubsDB_T. Note that this will show the presence of a particular name but not how many times that name appears.

4   Add iterators to each BST_T and associated procedures to use them. Note that there is an (i)terate options entry in the top menu but no code for it.

5   Consider the problem of deletion or retrieval of records with non-unique keys. We would need to have extra information in the parameters that identified the record uniquely. For example, if we wanted to delete the record for Brown from the NameRoll and we knew that there were several Browns then we would need to pass across the number key so that the operation could work through the Browns, checking until it found that key. We know where to search for the Browns' records. Devise a new delete procedure for the BST_T so that deletion can be done on the non-unique keys, with the unique key being one of the parameters for this procedure.

6   Complete deletion requires removing all KAPRec_Ts from the various BST_Ts *and* physically deleting the original DataRec_T. Design and implement this complete delete operation.

9.5 Summary

In this chapter we have covered the following:

- The concept of single-step iteration through a BT_T has been introduced.
- The ADT Iterator_T has been specified and implemented, based on the Stack_T.
- The Iterator_T is separate from the BT_T or BST_T it iterates over.
- A DataRec_T may be in several BST_Ts, or other container ADTs, at once but only have one physical instance.
- To use several BST_Ts with various keys to overlay structure we can pass functions as parameters.

CHAPTER 10

Searching and sorting

10.1 Introduction

Data structures are what we put data into. At some stage we want to get the data back again, so we have to *search* the structure for it. The example of the binary search tree shows that certain properties can allow us to devise easier and/or quicker algorithms to perform this search. The BST property ensures that the keys of the records are *sorted* in order. In this chapter we shall look at searching and sorting in other structures.

10.2 Defining the problems

This section defines the problems of searching and sorting. We assume that we are searching for and sorting records, each of which has a key. The key may be a single attribute of the record – e.g. student number in a student record – or perhaps a function of the record – e.g. a record may contain a stack of other elements and the key is the size of the stack.

The keys will be of type Key_T. Usually we shall use Key_T as a synonym for integer, but any *ordinal* type will do. An ordinal type is one on which we can define the relations of *strictly less than* – e.g. < in C++ for int – and *equals* – e.g. == in C++ for int. *Strictly greater than* is just *not strictly less than and not equals* but we sometimes have an explicit *strictly greater than* – e.g. in C++ for int x and y, x > y is equivalent to (!(x < y)) && (!(x == y)), which is equivalent to !(x < y || x == y). In the clubs example of Chapter 9, we had Q_Date_Before and Q_Dates_Equal for *strictly less than and equals*.

We need to clarify what we are going to search for or sort in the examples to follow. To concentrate on the algorithms I have simplified things by having the structures hold just integers which are their own keys. Later we shall adapt this to a record type with other fields besides the key field. The point is that once we can search for or sort keys then it is a short and obvious step to search for or sort the records with those keys.

10.2.1 Searching

In some applications the keys will be unique. For example, student record keys should be unique. There can only be at most one student record associated with a given student number. There may of course be none, since not all keys in the range allocated will be used. For example, student numbers often contain seven digits, and, despite appearances, no university has 9,999,999 students! In other applications the key may be non-unique because it is used to identify sets of records. For example, if we search a file of student records by course number, we want to get all the students in that file who are taking a particular course.

If we are doing a search on a unique key, then we may just want a single record corresponding to that key. Or we may require all the records whose keys are less than a certain value. Perhaps we want all the records whose keys lie between two values. A further possibility is that we just want to know whether or not there is such a record but not be concerned with its details. Each of these is a different type of searching operation. When we are searching on a non-unique key we may require all records whose keys match a given key. Or perhaps we want the first whose key matches a given key. The point is that given the nature of a key, there are a number of different types of search we might perform.

10.2.2 Sorting

As we have already seen, with the binary search tree, looking for elements in a structure can be quicker if the elements are sorted into order in some way within the structure. Clearly this is where the key comes in again. Thus a central theme in data structures concerns the algorithms for sorting elements in the different structures used.

10.3 Searching and sorting a linked list

To start we shall consider searching linear structures and the first of these is the linked list. The algorithms split into two classes, depending on whether the linked list is unsorted or sorted. In both cases, when you search either you are successful and find the key you want or you are not. In the binary search tree I had two distinct functions Q_BST_Present and BST_Retrieve_R, one to check if the element was there and one to retrieve it if it was. To illustrate a different approach I shall have functions that return a BOOLEAN, indicating whether or not the element is present, and include a variable argument that will hold information about the element if it is present. If the application required a lot of checking for the presence of a key but relatively little retrieval, then it would be best to design and implement two separate procedures as we had with the binary search tree.

In fact, the values are stored in a Sequence_T, whose underlying structure is a linked list. Since the operations on Sequence_T directly parallel those of a linked list, the issues of concern are clearly shown, and we can directly transform `Sequence_T` operations into direct linked list code using pointers. The `Sequence_T` is synonymed as `SearchDB_T`.

10.3.1 Searching an unordered list

Searching an unordered linked `SearchDB_T` is very simple. You start at the beginning and work through until you either find the element you are looking for or you reach the end. This is known as *sequential access* and is the way, for example, that we access external files on disk, in the examples in this book. Sequential search is demonstrated by `srchdemo.exe`, whose source can be found in `ch10\examples\linklist`. The files `searchdb.h/.cpp` contain various utilities for setting up `SearchDB_Ts`, containing random values, as well as the following procedure. This algorithm has been seen before, of course, since we have searched a linked `Sequence_T` before. What is new here is the addition of the variable parameter `Position`.

```
// PRE   NOT Q_Empty(DB)
// POST IF Value is in DB
//        Position is position of value in DB
//        RETURNS TRUE
//      ELSE
//        Position' is that of last in DB
//        AND Q_At_End(DB')
//        RETURNS FALSE
BOOLEAN
Q_PresentUnOrd(int Value, SearchDB_T DB, int &Position);

  Go_To_Head(DB);
  for (Position = 0;
       (!Q_At_End(DB)) && (Value != Get_Current(DB));
       Position++) {
   Go_To_Next(DB);
  }
  return(Value == Get_Current(DB));
}
```

The actual code should be easily understood by now, so look through it to make sure. What is of more interest here is how good the code is, in terms of time taken. We can take this to be the number of times the test in the control of the for loop is executed. Since `Position` starts at 0 and is incremented for each `Go_To_Next` as well as loop termination, then `Position` contains the number of times the test is performed. From this the following procedure is built:

```
void
Do_Multiple_Random_Searches(SearchDB_T SearchDB);
```

Choosing option u builds an unordered SearchDB_T, of size Size, specified by the user. The maximum possible element in the SearchDB_T is 2 * Size. s invokes Do_Multiple_Random_Searches. Here is an interaction.

```
Next request [0] ==> u
Please type in number of elements ==> 1000

Next request [1] ==> s
Please input maximum value to be searched for ==> 2000
Please input number of searches to be done ==> 1000
There were 757978 comparisons
There were 486 hits
Average of  757.978 comparisons
```

When the random SearchDB_T is set up by the u option invoking Make_UnOrdered_RandomDB, the maximum value is twice the size of the SearchDB_T. The s option, with the input above, has done 10,000 searches, each with a target value chosen at random, on a SearchDB_T of size 1000, and various statistics displayed. We can see that the number of comparisons is about 750, on average. This is to be expected since, if a value being sought is in the SearchDB_T, then on average we would look through half the elements, and if it is not, then through all the elements. Since we would expect about half the values to be in the SearchDB_T and half not, then in 1000 searches we would expect 500 * 500 + 1000 * 500 = 750,000 comparisons, or an average of 750 comparisons per search.

Exercise

1   If the maximum value to be searched for is increased greatly from 2 * Size, we get performance degradation. Here is an example.

```
Next request [1] ==> s
Please input maximum value to be searched for ==> 10000
Please input number of searches to be done ==> 1000
There were 941703 comparisons
There were 108 hits
Average of  941.703 comparisons
```

Explain this decrease in performance.

10.3.2 Searching an ordered SearchDB_T

Suppose that the SearchDB_T were in ascending order. If we were looking for 25, and we read the SearchDB_T as 4, 7, 12, 21, 27..., then, when we read 27 we can see that 25 is not in the SearchDB_T. So there is no point in searching beyond 27. With the unordered search we had to go right through the SearchDB_T to check that a value was not present. We can redesign the searching procedure as follows:

```
// PRE  DB is in ascending key order AND NOT Q_Empty(DB)
// POST IF Value is in DB
//         Position is position in DB
//         RETURNS TRUE
//      ELSE
//         IF at least one value in DB > Value
//           Position is that of the
//           next largest to Value
//         ELSE
//           Position is that of last in DB
//         RETURNS FALSE
BOOLEAN
Q_PresentOrd(int Value, SearchDB_T DB, int &Position) {

  Go_To_Head(DB);
  for(Position = 0;
    (!Q_At_End(DB)) && (Value > Get_Current(DB));
      Position++) {
    Go_To_Next(DB);
  }
  return(Value == Get_Current(DB));
}
```

To compare the performance of this search algorithm with that of the previous one, here is an interaction from using option o to build an unordered SearchDB_T. Once again s invokes Do_Multiple_Random_Searches, a flag being set by the o option to indicate that the SearchDB_T is ordered.

```
Next request [2] ==> o
Please type in number of elements ==> 1000

Next request [3] ==> s
Please input maximum value to be searched for ==> 2000
Please input number of searches to be done ==> 1000
There were 502761 comparisons
There were 520 hits
Average of  502.761 comparisons
```

The results suggest that the number of comparisons is about half the size of the array. This makes sense. Suppose that there are n keys in the search array SA. If they randomly but uniformly distributed across the possible range of keys, then the chance that a new random key will be

- less than or equal to `SA[0]` is `1/(2*n)`;
- more than `SA[i]` but less than `SA[i+1]` for `i = 1` to `n-2` is `1/n`;
- more than `SA[n-1]` is `1/n`.

So the expected number of comparisons is

```
1*1/(2*n) + 2 * 1/n + ... + (n-1)*1/n + n*1/(2*n)
= (n²-1)/(2*n)
```

This gets nearer to `n/2` as n gets big, which confirms our findings above. Figure 10.1 illustrates this but be aware that the above reasoning is based on an idealisation that is extremely unlikely to hold. It is sufficiently good to give us an estimate over the long term for repeated trails.

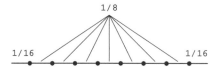

Figure 10.1 Ideally distributed, eight keys in the range would divide it into two sub-ranges of 1/16 and seven sub-ranges of 1/8.

Exercises

1   Design, implement and test `Select_Range`. Put it in `searchdb.h/.cpp`. In `srchdemo.cpp`, you will need a 'wrapper' procedure for IO and to call `Select_Range`, and use `Print_All_Values` for testing.

```
// PRE   DB is in ascending key order
//       AND Lo <= Hi
// POST  RETURNS SearchDB_T whose elements are all
//       those of SearchDB between Lo and Hi inclusive
SearchDB_T
Select_Range(int Lo, int Hi, SearchDB_T SearchDB);
```

2   Dispense with `sequence.h/.cpp` and transform all its operations, used in `searchdb.h/.cpp` and `srchdemo.cpp`, into pointer-based code.

10.3.3 Sorting a linked `SearchDB_T`

The ordered `SearchDB_T` searching demonstration program of Section 10.3.2 requires a sorted `SearchDB_T`. This is built up from a sequence of random numbers, given by the `stdlib.h` operations `rand()`. Each number is inserted into the `SearchDB_T` of random numbers already generated, which is in order, in such a way that the resulting `SearchDB_T` is in order. This is done with the following procedure:

```
// PRE  Keys in DB are in ascending order
// POST DB! = DB with NewRec added
//         AND keys in DB' are in order
void
Add_Value(int Value, SearchDB_T DB);
```

Since a `SearchDB_T` with no elements – that is an empty `SearchDB_T` – is in order (well which elements are out of order?) we can see how easy it is to build up an ordered `SearchDB_T` from the following two examples.

```
Add_Value(4, ())  ==> (4)
Add_Value(9, (3, 4, 6, 15, 29)) ==> (3, 4, 6, 9, 15, 29)
```

The code is similar to `Q_PresentOrd`, with extra instructions for the insertion.

```
if (Q_Empty(DB)) {
  Append_After_Current(Value, DB);
  }
  else {
    Go_To_Head(DB);
    for (;
      (!Q_At_End(DB)) && (Value > Get_Current(DB));){
      Go_To_Next(DB);
    }
    if (Value <= Get_Current(DB)) {
      Insert_Before_Current(Value, DB);
    }
    else {
      Append_After_Current(Value, DB);
    }
  }
}
```

Exercise

1   Design, implement and test `SortDB`. Put it in `srchdemo.cpp`. You will need a 'wrapper' procedure for IO and to call `SortDB`, and use `Print_All_Values` for testing.

```
// PRE  TRUE - SearchDB is not necessarily in order
// POST RETURNS SearchDB_T whose elements are all
//       those of SearchDB in ascending order
SearchDB_T
SortDB(int Lo, int Hi, SearchDB_T SearchDB);
```

10.3.4 Heuristic methods for sequential searching

For very many applications involving information retrieval, it is often found that a disproportionately small number of items account for a large number of retrievals. For example, librarians may refer to the 80–20 rule. Over a period of time they notice that about 80% of borrowings are accounted for by the most popular 20% of books. This is an empirical rule, though such quantitative rules can be derived from plausible assumptions about the model of borrowing using standard probability. In a database application it may well also be the case that a relatively large number of retrievals are for a relatively small number of records.

There may be a further factor, which is that once a record has been retrieved, then its probability of being retrieved again 'soon' is increased. For example, suppose that a student is borderline for her class of degree. Then her record may be accessed for the first time by her tutor, who then e-mails the course tutor. The course tutor then accesses the record, and phones the dean, who also accesses the record, as does the chief examiner. The point is that a record is accessed because it is of interest, and this interest may cause a flurry of accesses.

We could exploit either or both of these tendencies by having a rule that whenever a record is accessed, it is relocated to the front of the sequence. Suppose that record R, in position 205, is retrieved. It goes to the front of the sequence. Another half-dozen records are accessed and in their turn are put at the front. Record R is required again, and is now found in position 7, rather than 205.

This is demonstrated by srchdemo in ch10\examples\heurist. The same kind of unordered SearchDB_T is set up as before. The difference is that when choosing the Targets at random, the lines

```
Target = 1 + rand() % MaxVal;
for (; (Q_LowFrequencey(Target,
      LowFrequenceyFactor))&&(rand() % 8 < 7);) {
  Target = 1 + rand() % MaxVal;
}
```

mean that if LowFrequencyFactor equals 20 then all Target values between the bottom $\frac{1}{20}$th – that is 5% – and top $\frac{1}{20}$th – that is 5% – of the range are regarded as 'low frequency'. The loop, with the rand() % 8 < 7, means that, whereas low frequency values are expected to make up 90% of the values, the proportion chosen as targets in a long run of searches is 9/17 = 0.529 to 3 d.p. In the run below, 88% of values are low frequency, those with values between 11 and 189. The values occurring with higher frequency are indicated by a <.

```
Next request [32] ==> u
Please type in number of elements ==> 100
Next request [33] ==> r
Please type in LowFrequenceyFactor > 2 ==> 20
Next request [34] ==> p
```

```
Values of the table are as follows
 63    146 <194  158  166  147  13   186  134  160  189
 104   81   176  143  30   174  76   127 <191  159  56
<10    98   53   82   107  110  46  <198  140  14   23
 87    25   116  182  142  70   33   92   47   124  27
<5     29   157  31   133  11  <196  41   105  88   18
 14    112  141  89   61   161  69   136  64   90   129
<7     185  54   122  135 <3   71   58   177  99   165
<193   153  32   172  74   118 <200  180  57   55   130
 52    21   170  22   95   132  51   37  <192  171  12
<8
88 are low frequency queries
45 of first 50 are low frequency queries
```

A multiple search using the s option gives us the following:

```
Next request [35] ==> s

Please input number of searches to be done ==> 100000

There were 6.53629e+06 comparisons
There were 53104 hits
Average of   65.3629
51509 targets were from low frequency values - average of
0.51509
```

A further printout shows the change in balance.

```
Next request [36] ==> p
Values of the table are as follows
 29    74   61   171  122 <193 <10  <198 <192 89   30
 124   70   51   76  <5    58  <200 <196 <8   <194 135
<3     88   92  <7    95   158  18   12   82   132  161
 71    99   146  140  182  56   147  170  52   23   160
 11    180  141  133  186  14  <191  153  112  130  174
 55    177  157  172  25   136  32   54   69   90   105
 41    53   104  134  127  107  159  22   98   116  189
 57    129  63   33   148  87   143  46   166 31    64
 37    185  21   13   142  27   81   47   110 176   165
 118
88 are low frequency queries
39 of first 50 are low frequency queries
```

All but one of the 12 more frequently accessed values are in the first half of the sequence. Note that the average number of comparisons is just over 65. This is not as good as searching an ordered sequence but better than searching an unordered sequence. However, this example serves to show that there may be other considerations to efficiency than the pure structure of data.

10.3.5 Limits of searching and sorting algorithms on linked lists

A linked list, or indeed any linear structure with sequential access, such as Sequence_T, however we implement it, is limited by the sequential access mode. An array allows *direct access*. That is to say that we can go directly to element n, by the usual access operator – for example MyArray[n] – rather than plodding through all the preceding elements. We can get some improvement with sorted data or by using heuristic methods, but if the application requires a lot of retrieval operations, then sequential access on linear structures is really not effective for large amounts of data and either a non-linear structure – e.g. the BST_T – or a structure allowing direct access, such as the array, should be used.

10.4 Searching an array

There are similar considerations for sequential searching of an array as for a linked list. As we shall see there are better ways of searching an ordered array. Sorting an array, however, is a problem with many algorithmic solutions.

10.4.1 Sequential searching of an unordered array

If the array is not ordered then start at the beginning and work through, until you find the target or the end.

Exercises

1   Create a new directory arr_srch. Copy the original files from ch10\examples\linklist. Delete sequence.h/.cpp. In searchdb.h redefine SearchDB_T as follows:

```
typedef struct {
  Element_T Recs[MaxElements];
  int CurrentElement,
      NumberElements;
} SearchDB_T;
```

For all options associated with unordered SearchDB_Ts, replace all calls to the original Sequence_T operations by new fragments of code, based on the new type definition of SearchDB_T. Comment out all other calls to the original Sequence_T operations, else it will not compile! This will be uncommented to complete the exercise in Section 10.4.2 below.

2   Run your new program and use the s option to confirm that the searching performance is about the same as before.

10.4.2 Sequential searching of an ordered array

If the array is ordered then work through until you find the target or a value greater than the target.

Exercises

1 Finish off the work from Exercise (1) in Section 10.4.1 as follows. For all commented-out code, replace all calls to the original Sequence_T operations by new fragments of code, based on the new type definition of SearchDB_T.

2 Run your new program and use the s option to confirm that the searching performance is about the same as before.

10.4.3 Binary search of an ordered array

If the array is ordered, then sequential searching is by no means best! Recall the telephone directory example of recursion from Section 6.2. Sequential searching would be like starting at page 1 and plodding on, until you finally reached Zetterman or Zipf or whatever. We can use the structure of our own practical algorithm for finding names, to find a value, or its absence, in an array of values. Here is the pseudo-code.

```
Q_BinSearchPresent_R(Target, Array, First, Last)
   IF First > Last
     RETURN(FALSE)
   ELSE
     Set Middle to (First + Last)/2
     IF Target = Array[Middle]
       RETURN(TRUE)
     ELSE
       IF Target < Array[Middle]
         RETURN(Q_BinSearch_R(
                Target, Array, First, Middle - 1))
       ELSE
         RETURN(Q_BinSearch_R(
                Target, Array, Middle + 1, Last))
```

To explain this, suppose that we have an array of 18 elements and we want to see if the Target element 26 is in the array. A run of the demonstration program srchdemo in ch10\examples\array has been used to show this in Figure 10.2. The italicised elements are the index numbers of the array, while the contents of the array cells so indexed are non-italics. On the first call $(0 + 17)/2 = 8$. The

```
Next request [22] ==> b
Type in target element ==> 26
  0  1  2  3  4  5  6  7  8  9 10 11 12 13 14 15 16 17
  1  4 10 11 15 16 19 20 21 22 25 26 27 29 31 32 35 36
                             9 10 11 12 13 14 15 16 17
                            22 25 26 27 29 31 32 35 36
                             9 10 11 12
                            22 25 26 27
                                11 12
                                26 27
```

Figure 10.2 Binary search locates the value 26 in an ordered array.

value at position 8 is 21, smaller than 26, so we shift attention to cells indexed 8 + 1 = 9 to 17. (9 + 17)/2 = 13. The content of cell 13 is 29, bigger than 26, so we now turn to cells 9 to 13 - 1 = 12. (9 + 12)/2 = 10. Cell 10 contains 25, which is less than 26. Attention now turns to cells 10 + 1 = 11 to 12. (11 + 12)/2 = 11. And, bingo, in cell 11 we find 26!

Figure 10.3 shows an example of what happens if Target is not in the array.

If Target is not present then inevitably the search narrows to a one- or two-element sub-array. In the first case we have First = Last, and Middle = (First + Last)/2 = First = Last. So the next interval is either First...First - 1, or Last + 1...Last, depending on whether Target < Array[Middle] or Target > Array[Middle]. In the second case we have Last = First + 1, and Middle = (First + Last)/2 = (First + First + 1)/2 = First. So the next interval is either First...First - 1, or First + 1 ...Last = Last...Last, depending on whether Target < Array[Middle] or Target > Array[Middle]. In both sub-cases of the first case we encounter the termination condition First > Last, on the next recursive call, leading to a FALSE return. This is also true of the first sub-case of the second case. The second sub-case (Last...Last interval) reduces to the first main case, already considered.

The code in ch10\examples\array\srchdemo.cpp has some extra parameters for IO to show progress as in Figures 10.2 and 10.3. Use option o to set up

```
Next request [26] ==> b
Type in target element ==> 12
  0  1  2  3  4  5  6  7  8  9 10 11 12 13 14 15 16 17
  1  4 10 11 15 16 19 20 21 22 25 26 27 29 31 32 35 36
  0  1  2  3  4  5  6  7
  1  4 10 11 15 16 19 20
              4  5  6  7
             15 16 19 20
              4
             15

Target 12 is not in array
```

Figure 10.3 Binary search shows that the value 12 is not in an ordered array.

the sorted array and then option b to do the binary search. There are two binary search procedures, in fact. BinarySearchPrinting_R produces the output we have seen and is best used with small arrays of size 20 or less. BinarySearch_R does not do any printing and is used for statistics, as the next section shows.

10.4.4 Efficiency of binary search of an ordered array

In each call to BinarySearch_R, a variable parameter Comps is incremented. This gives a measure of the efficiency of the procedure. Once again option s gives a measure.

```
Next request [31] ==> o
Please type in number of elements ==> 1000

Next request [32] ==> s
Please input maximum value to be searched for ==> 2000
Please input number of searches to be done ==> 10000
There were 100060 comparisons
There were 4935 hits
Average of  10.006 steps
```

Table 10.1 shows a table of runs, using s. Column 1 shows the size of the array. In each case 10,000 searches were done on the array, with values in the same range as the array elements 1...2000, so there was a 1 in 2 chance that any particular value would be found in the array. Column 2 shows the average number of comparisons, which is the same as the average number of calls to BinarySearch_R. Column 3 is $Log_2(n)$, where n is the array size. You will notice that these figures are very near to those of column 2.

This shows the great advantage of the binary search. The time taken only goes up as the logarithm of the array size. Sequential searching was proportional to either 75% (unordered) or 50% (ordered) of the array size. Of course the sequential search employed only simple steps like moving from one array element to the next as opposed to a recursive call. But suppose that each step of ordered

Table 10.1 Binary search performances on arrays of different sizes.

n = Array size	c = Average comps	$Log_2(n)$
10	3.95	3.32
50	5.82	5.64
100	6.80	6.64
200	7.75	7.64
500	9.01	8.97
1000	9.99	9.97
2000	10.96	10.97
10000	13.3	13.29
15000	13.88	13.87

sequential search (SS) took up p units of time, while each step of binary search (BS) took q units of time. Then SS would take time $p*n/2$, while BS would take time $q*Log_2(n)$. If n were small and q much bigger than p then SS would be better. But we can always find a value for n at which BS is better for all array sizes greater than or equal to n, as follows:

$$p*n/2 \; > \; q*Log_2(n) \;\; ==> \;\; n/Log_2(n) \; > \; 2*q/p$$

Once we find a value of $n > 1$ for which this is true, then it is true for all values of n greater than this, and binary search will be a better-performing algorithm, on average, than sequential search.

Exercises

1   What is wrong with using the binary search idea on a sequential access structure, such as a linked list or Sequence_T? There are at least two ways of doing this but there are reasons why each of them is not really sensible.
2   Design and implement an iterative version of binary search.

10.5 Sorting an array

We shall look at three ways of sorting an array. The three ways represent very different approaches but all rely on comparisons of elements.

10.5.1 Bubblesort

Bubblesort is usually a poor algorithm for searching but because it is relatively simple to explain, it is useful as a first look at array sorting. The idea is this. Suppose we have an array with indices $0...n-1$. If we can get the biggest element to position $n-1$, then get the next biggest to position $n-2$ and so on, this will have sorted the array. Figure 10.4 shows an example. Elements are 'bubbled up' to their proper place.

```
8 12 10   1   9   3 |
8 10   1   9   3 12 |
8   1   9   3 10 |  12
1   8   3   9 |  10 12
1   8   3 |    9 10 12
1   3 |    8   9 10 12
```

Figure 10.4 Elements are 'bubbled up' in order of size to their correct positions.

```
START      8 12 10  1  9  3
NO SWAP    8 12 10  1  9  3 |
SWAP       8 10 12  1  9  3 |
SWAP       8 10  1 12  9  3 |
SWAP       8 10  1  9 12  3 |
SWAP       8 10  1  9  3 12 |
NO SWAP    8 10  1  9  3  |  12
SWAP       8  1 10  9  3  |  12
SWAP       8  1  9 10  3  |  12
SWAP       8  1  9  3 10  |  12
SWAP       1  8  9  3  | 10 12
NO SWAP    1  8  9  3  | 10 12
SWAP       1  8  3  9  | 10 12
NO SWAP    1  8  3  |  9 10 12
SWAP       1  3  8  |  9 10 12
NO SWAP    1  3  |  8  9 10 12
FINAL      1  3  8  9 10 12
```

Figure 10.5 Bubblesort in action.

How is this done? The full picture is shown in Figure 10.5. The kth 'bubble', 1
<= k <= n - 1, starts by comparing the elements in positions 0 and 1, and
swapping them if they are in the wrong order, but otherwise leaving them.
Elements in positions 1 and 2 are then compared, and swapped if necessary. The
element in position 1 may have just been swapped there, from position 0, of
course. This is how the 'bubbling' mechanism does its stuff. The kth bubble
continues by repeating on up to elements in positions n-k and n-k+1. n-k
comparisons are done in all. The | shows the division between the unsorted and
sorted portions of the array.

Here is the pseudo-code for Bubblesort. Q_Sorted is used to cut short the
process if the array turns out to be sorted before the maximum number of
comparisons has been done. Before entering the outer loop, Q_Sorted is set to
FALSE. The outer loop carries on while Q_Sorted is not TRUE. Once inside this
loop, Q_Sorted is set to TRUE. Then, in the inner loop, Q_Sorted is reset to
FALSE if any swapping has to be done. If no swapping has to be done, then the
interval of array worked by the inner loop must have been in order and so
Q_Sorted is left as TRUE. LoSorted is the index of the first cell of the last part of
the array – that is the sorted part. This is initially equal to the Size of the array,
but because we count from 0 here, this merely indexes a non-existent cell. After
each run of the outer loop, the sorted part of the array extends (at least) one cell
further to the left, and so LoSorted is decremented by 1.

```
Bubble_Sort(Array, Size)
  SET Q_Sorted TO FALSE
  SET LoSorted TO Size
  FOR NOT Q_Sorted
    SET Q_Sorted TO TRUE;
```

```
FOR Index = 0 TO LoSorted - 2
  IF Array[Index] > Array[Index + 1]
    SET Temp TO DB[Index]
    SET DB[Index] TO DB[Index + 1]
    SET DB[Index + 1] TO Temp
    Q_Sorted TO FALSE
DECREMENT(LoSorted)
```

So how good is Bubblesort? Here are the final statistics from a run with an array of 100 elements.

```
4797 comparisons were made resulting in 2478 swaps
```

Suppose that the outer loop is executed the maximum possible number of times. This is n-1 times for an array of size n. The first time the inner array is executed n-1 times, then n-2 times down to 1 time. So the total number of comparisons is

```
(n-1) + (n-2) + (n-3)...+ 1 = n*(n-1)/2
```
(This uses the arithmetic progression formula from mathematics.)

This gives the maximum possible number of comparisons. Plugging in our value of n = 100 from the example we get 4950 for the number of comparisons, not much greater than the number in the example. The difference is accounted for by the fact that there is a very good chance that the array will be in order, due to the repeated 'bubbling' by the time we get to the last few runs of the outer loop, and the use of Q_Sorted allows termination of the loop at this point. However, it does not save much, judging by this example. As we shall see, there is a better alternative.

Exercises

1 In ch10\examples\array, the program sortdemo contains code for Bubblesort, with some extra instructions for display purposes. Run this a few times, using u to set up an unsorted array and b to sort it. Once sorted you need to set up a new unsorted one each time of course! Use small arrays, size under 20, else the display is not terribly helpful.

2 Comment out the display instructions as indicated in the body of BubbleSort. Run the new program for quite large array sizes – up to 30,000 depending on your computer. Note that the comparison and swap counters are double to be able to do their counting. Does the n*(n-1)/2 rule still seem to hold?

3   Set up a new option to build a sorted array in *reverse order*, using an adaptation of `BubbleSort`, and then run `BubbleSort` on it to see the worst-case scenario, in terms of swaps.

4   Set up an `s` option, as with the binary search demonstration, to check that the single-array sorts done are not exceptional. You will need to re-randomise the array each time around the loop.

10.5.2 Quicksort

The Quicksort algorithm presents a very different approach to sorting an array. Imagine that we had the following procedure implemented:

```
// PRE  Lo <= Hi AND SortArray[Lo] = Pivot
// POST Elements of SortArray' = elements of SortArray
// AND Lo' = Lo
// AND  Hi' = Hi
// AND (SortArray'[Lo...PivotIndex-1] < Pivot
// AND SortArray'[PivotIndex] = Pivot
// AND (SortArray'[PivotIndex+1...Hi] > Pivot
void
Partition(SortArray, Lo, Hi, PivotIndex);
```

Never mind the implementation for now! What's the contract here? As long as the interval `SortArray[Lo..Hi]` contains at least one cell and the value in `SortArray[Lo]` is `Pivot`, then after completion, `Pivot` has been put in `SortArray`, such that all the values to the left are less than `Pivot`, and all those to the right are greater than or equal to `Pivot`. In short `Pivot` is in its rightful place if `SortArray` is fully sorted. The top three lines of Figure 10.6 show this.

If we then `Partitioned` the two sub-arrays to the left and right of `Pivot`, then two more elements would be in place. The bottom three lines of Figure 10.6 illustrate this for the left sub-array. And so on. Every call to `Partition` puts an element in place and this element has the > relationship to those on its left and the <= relationship to those on its right. Eventually, along all lines of recursion, for that is what it is, there would be an attempt to partition a sub-array of no elements or of one. In both cases the recursion stops. From this we can simply write the code for Quicksort.

```
Lo is 0  -  Hi is 11
L20  14  21   7  20  16   2   1  19   7  23 H23
  7  14   7  16   2   1  19 P20  20  21  23  23

Lo is 0  -  Hi is 6
L7  14   7  16   2   1 H19  20  20  21  23  23
  1   2  P7  16  14   7  19  20  20  21  23  23
```

Figure 10.6 Two successive calls to `Partition`.

```
void
QuickSort_R(SortArray_T SortArray, int Lo, int Hi) {
  int PivotIndex;

  if (Lo < Hi) {
    Partition(SortArray, Lo, Hi, PivotIndex);
    QuickSort_R(SortArray, Lo, PivotIndex - 1);
    QuickSort_R(SortArray, PivotIndex + 1, Hi);
  }
}
```

Figure 10.7 shows a run of QuickSort_R on an array of 12 elements. As before the lines come in pairs. The first shows the state at the beginning of Partition, with Lo and Hi marked L and H. The second shows the state at the end of Partition with the pivotal element marked P. This table is abstracted from a run of srtdemo in ch10\code\examples\qsort using option u, choosing a size of 12, followed by q, choosing the array demonstration feature with a y, on first prompt, and n on second prompt.

```
L10  15   20    1    8    3   13    3   16   15    6  H21
  6    1    8    3    3  P10   13   20   16   15   15   21
 L6    1    8    3   H3   10   13   20   16   15   15   21
  3    1    3   P6    8   10   13   20   16   15   15   21
 L3    1   H3    6    8   10   13   20   16   15   15   21
  1   P3    3    6    8   10   13   20   16   15   15   21
  1    3    3    6    8   10  L13   20   16   15   15  H21
  1    3    3    6    8   10  P13   20   16   15   15   21
  1    3    3    6    8   10   13  L20   16   15   15  H21
  1    3    3    6    8   10   13   15   16   15  P20   21
  1    3    3    6    8   10   13  L15   16  H15   20   21
  1    3    3    6    8   10   13  P15   16   15   20   21
  1    3    3    6    8   10   13   15  L16  H15   20   21
  1    3    3    6    8   10   13   15   15  P16   20   21
```
This QuickSort took 15 recursive calls
and 67 moves on an array of size 12

Figure 10.7 A complete run of QuickSort.

10.5.3 Partition

QuickSort_R is an elegant piece of code. But it is built on a 'what if?' Nothing has been said about the 'how' of Partition. In fact Partition is the key to the performance of QuickSort. Now it is relatively easy to think of various partitioning algorithms on an array Array. For example, we have two auxiliary arrays, Less and More. Choose pivot Pivot = Array[PivotIndex] as you like. Work though Array and, except for Index = PivotIndex, assign Array[Index] to the next place in Less or More, depending on whether Array[Index] is less than Pivot or greater than or equal to Pivot. Then read

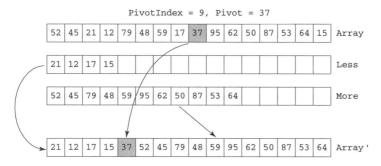

Figure 10.8 An obvious but not very efficient way of Partitioning.

all the elements of Index into Array, from cell 0 upwards, overwriting what is there already. Then read Pivot into Array in the next position. Finally read all the elements from More into Array from the position after PivotIndex, upwards. Figure 10.8 shows an example of this.

This works but it involves moving all the elements twice, except for Array[PivotIndex], which moves just once. More efficient Partitions are usually based on swapping the elements around in the same array, but keeping this swapping to an 'acceptable level'. Such an algorithm is illustrated in Figure 10.9.

	0	1	2	3	4	5	6	7	8	9	10	11	12	13	14
1	52	45	21	12	79	48	59	17	37	95	62	50	87	23	64
2	52	45	21	12	79	48	59	17	37	95	62	50	87	23	64
3	52	45	21	12	79	48	59	17	37	95	62	50	87	23	64
4	52	45	21	12	79	48	59	17	37	95	62	50	87	23	64
5	52	45	21	12	79	48	59	17	37	95	62	50	87	23	64
6	52	45	21	12	48	79	59	17	37	95	62	50	87	23	64
7	52	45	21	12	48	79	59	17	37	95	62	50	87	23	64
8	52	45	21	12	48	17	59	79	37	95	62	50	87	23	64
9	52	45	21	12	48	17	37	79	59	95	62	50	87	23	64
10	52	45	21	12	48	17	37	79	59	95	62	50	87	23	64
11	52	45	21	12	48	17	37	79	59	95	62	50	87	23	64
12	52	45	21	12	48	17	37	50	59	95	62	79	87	23	64
13	52	45	21	12	48	17	37	50	59	95	62	79	87	23	64
14	52	45	21	12	48	17	37	50	23	95	62	79	87	59	64
15	52	45	21	12	48	17	37	50	23	95	62	79	87	59	64
16	23	45	21	12	48	17	37	50	52	95	62	79	87	59	64

Figure 10.9 An example of a Partition algorithm at work.

The table shows the step-by-step partitioning of an array. The array indices 0...14 go across the top, while the steps 1 to 16 in the partition are indexed by the numbers down the left-hand side. The Pivot is 52, which occupies the first cell for all but the last step. From step 3 onwards the light grey sub-array is the portion of the array known to be less than Pivot. From step 5 onwards the dark grey sub-array is that portion of the array known to be greater than or equal to Pivot, with the exception of the pivot value in cell 0. In each row, the first italicised and bold element is in position LastLessThanPivot, except where it is in position 0. This shows the last cell in the sub-array of values known to be less than Pivot. This cell is, of course, light grey. The second italicised and bold element is NextToBePlaced. This is the first element of the unknown region, which may be less than, equal to or greater than the pivot. NextToBePlaced is incremented each step but, as can be seen, LastLessThanPivot may 'get stuck' for several steps at a time.

Clearly the algorithm to do this involves a loop, and we can establish an invariant on this loop that captures what is happening in the example and can be used generally. It is as follows:

```
Array[1...LessThanPivot] < Pivot AND
Array[LessThanPivot...NextToBePlaced-1] ≥ Pivot
```

If this is so, then, as NextToBePlaced increases each time around the loop, sooner or later NextToBePlaced = Hi + 1, and, if the invariant is true then the array is partitioned, so the loop can terminate with success.

Now what is required is to work out how this can be done – the 'clever part'. Look again at Figure 10.9. Consider step 8. The next element to be considered, 37, is less than 52, so it must become part of the light grey array. All we do is swap it with 59, the first element in the dark grey array, and increment LessThanPivot. In step 9 there is no need to do this as 95 is larger than 52. We start out with LessThanPivot = 0, showing that there are no light grey cells. The loop, for the general cases – exemplified by steps 8 and 9 – would be performed by the following pseudo-code:

```
FOR NextToBePlaced <= Hi
  IF Array[NextToBePlaced] < PivotValue
    Swap(Array[NextToBePlaced],
        Array[LastLessThanPivot + 1]);
    LastLessThanPivot++;
  NextToBePlaced++;
```

But does this work at the start, where NextToBePlaced = 1 and LastLessThanPivot = 0? Let Array be of length n. As long as the elements encountered were >= Pivot, then NextToBePlaced is just incremented. If all elements are >= Pivot, then it just runs through and terminates. The invariant is true at termination. If it initially meets an element < `Pivot` at position 1, then it swaps that element with the one at `LastLessThanPivot+1` – that is at position 1, so the swap is somewhat redundant but not wrong. This is what happens here. `LastLessThanPivot` is now incremented to 1. If all the elements after that were also < `Pivot`, then repeated redundant swaps lead to the original array ordering being kept. Since `Array[0] = Pivot` is clearly in the wrong place then it needs to be swapped with `Array[LastLessThanPivot]`, which is `Array[n - 1]`. Thus a line

```
Swap(Array[Lo], Array[LastLessThanPivot]);
```

is required after the loop terminates. The first more general case is as follows. If one or more of the elements from `Array[1]` onwards are >= `Pivot`, but at last an element < `Pivot` is encountered in `Array[NextToBePlaced]`, then this is swapped with `Array[LastLessThanPivot + 1]`, which is `Array[1]` on the first occasion, and so must be an element >= `Pivot`. `LastLessThanPivot` is incremented. This maintains the invariant, as will further encounters with elements < `Pivot`. In the second more general case, if one or more of the elements from `Array[1]` onwards are < `Pivot`, then redundant swapping and increment-ing of `LastLessThanPivot` extends the region. If at last an element >= `Pivot` is encountered in `Array[NextToBePlaced]`, then `LastLessThanPivot` is not incremented and a region of elements known to be >= `Pivot` is started. See steps 4 to 5 in Figure 10.9. In both more general cases the invariant is maintained and we exit the loop needing to swap `Array[0]` with `Array[LastLessThanPivot]` to finish off the work. The first two cases are in Exercise (1)(a) and (b) below, and the first general case is in Exercise (1)(c). So this discussion has finished off the details of what seems like an algorithm for `Partitioning` and provided an outline proof of its correctness, based on use of the loop invariant.

Remember that `Partition` works on sub-arrays. So, for clarity, I showed `Array` as being indexed from 0 in Figure 10.9. Of course it will be a sub-array, whose first index is not generally 0.

I did not devise this algorithm, but I found that constructing the example was useful to understand it. Then considering the cases and the loop invariant, I was able to work through and prove to myself that it was true. More detail is needed if you are not convinced. See Exercise (2) below.

Why choose position 0 in `Array` to be the one holding the `Pivot` value? Having it in position 0 makes it easier but there might be some circumstance whereby the first element was always the smallest or largest, which might cause bad performance, as discussed in the next section. The easiest thing to do is to decide on an algorithm for choosing any element in `Array` for the `Pivot` value and then swapping this with the value in `Array[0]`.

Exercises

1   Work through `Partition` with the following values of `Array`:
(a)

34	54	77	58	93	76	82	84	65	44	39	89	87	69	47	60

(b)

78	54	77	58	39	76	22	36	65	44	39	27	59	69	47	60

(c)

34	54	77	58	93	22	82	33	12	44	39	89	87	69	47	19

2   Work through the informal discussion and proof above and see if you follow the steps. If something seems left out then perhaps I have thought it 'obvious'. Add the missing detail to be sure that you understand.

3   If you examine the code for `Partition` in `srtdemo.cpp`, you will find that there is extra stuff for displaying the states of `Array` either before and after every partition, or after every swap as well. Add extra code that will also show the state at every comparison and indicate the `NextToBePlaced` and `LastLessThanPivot` with characters X and N, just as `Lo` and `Hi` are marked. You will need to add an extra two parameters to `Print_HighLightedArray` in `sortdb.h/.cpp`.

10.5.4 Performance of Quicksort

To get a feel for Quicksort's performance, there are three options in `sortdemo. o` sets an array in ascending order, `r` sets up an array in descending, or reverse, order and `s` does multiple sorts on randomly created arrays. Figure 10.10 shows the `s` option being used to find the average of sorts on 100 arrays. Compare this with the single-array sample for Bubblesort of 4797 comparisons and 2478 swaps.

If the array is sorted then things are a little different, as shown in Figure 10.11. Comparisons are way up, slightly worse than the sample Bubblesort, but swaps are down.

```
Please type in number of elements ==> 100
Please input number of searches to be done ==> 100
There were 13400    calls
Average of   134    calls per sort
There were 64886    comparisons
Average of   648.86 comparisons per sort
There were 37676    swaps
Average of   376.76 swaps per sort
```

Figure 10.10 Average performance of Quicksort on 100 unsorted arrays.

```
Next request [1] ==> o
Please type in number of elements ==> 100
Next request [2] ==> q
Do you want the array displayed at every partition?
This QuickSort took 199 recursive calls
and 4950 comparisons
and 99 swaps on an array of size 100
```

Figure 10.11 Quicksort on an array already sorted in ascending order.

An array sorted into reverse order produces the worst results, as shown in Figure 10.12.

```
Next request [3] ==> r
Please type in number of elements ==> 100
Next request [4] ==> q
Do you want the array displayed at every partition?
This QuickSort took 183 recursive calls
and 4469 comparisons
and 2343 swaps on an array of size 100
```

Figure 10.12 Quicksort on an array already sorted in descending order.

It can be shown that the average performance of Quicksort is proportional to n*Log(n-1), where n is the size of the array. In the worst case it can be nearly as bad as Bubblesort. However, this is when the array is nearly sorted, or reverse sorted, already. This is extremely unlikely with genuinely random data, but if you suspect that the keys may show some 'sortedness', then you could either exploit this with other methods, or if that is not really feasible, randomise them.

Exercises

1   It can be shown that if the pivot is chosen nearer to the median value of the elements in the sub-array, then the performance will be better. Unfortunately, finding the median involves sorting! However, there are reasonably good estimators. Add a new function to sortdemo.h/.cpp.

```
// PRE   TRUE
// POST RETURNS a value in range Lo..Hi
int
Get_Pivot_Position(SortArray_T Array, int Lo, int Hi);
```

In Partition insert code before the line

```
PivotValue = Array[Lo];
```

which uses Get_Pivot_Position to find the position of a pivot value, then swaps that value with Array[Lo]. Now think up some cunning code to find this pivot position. For example, you could look at five elements at random, find the median of those and make this the pivot value, returning its position in Array.

2 Run the original sortdemo.

(a) Choose o, then 5, and q, then n, to run Quicksort on an ordered array of size 5 without display. Note the statistics. Now choose o, then 5, and q, then y and y, for a full display of the run. From the essential code – i.e. without the lines for display – try to work out why there are those particular numbers of recursive calls, comparisons and swaps.

(b) Make a prediction for running Quicksort on an ordered array of size 7.

(c) Repeat (a) for an array of six elements.

(d) Make a prediction for running Quicksort on an ordered array of size 8.

3 Repeat Exercise (2) for reverse ordered arrays using option r.

10.5.5 Quicksort, binary search and the binary search tree

In Exercise (1) at the end of Section 10.4.4, it was asked why binary search on a sequential access structure, such as a linked list or Sequence_T, was a bad idea. Assuming an ordered list Sequence, one way to do it would be to count along to find the elements in various positions. Suppose that Sequence contained the values

```
{2, 5, 9, 23, 25, 34, 35, 46, 48, 57, 60, 64, 71, 78, 89}
```

If we want to see if 9 is in Sequence we must first look at element in position $(0 + 14)/2 = 7$, Sequence being 15 elements long. Eight 'hops' (1 Go_To_Head + 7 Go_To_Nexts for Sequence_T) take us to element 7. Finding 46, we see that we need to go to element $(0 + 6)/2 = 3$. This takes four 'hops'. Then we have to look at the element in position $(0 + 2)/1 = 1$. This takes two 'hops'. Finally we have to look at the element in position $(2 + 2)/2 = 2$. This requires just a single 'hop' (1 Go_To_Next). Total 'hops' = $8 + 4 + 2 + 1 = 15$. This is a worst case, but relatively simple maths shows that the average search time, in terms of hops, is about $\frac{2}{3}n$, where n is the size of the array. (We also have to count the elements in Sequence, but this need only be calculated once or just updated as new additions or deletions are made.) This is better than sequential search, but not as good as the previous algorithm for searching an ordered sequential access structure. Alternatively we could have a parallel array, each element containing a key and a pointer, in the form of a KAPRec_T, to the relevant element in the Sequence, and use this for the sorting and searching mechanism. But this is not

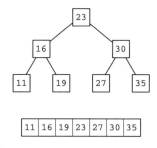

Figure 10.13 `BST_T` and `SortArray_T`.

really solving the problem. All we are doing is sorting an array of `KAPRec_T`s, and this will be subject to the usual problems that arrays encounter, when trying to represent rapidly changing dynamic data structures.

However, the idea of binary search can be applied to non-linear structures. This is, of course, what happens with the binary search tree. Figure 10.13 shows a balanced `BST_T`, with just keys, and the `SortArray_T` that it 'flattens into'. A search for a particular key in one will follow the same sequence of keys, on its path, as does the search for the same key in the other. This is a 'neat' example. Since there are many ways of building a `BST_T` out of the same set of *n* keys, for *n* > 1, there are many `BST_T`s for any single `SortArray_T`.

If we had a sequence of keys read into a `BST_T`, then the first plays the same role as the pivot in Quicksort. All keys following are divided into two sequences, the 'less thans' and the 'greater than or equals'. A slight difference is that Quicksort rearranges both sequences, and this rearrangement is dependent on the particular implementation of `Partition`, so that there is not a neat correspondence.

The important thing in looking at the relationships of these different structures and processes is to see how the same problem sets up correspondences between the structures and processes. The work done by this pattern of structure here is done by that pattern for processes there.

10.5.6 Merging sorted arrays

Suppose that we had two arrays already sorted into order. If we wanted to have the sorted array containing the elements of both of these arrays then it is a simple matter to read the elements from them into a third array. You can imagine that the two streams of integers merge something like two streams of traffic. Figure 10.14 shows this. Suppose that each of the two sorted arrays on the right has an index moving from 0 to the maximum value of its array. Then we could describe the algorithm to do the merging as follows, where `Array1` and `Array2` are the original arrays and `NewArray` is to contain the result of merging `Array1` and `Array2`:

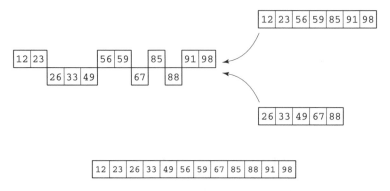

Figure 10.14 Merging the elements from two sorted arrays by taking the larger of the two next elements, one from each array.

```
Merge(Array1, Array2, NewArray)
SET Index1 TO 0
SET Index2 TO 0
SET NewIndex TO 0
FOR Index1 < Size(Array1) AND Index2 < Size(Array2)
   IF Array1[Index1] < Array2[Index2]
      SET NewArray[NewIndex] TO Array1[Index1]
      SET Index1 TO Index1 + 1
   ELSE
      SET NewArray[NewIndex] TO Array1[Index2]
      SET Index2 TO Index2 + 1
   SET NewIndex TO NewIndex + 1

FOR Index1 < Size(Array1)
   SET NewArray[NewIndex] TO Array1[Index1]
   SET Index1 TO Index1 + 1
   SET NewIndex TO NewIndex + 1

FOR Index2 < Size(Array2)
   SET NewArray[NewIndex] TO Array2[Index2]
   SET Index2 TO Index2 + 1
   SET NewIndex TO NewIndex + 1
```

So we have a sequence of three FOR loops. Only one of the last two gets executed in any application of the algorithm. Try to work out why before continuing.

What happens is that the algorithm keeps looking at the two values indicated by the two indices Index1 and Index2. It picks the smaller and puts that in the next position on NewArray and then increments the index of the array it came from. If either of the indices goes past the end, by being equal to the size – remember we index from 0 – then the first loop ends. The next two loops just read off elements from each of `Array1` and `Array2` in turn. However, if `Index1` has become equal to `Size(Array1)` then it never gets involved with the loop of the second `FOR` and goes straight to the third `FOR`. On the other hand, if `Index2` was the one that finished first, then the algorithm goes to the second `FOR` and reads off any elements left in `Array1` before going to the third `FOR` and then not entering the loop.

10.5.7 Mergesort

So sorting an array is simple. We split it into two, sort both halves and then merge. But how do we sort both halves? Well we do the same on them of course! This is a recursive algorithm! When do we stop? An array of length 1 is sorted so this is a good time to stop. This suggests the following:

```
MergeSort_R(Array)
IF Array has more than 1 element
   Split array into LeftArray and RightArray
   MergeSort_R(LeftArray)
   MergeSort_R(RightArray)
   Merge(LeftArray, RightArray, ?)
```

We can see that, as long as the split always produces two arrays each smaller than the original, then sooner or later each and every branch of the recursion reaches a state where `Array` has one element or less and halts. There is a question about where we are going to put the result of `Merge` – see ? mark. The easiest thing to do is to put it in the original array. In fact what we shall do is to use only the original array and an auxiliary array to do scratchpad work in. As before we shall work with intervals of the array. Here is a specification for `Merge`.

```
// PRE  Elements SortArray[LeftLo...LeftHi] are in
//      ascending order
//      Elements SortArray[RightLo...RightHi] are in
//      ascending order
// POST Elements SortArray[LefttLo...RightHi] are in
//      ascending order
void
Merge( SortArray_T Array, SortArray_T TempArray,
       int LeftLo, int LeftHi,
       int RightLo, int RightHi, int DBSize);
```

`TempArray` is passed across as the scratchpad array. Since in our demonstration programs we allow the user to set the size of the array, we do not want to constantly allocate and deallocate an array every time `Merge` is called. So this is done once and then `TempArray` is passed around as a parameter. The original algorithm is changed in that `Array1` and `Array2` are intervals in the main array, `Index1` goes from `LeftLo` to `LeftHi` and `Index2` from `RightLo` to `RightHi`, and the results are put into TempArray and then copied back at the end. DBSize is used in the demonstration program to print out the array and is not an essential part of the algorithm.

```
Merge(Array, TempArray,
      LeftLo, LeftHi, RightLo, RightHi)
SET Index TO LeftLo
SET Index1 TO LeftLo
SET Index2 TO RightLo
FOR Index1 <= LeftHi AND Index2 < RightHi
  IF Array[Index1] < Array[Index2]
    SET TempArray[Index] TO Array[Index1]
    SET Index1 TO Index1 + 1
  ELSE
    SET TempArray[Index] TO Array[Index2]
    SET Index2 TO Index2 + 1
  SET Index TO Index + 1

FOR Index1 <= LeftHi
  SET TempArray[Index] TO Array[Index1]
  SET Index1 TO Index1 + 1
  SET Index TO Index + 1

FOR Index2 < RightHi
  SET TempArray[Index] TO Array[Index2]
  SET Index2 TO Index2 + 1
  SET Index TO Index + 1

SET Index TO LeftLo
FOR Index <= RightHi
  SET Array[Index] TO TempArray[Index]
  SET Index TO Index + 1
```

The big difference is that we are working on two (adjacent) intervals Array[LeftLo...LeftHi] and Array[RightLo...RightHi], storing results in TempArray and then, at the end, copying the results back into Array.

This is implemented in ch10\code\examples\merge\sortdemo. Here is a typical run.

```
Next request [3] ==> u
Please type in number of elements ==> 13
Next request [8] ==> g
 #14 *10  15   9  13  11  21  23   2  25  16   7  26
  10  14 #15  *9  13  11  21  23   2  25  16   7  26
 #10  14  *9  15  13  11  21  23   2  25  16   7  26
   9  10  14  15 #13 *11  21  23   2  25  16   7  26
   9  10  14  15 #11  13 *21  23   2  25  16   7  26
  #9  10  14  15 *11  13  21  23   2  25  16   7  26
   9  10  11  13  14  15  21 #23  *2  25  16   7  26
```

```
  9  10  11  13  14  15  21  #2  23 *25  16   7  26
  9  10  11  13  14  15  21   2  23  25 #16  *7  26
  9  10  11  13  14  15  21   2  23  25  #7  16 *26
  9  10  11  13  14  15  21  #2  23  25  *7  16  26
 #9  10  11  13  14  15  21  *2   7  16  23  25  26
  2   7   9  10  11  13  14  15  16  21  23  25  26
```

The # indicates `LeftLo` and the * `RightLo`. So, for example, in line 6 of the array printout, the four elements after # have already been sorted, as have the three elements after *. In the next line you see the result of the merge.

Given the size of `Array`, Mergesort always has the same performance whatever the original ordering. This is better than Quicksort's worst time, though not as good as Quicksort's average time. Mergesort can also be used with external files. However, it does require the temporary array, so this might be a problem if space is short.

Exercises

1   Why is the performance of Mergesort always the same for a given `Array` size?

2   Implement the equivalent of `Do_Multiple_Random_Sorts` for `MergeSort_R` to perform the same empirical performance analysis as we have done for other sorting techniques.

10.6 Radix sort

So far all the sorting methods considered have used comparisons of elements. A radically different approach is that used in radix sort. A *radix* is the base of a number representation system. The radix 2 system is the binary system, the radix 10 system is the denary system, and the radix 26 system is that of the Latin alphabet. You might not think of an alphabetical system as being numerical but that is just what we use it for when we use alphabetical keys, such as surnames. So, in general, radix n uses n different digits.

10.6.1 How radix sort works

The idea is that we use a sequence of sequences, one for each digit used by the radix, to sort a sequence of keys. Suppose the largest key has k digits. Then, for each i, 0 <= i <= k, we go through the sequence of keys and put each key at the end of the sequence corresponding to its ith digit from the right.

Here is the first stage on a sequence of keys, using the least significant digit, the 1st from the right – that is the rightmost digit.

345, 213, 465, 218, 892, 965, 371, 820, 067, 723, 699, 216, 562, 013, 248, 927, 004, 801, 672, 933, 122, 637

0	1	2	3	4	5	6	7	8	9
820	371	892	213	004	345	216	067	218	699
	801	562	723		465		927	248	
		672	013		965		637		
		122	933						

Now we read the keys out of the digit-based sequences into another sequence of keys, maintaining the order just established.

820, 371, 801, 892, 562, 672, 122, 213, 723, 013, 933, 004, 345, 465, 965, 216, 067, 927, 637, 218, 248, 699

The next step is to repeat the first stage but using the least but one significant digit.

0	1	2	3	4	5	6	7	8	9
801	213	820	933	345		562	371		892
004	013	122	637	248		465	672		699
	216	723				965			
		218	927			067			

Once again the keys are read out into another sequence, maintaining order. Notice how, if we just look at the last two digits in each key, there is complete ordering. But we still need to do something about the first digit.

801, 004, 213, 013, 216, 218, 820, 122, 723, 927, 933, 637, 345, 248, 562, 465, 965, 067, 371, 672, 892, 699

The next, and here last, step is to repeat the process on the least significant digit.

0	1	2	3	4	5	6	7	8	9
004	122	213	345	465	562	637	723	801	927
013		216	371			672		820	933
067		218				699		892	965
		248							

This gives the sorted sequence

```
004, 013, 067, 122, 213, 216, 218, 248, 345, 371, 465, 562,
637, 672, 699, 723, 801, 820, 892, 927, 933, 965
```

10.6.2 Implementing radix sort

First we need a function that picks out digits from the key.

```
// PRE   Integer >= 0
// POST  RETURNS Nth least significant digit
// e.g.  Get_NLSD(1, 758) -> 8
//       Get_NLSD(2, 758) -> 5
//       Get_NLSD(3, 758) -> 7
//       Get_NLSD(4, 758) -> 0
int
Get_NLSD(int N, int Integer);
```

Then we need a data structure for the sequence of sequences. Since the radix value is fixed, we can use an array of Sequence_Ts.

```
typedef Sequence_T RadixTable_T[Radix];
```

The pseudo-code for RadixSort is then fairly straightforward if you have followed the example above. Note that the parameter Sequence is repeatedly emptied and filled and that the Sequence_Ts in RadixTable are also reused. It is necessary initially to create these Sequence_Ts in RadixTable and finally to free up the memory dynamically allocated by this initialisation. Sequence, being the parameter passed across, does not require the procedure to deal with these aspects of its existence.

```
// PRE   NOT Q_Empty(Sequence)
// POST  Sequence is in order
RadixSort(Sequence)
RadixTable_T RadixTable

SET DigitCount TO number of digits in maximum key in Sequence
SET all fields of RadixTable TO empty Sequence
FOR SigDigitPlaceIndex = 1 TO DigitCount
  Go_To_Head(Sequence)
  FOR NOT Q_Empty(Sequence)
    SET NextElement TO Get_Current(Sequence)
    Delete_Current(Sequence)
    SET SigDigit TO
        Get_NLSD(SigDigitPlaceIndex, NextElement)
    Append_After_Current(NextElement, RadixTable[SigDigit])
    IF NOT Q_At_End(RadixTable[SigDigit])
       Go_To_Next(RadixTable[SigDigit])
```

```
FOR Digit = 0 TO Radix - 1
  Go_To_Head(RadixTable[Digit]);
  FOR NOT Q_Empty(RadixTable[Digit])
    SET NextElement TO
      Get_Current(RadixTable[Digit])
    Delete_Current(RadixTable[Digit])
    Append_After_Current(NextElement, Sequence)
    IF NOT Q_At_End(Sequence)
      Go_To_Next(Sequence)
Free memory in all fields of RadixTable
```

This is implemented in ch10\code\examples\radix. The procedure RadixSort also contains code for displaying progress of the sort. Here is part of a run of srtdemo.

```
Next request [0] ==> u
Please type in number of elements ==> 49
Next request [1] ==> r
Sequence is 53 33 7 13 93 62 54 46 17 61 87 55 44 69
23 66 22 58 72 82 37 70 51 14 80 21 24 52 74 11 81 60
78 19 47 41 31 73 98 3 91 25 77 56 4 63 64 39 42
Significant digit place index is 1
subsequence 0 is 70 80 60
subsequence 1 is 61 51 21 11 81 41 31 91
......................
subsequence 9 is 69 19 39
Sequence is 70 80 60 61 51 21 11 81 41 31 91 62 22 72
82 52 42 53 33 13 93 23 73 3 63 54 44 14 24 74 4 64 55
25 46 66 56 7 17 87 37 47 77 58 78 98 69 19 39
Significant digit place index is 2
subsequence 0 is 3 4 7
subsequence 1 is 11 13 14 17 19
......................
subsequence 9 is 91 93 98
Sorted sequence is 3 4 7 11 13 14 17 19 21 22 23 24 25
31 33 37 39 41 42 44 46 4 7 51 52 53 54 55 56 58 60 61
62 63 64 66 69 70 72 73 74 77 78 80 81 82 87 91 93 98
```

10.6.3 Performance of RadixSort

There are three factors to consider when looking at the performance of radix sort. There is n, the number of elements to be sorted. Then there is the length of the biggest element l. Finally there is the value of the radix r. If we look at the pseudo-code then we see that we have an outer loop performed l times. Inside there are two loops, performed one after the other, the first reading all the elements from Sequence into RadixTable and the second reading them back (rearranged somewhat) again. Each of these is performed n times and each requires a Delete_Current and an Append_After_Current, both significant operations. The number of steps is then proportional to n*l. l might not be much of a problem for integer keys in many cases, but it might be an issue where long strings – for example library book titles – are concerned. The value of r affects the value of l, in that larger radices require fewer digits for value – e.g. 9 radix 10 is 1001 radix 2. r directly affects the size of RadixTable_T, but this is a single structure and the total length of all the Sequence_Ts it contains is n – that is, bounded. If radix sort were performed based solely on arrays with something like the following data structure then this might be an issue, because the space required is Radix*MaxNumElements.

```
typedef Key_T RadixSequence_T[MaxNumElements];
typedef RadixSequence_T RadixTable_T[Radix];
```

Exercises

1   The s option on srtdemo gives silly results. Fix it and investigate RadixSort's behaviour for various sizes of initial sequence, counting Delete_Current and Append_After_Currents.

2   Reimplement RadixSort using arrays, as indicated in the discussion on performance. The parameter to RadixSort will be an array. For each array in RadixTable you will also need to keep an index value showing its next free member. Change the s option to count adding elements to the arrays. Why do you not need to count deletions from the arrays?

3   Design and implement the following function.

```
// PRE   l > 0
// POST RETURNS a random string over [a...z} of length l
char
* Make_RandomString(int l);
```

You may want to use the following line, where Result is the local variable in which you build up the random string.

```
Result[Index] = (char) (rand()%26 + (int) 'a');
```

Now to amend the srtdemo code, for RadixSort, so that it does its stuff with strings rather than integers. You will need to do this in stages and comment out code that you have not yet amended. First, get the u option to set up a sequence of random strings, instead of integers. Ask yourself questions like does Print_All_Values need changing? Then work out what changes need to be made to RadixSort and its supporting operations.

10.7 Hashing

Suppose that my filing system consisted of 17 cardboard boxes from the photocopier room. I keep getting bits of paper and each is identified uniquely with a number between 0 and 999,999. I now have 1377 bits of paper. If I put them in the boxes at random then the best I can do to recover them is sequential search – average search time proportional to `(1 + 1377)/2 = 689`. But if I knew which box a bit of paper was in, then I would only have to sequentially search that box. If the bits of papers were fairly evenly distributed I would only have to look through `1377/17 = 81` bits of paper. But if they were not evenly distributed – suppose that one box had 1361 bits of paper and the others just 1 each – then I would not gain much benefit. For, assuming that I am as likely to need one bit of paper as another, the search time is proportional to `1361/1377*(1361 + 1)/2 + 16/1377*1 = 673.6`. I need a way to distribute them uniformly. One approach is to number the boxes 0 to 16. Then, when I get a bit of paper with key `Key`, I work out `Key modulus 17`, giving a number between 0 and 16. So I put the bit of paper in that box. As long as the key values are randomly but uniformly distributed, I could expect almost all boxes to have around 17 bits of paper in, with perhaps one or two with significantly more or fewer. This is the basic idea behind *hashing*, a method which presents an alternative to searching sorted structures for data to be retrieved.

10.7.1 Hash tables and hash functions

The set of boxes are a *hash table*. The function is called a *hash function*. The idea of a hash table is a little more general than the example suggests. We might be happy to have an array of 100 cells but only require to store 50 elements in it. If the keys of the elements are in the range 0 . . . 9999, then clearly we need to find a mapping from the key to an index in the range 0 . . . 99. A hash table is a set of locations such that we use a function, the hash function, on the key to determine where an entry goes. We might attempt to store more than one data item in a particular location. This is called a *collision*. Collisions are much more likely than 'common sense' suggests. Suppose that we put 12 elements into the table. What is the probability of a collision? First, we work out the probability that there is not a collision. The first element can go anywhere. The second can choose 99 out of 100 places to avoid a collision. The third can choose 98 out of 100 places to avoid colliding with either of the two already there. And so on. This gives a probability of

$$\frac{99}{100} * \frac{98}{100} * \frac{97}{100} * \frac{96}{100} \cdots \frac{90}{100} * \frac{89}{100} = 0.503$$

so the probability of a collision with just 12 elements is `1 - 0.503 = 0.497`. The single-file program `collide.cpp`, in `ch10\code\examples\hash` illustrates this. It shows the probabilities of a collision for `Index` elements inserted into an array of `Size` cells, at random. Table 10.2 shows how many elements are required

Table 10.2 Number of elements required to have an evens
chance of a collision.

Number of cells	Number of elements	Elements/cells ratio
10	4	0.4
100	12	0.12
1000	38	0.038
10000	118	0.0118
100000	373	0.00373
1000000	1178	0.001178

in arrays of different numbers of cells to make the probability of a collision greater than 0.5. The proportion of elements to the number of cells decreases as the number of cells increases. Clearly, even if we do not mind wasting a proportion of cells, we still have collision problems.

There are two main ways of dealing with this problem. The first is to find another empty place in the table, by, for example, rehashing on the result of the hash function. The second, which we shall consider briefly, is to place another data structure, for example a linked list, at each of the locations and then to insert the element into this list, when the hash function indicates the location where the list is at. This is called *collision resolution by chaining*.

10.7.2 Implementing hash tables

A simple hash table is implemented in ch10\code\examples\hash in files hashtab.h/.cpp, and demonstrated by hashdemo.cpp. HashTable_T is implemented as an opaque type with the 'real' declarations being as follows:

```
typedef Sequence_T Bucket_T;

typedef struct {
  Bucket_T *Buckets;
  BOOLEAN  Q_Empty;
  int      NumLocations;
  int      NumUsedLocations;
} HashTableRec_T, *HashTableRec_Ptr_T;
```

The hash function Hash_Key is not a declared operation on HashTable_T ADT, and is internal in hashdemo.cpp. In this case it is a very simple function.

```
// PRE   TRUE
// POST Key is hashed to a value in range [0...NumLocations-1]
int
Hash_Key(Key_T Key, int NumLocations) {

  return(Key % NumLocations);
}
```

Exercises

1   Implement and test the following function:

```
// PRE   TRUE
// POST RETURNS number of items in HashTable
int
Find_Size(HashTable_T HashTable);
```

2   Implement and test the following procedure:

```
// PRE   Q_PresentValue(Value, HashTable)
// POST HashTable' = HashTable with Value removed
void
Delete_Value(int Value, HashTable_T HashTable;
```

3   Reimplement `HashTable_T` using `BST_Ts` instead of `Sequence_Ts`. Note that because of the implementation of `BST_T` we have used, you will have to make the `HashTable_T` parameter a variable parameter in update procedures – e.g.

```
Add_Value(int Value, HashTable_T &HashTable)
```

This is to allow the very first element to be inserted.

10.7.3 Choosing the hash function

The example has a very simple hash function which meets the first criterion for a hash function, which is that it should be easy to compute. The second criterion is that it should distribute the keys that arise in practice evenly across the locations – in the example the indices of the array. This means that 'most' locations should contain 'about the same number' of keys. (Look again at the cardboard box filing system.) Our simple function does that but this is because the keys are generated randomly and uniformly. Suppose that we had 1000 locations and keys in the range $0 \ldots 99,999$ for employees. If the first two digits of a key gave the employee's department, and the last three digits gave the number within that department, which was recycled when an employee left, and that there were 12 departments and the largest contained 373 people, then our simple function will fail to meet the second criterion. The reason is that using `Key modulus 1000` will generate lots of locations up to 373, with not so many keys going to higher numbers in this range, and no locations at all from 374 to 999. Because the keys are not uniformly distributed in the key range, this hashing function fails to distribute uniformly. This where we start to think about real hashing! We want to use all the information in the key but avoid the bias implicit in the way the key has been structured. One way to do this might be, for example, to make up two integers taking the digits in odd and even positions respectively, multiply them together, add the original number, then take the result `modulus 100`.

```
Hash_Key(09034) = (004 * 93 + 09034) modulus 100 =
9406 modulus 100 = 406
```

This is called *folding*. Is it any better? We might be able to spot a flaw in this by reasoning about it. Alternatively we can just run this on real-world keys and look at the distribution.

Often using a non-prime number for the modulus can generate patterns which produce non-uniformity. So it might be better to sacrifice three locations and take `modulus 97` instead.

Getting the hash function right can make a radical improvement to the performance of an information system. Seeing that we have got it right depends on considering the nature of the keys to start with, working out schemes to use the maximum amount of information in the key without being biased by how the structure of that information represents the real-world problem, and testing the function on real data.

Exercises

1 (a) Design and implement a function to return random keys that are as follows. The first two digits show department number, and the last three digits show employee number. The maximum employee number in each department is shown below.

DeptNo	MaxNum	DeptNo	MaxNum	DeptNo	MaxNum
1	24	5	36	9	41
2	67	6	74	10	209
3	231	7	373	11	35
4	4	8	70	12	11

So 02037 is employee 37 in department 2.

The simplest way is to find the total number of the `MaxNum`s, which is 1175. Generate a random number in the range 0...1175 by `1 + rand()%1175`. Suppose this is 103. Then this would be in department 3 because 24 + 67 < 103 <= 24 + 67 + 231. This gives you the first two digits – here 03. Now get a random number in the range `1 + rand()%MaxNum` for the particular department. Here this would be `1 + rand()%231`. Suppose this is 79. Then the whole key is 03079.

(b) Write the new body of code for `Hash_Key` to implement the folding scheme suggested above. Add a new procedure `Print_Size_Of_Buckets` to `hashtab.h/.cpp`, which prints out the size of each `Bucket_T` but not the values in the bucket.

(c)   You can now test the suggested folding hash function by generating lots of numbers, according to the scheme in (a), inserting them with Hash_Key.

2   Reimplement hashtab.h/.cpp so that it works with strings as keys rather than integers. Some changes to hashdemo.cpp will be required for testing. Use the random string generator from Exercise (3), Section 10.6.3 for testing.

10.8 What about the rest of the data?

In this chapter we sorted and searched for keys alone. This is to bring out the essential features of the structures and algorithms. But in reality, of course, we usually need more than the key. Here we demonstrate that all that has gone before addresses the main problem, and that 'tweaking' solutions so that we can store and retrieve records properly is a relatively simple step. A 'with records' version, using KAPRec_Ts, of the search of an ordered sequential structure is presented in ch10\code\examples\withrecs. The records are loaded from test1.dat. Note the post-conditions of Q_PresentOrd in searchdb.h/.cpp, which mean that retrieval is a simple step after checking for the presence of a key. This is shown in Check_ValueOrd(SearchDB_T DB) in srchdemo.cpp.

Exercises

1   Adapt the files in ch10\code\examples\array along the same lines so that records are loaded from file and searched for with binary search. This will involve reimplementing Bubble_Sort to handle KAPRec_Ts but not changing the basic algorithm at all.

2   Do the same for ch10\code\examples\qsort. Once again the basic algorithms are not changed.

3   Do the same for ch10\code\examples\heurist.

4   Do the same for ch10\code\examples\radix.

5   Do the same for ch10\code\examples\hash.

6   Take any one of the sample programs for searching or sorting and adapt it to use the Name field of DataRec_T as the search or sort key. This will not be unique, of course.

10.9 Summary

In this chapter we have covered the following:

- The problems of searching and sorting have been defined with respect to the concept of a record key and the ordinal relationships.
- Sequential, ordered and heuristic methods have been presented for searching a sequentially accessed structure, such as a linked list.
- Sequential and ordered search methods on the array have been given as exercises.
- Bubblesort, Quicksort and Mergesort have been presented as three very different approaches to sorting an array.
- The relationships between binary search, Quicksort and the binary search tree have been discussed.
- Radix sort has been presented as a different method of sorting from comparison-based methods.
- A simple example of hashing with hash table and hash function has been introduced and implemented.
- The step from using any of the foregoing methods with integers to using whole records with different types of keys has been discussed.

CHAPTER 11

The Graph_T *ADT*

11.1 Introduction

In this chapter we introduce the most general non-linear data structure that most programmers will come across, in the form of the ADT Graph_T. First we look at a number of problems to motivate its use. From the problems we develop a specification for Graph_T. Then we implement Graph_T, using previous ADTs. Finally we look at a typical example of an algorithm on a graph.

11.2 Trains, bridges and graphs

Consider the problems of running a railway network. This consists of a set of stations and advertised journeys between them at particular times. How do we go about specifying and designing an information system that can cope with all this?

First, we must consider the basic data that is required – the stations and all the data associated with each, and the advertised journeys and all the information associated with them. This gives a basic information service from which we can find, for example, that there is a train from London Paddington to Oxford, departing at 9.15, arriving at 10.21; a standard return costs £18.60 or there is a car hire service at Oxford.

Second, we shall want to make queries with more complex answers. For example, I may wish to get to Glasgow by 9.00 p.m. for a conference the next day, but I want to leave Oxford as late as possible. This involves using an algorithm on the basic data.

We need a data structure for the basic information. So we shall specify it in the form of an ADT and then use familiar ADTs to implement the ADT.

11.2.1 Abstracting and representing the essential entities

When we approach such a problem we look for the essential entities, that is things which are the backbone of the situation and which have attributes or properties. Then we are interested not just in what those attributes may be but also in the relationship of the entities to each other. Here there are two types of entity –

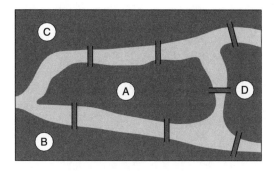

Figure 11.1 The map of bridges of Königsberg.

stations and *journeys*. The relationship is fairly simple. Any journey starts at one station and ends at another. For our purposes here, I am taking it that a trip from A to E, stopping at B, C and D, is in fact four journeys. Between any two stations there may be a number of journeys.

To see how to represent this let us turn to an older problem called 'The Bridges of Königsberg'. Königsberg is a town in the former East Prussia and was home to the philosopher Immanuel Kant. It was situated on both banks and two islands on the River Pregel. Seven bridges connected the different parts of Königsberg, as shown in Figure 11.1. The problem of the bridges of Königsberg was to start somewhere and cross each bridge, once and once only, in a single walk. This did not have to be a circuit. Thus it was a favourite Sunday occupation of the good citizens of Königsberg to try to solve this problem, until it was all ruined for them by the mathematician Leonhard Euler (1707–1783), a contemporary of Kant.

Euler formalised the problem with a *graphical representation*, as shown in Figure 11.2. The details of the distances and other matters that are essential to the usual geographical map are completely absent. Instead we have points, which we shall call *vertices*, to represent the different pieces of land – two banks and two islands – and lines, which we shall call *arcs*, to represent the bridges. The whole collection of arcs and vertices is called a *graph*. From this *representation*, Euler was able to solve the Königsberg bridge problem and deduce a more general

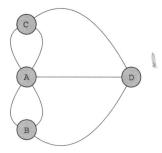

Figure 11.2 The abstracted bridges of Königsberg.

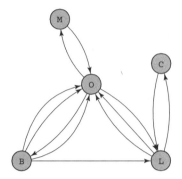

Figure 11.3 A graphical representation of (some of) the UK railway system.

result. Because he had *abstracted* the essential features of the problem, he was able to apply logical reasoning.

Similarly, it may become much easier to develop programming solutions to real-world problems, such as our railway system, if we adopt a graphical representation, as shown in Figure 11.3. Here I have treated London as one big station, for the purposes of keeping the example simple, and the others are Oxford, Bristol, Cambridge and Manchester. Unlike the Königsberg graph each arc has a direction, shown by an arrow. This is because each arc represents a journey, at a particular time, from one place to another. We cannot 'go backwards' on the journey at that time. The Königsberg arcs represent bridges with no time involved. A Königsberger can go back and forward on a bridge anytime he or she wants. The difference is that the Königsberg graph is *undirected*, whereas the railway graph is *directed*. The ADT we shall develop is a directed graph. If we want an undirected graph, then for every arc from X to Y we put in an arc from Y to X, so the directed graph is the more general of graphs.

11.2.2 Two more examples

Because computing is very much concerned with locations, states and flow, many computing diagrams are graphs. For example, we have *flowcharts*, *data flow diagrams* and *state transition diagrams*.

A state transition diagram is shown in Figure 11.4. This shows how to recognise a sequence of symbols as either an integer, a sequence of one or more

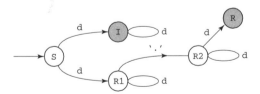

Figure 11.4 A state transition diagram to recognise integers or real numbers.

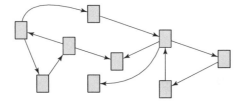

Figure 11.5 A fragment of the World Wide Web represented as a graph.

digits, or a real number, a sequence of one or more digits, followed by a decimal point '.', followed by a sequence of one or more digits. If we read the sequence and end up in either of the two shaded-circle states I or R, then the string is accepted as being either an Integer or a Real.

The World Wide Web is a graph, based on the Internet, another graph at another level (see Figure 11.5). Designing the structure of websites involves thinking graphically. Developing searching and retrieval software involves programming to traverse graph structures.

11.2.3 A formal definition of a graph

If you look in any discrete maths book you will find a formal definition of a directed graph something like the following:

> A directed graph (digraph) consists of a pair of sets (*V*, *E*), for vertices and arcs, with a pair of functions *i* and *f*, initial and final, from *E* into *V*.
>
> If $i(e) = x$ and $f(e) = y$ then *e* is an edge from *x* to *y*.
> *y* is a *successor* of *x* and *x* is a *predecessor* of *y*.

Figure 11.6 shows an example of a directed graph in line with this definition. Note that all arcs must have an initial vertex and a final vertex. However, it is quite all right for a vertex, like 4, to have no arcs going to or coming from it.

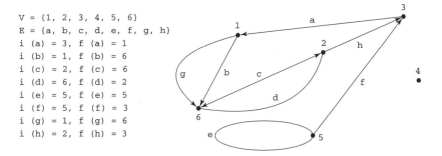

```
V = {1, 2, 3, 4, 5, 6}
E = {a, b, c, d, e, f, g, h}
i (a) = 3, f (a) = 1
i (b) = 1, f (b) = 6
i (c) = 2, f (c) = 6
i (d) = 6, f (d) = 2
i (e) = 5, f (e) = 5
i (f) = 5, f (f) = 3
i (g) = 1, f (g) = 6
i (h) = 2, f (h) = 3
```

Figure 11.6 An example of a directed graph, according to the definition.

This definition will be reflected in the specification and implementation of Graph_T.

11.3 Specifying the Graph_T

There are three parts to the specification of the Graph_T.

First, we want to specify the ADTs that are the components of the Graph_T, the vertices and the arcs. A vertex – e.g. representing a station – will have various sorts of associated data. Similarly an arc – e.g. representing a journey – also has data. Part of this data is structural. Each vertex has an identifier. Each arc has an identifier, and also some reference to the source vertex – the one it goes from – and the sink vertex – the one it goes to. In a real-world application, such as the railway network, most of the data associated will be stuff like station names, whether there is a car hire facility, times of arrival and departure. We need to make ADTs for these data records.

Second, we want to be able to build the Graph_T. That is, we want to add data records for vertices and arcs, and make the right connections, and be able to go through this data systematically.

Third, we want to explore the Graph_T. There must be some means by which we can start at a particular vertex and then move along any of the arcs from it to another and so on. It must also be possible to design and code algorithms that can do this automatically to search for shortest trips, for example.

We shall look at each of these parts in turn. The code for Graph_T is in ch11\examples\graph. For the specification have the .h files to refer to and for the implementation have the .cpp files to refer to.

11.3.1 Vertex and arc types VertDataRec_T and ArcDataRec_T

If you look at vertdata.h and arcdata.h, you will find the specification for the VertDataRec_T and the ArcDataRec_T in pre- and post-condition form. These are much the same as previous types of record and, for the demonstration, contain only name fields for the 'real-world' data. If you wanted to use Graph_T for the railway system example, you would add considerably to these records. ArcDataRec_T has fields for the initial and final vertices.

As before we shall use key/address pairs. Since there are two key/address pair types there are separate ADTs. These are specified and implemented in astore.h/.cpp, for the ArcKAPRec_T, and vstore.h/.cpp, for the VertKAPRec_T. Because there are two ADTs we have to particularise the names for each so that we have MakeArcKAPRec and MakeVertKAPRec as two separate operations, one for each ADT. Note also that we have added two fields to ArcKAPRec_T because the source, FromVertKey, and sink, ToVertKey, vertex keys are important structural information.

Exercise

1   For each ADT, read the pre- and post-condition specifications in the source files and then see how the implementation for each procedure meets the specification.

11.3.2 Graph_T

The operations for Graph_T come in several sections. These are specified in graph.h under the different sections.

First, there are four operations to create and build a Graph_T. They are Create_Graph, Make_Empty, Add_Vert and Add_Arc.

Second, there four query operations on the status of the graph. They are Q_EmptyGraph, Q_NoArcs, Get_Size and Get_Number_Of_Arcs.

Third, there are four query operations on vertices and arcs. They are Q_VertPresent, Retrieve_Vert, Q_ArcPresent and Retrieve_Arc.

Fourth, there are 12 iterated traversal operations. These are divided into two sets of five operations each to iterate through the vertices and arcs respectively, and two other operations to mark or unmark vertices. The order of iteration of either the vertices or arcs is that of their keys and bears no relationship to the actual relationship of vertices and arcs in the graph. The marking and unmarking operations are used by algorithms that must avoid getting in a loop as they seek paths through the graph. The operations are Q_FirstVert, Q_LastVert, Go_To_FirstVert, Go_To_NextVert, Get_CurrentVert – vertex traversal operations; Q_FirstArc, Q_LastArc, Go_To_FirstArc, Go_To_NextArc, Get_CurrentArc – arc traversal operations; Set_CurrentMark, UnSet_CurrentMark and Q_CurrentVertMarked – marking and unmarking operations.

The fifth set of operations consists of the single Load_Graph_From_File operation.

This seems like a lot of operations but bear in mind that we have two sets of things – vertices and arcs – to deal with. In the BST_T we just had nodes. So we end up with, very roughly, two sets of the same types of operations as on the tree. In fact we have not yet finished, for whereas we could travel around a BST_T, going left or right, we only have key order traversal at present. This is remedied in the next section.

11.3.3 Traveller_T

Also in graph.h we specify operations on Traveller_T. A Traveller_T is an ADT associated with a Graph_T that travels from vertex to vertex along the arcs, being able to work through the set of arcs at each vertex.

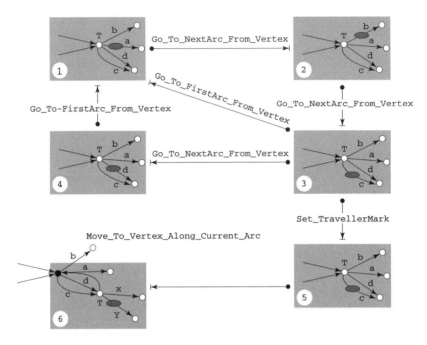

Figure 11.7 The Traveller_T T and some of its operations.

The idea is that a Traveller_T sits on a vertex, like a spider, and considers what to do next, or rather the algorithm controlling the Traveller_T does. Figure 11.7 illustrates this. T is the Traveller_T, in diagram 1 originally sitting at a vertex with arcs from it labelled a, b, c and d. The vertex is white, showing it unmarked. The alphabetical order shows the order in which T will 'consider' the arcs. The grey oval marks a as the current arc of consideration. The operation Go_To_NextArc_From_Vertex(T) makes the arc b the current arc, taking us to diagram 2. Repeating this operation takes us to diagram 3, where c is the current arc. As shown here, we can get back to the first a as current anytime by invoking Go_To_FirstArc_From_Vertex(T). We can use Go_To_NextArc_From_Vertex(T) to make d the current arc, as shown in diagram 4, and then invoke Go_To_FirstArc_From_Vertex(T) to make a the current arc, thus returning to diagram 1. So far T has just 'flipped through' the arcs that it might travel along. If it was decided that T was to travel down an arc, then we need another operation. We might also want to mark the vertex, where T moves from, so as to indicate that it had been visited. So, invoking Set_TravellerMark(T) marks the vertex, as shown in the transition from diagram 3 to diagram 5. Then Move_To_Vertex_Along_Current_Arc(T) performs the move, as shown in the step from diagram 5 to diagram 6.

In all there are 16 operations on Traveller_T in several sets. These operations are specified in graph.h.

In the first set there are five operations concerned with creating, resetting, copying and destroying a traveller. Create_Traveller, Q_Vert_For_ Traveller, Start_Traveller, ReSet_Traveller and Destroy_Traveller are these operations.

The second set of three operations are query operations, getting the key value, getting the key/address pair record, or seeing if the vertex, where the Traveller_T sits, has no arcs going out of it. They are Get_TravellerVertKey, Get_TravellerVertKAPRec and Q_End_Of_Path.

Operations dealing with examining the choices available for the next move and making that move make up the third set of five operations. Some of these are featured in Figure 11.7. It is important to realise that, unless there are no outgoing arcs – that is Q_End_Of_Path(Traveller) – the Traveller_T has one or more arcs to consider moving down. It has to be able to examine each in turn, using Go_To_FirstArc_From_Vertex to move to the first one, Go_To_ NextArc_From_Vertex to move to the next one, and Get_CurrentTraveller_ ArcKAPRec to retrieve the key/address pair for the arc, thus being able to access information about the arc. If it has reached the last of the arcs from its current vertex then Q_No_More_Arcs will be true. This set of operations allows the Traveller_T to 'browse' the arcs of which it is the source or 'from' vertex, until it can make a decision about what to do (or rather the algorithm using the Traveller_T does). If the decision is to move on then this is done with Move_To_Vertex_Along_Current_Arc.

Finally there are three operations for letting the Traveller_T mark vertices as it goes around the Graph_T. They are Set_TravellerMark, UnSet_ TravellerMark and Q_Traveller_At_MarkedVert.

11.4 Implementing Graph_T

From the specification there are a number of reasonably useful ways to implement Graph_T. The implementation here is chosen because it offers an opportunity to see the reuse of other ADTs, albeit in a slightly amended form. Please remember that these ADTs are the underlying structure for this particular implementation and the Graph_T, both as specified above and explored in Figure 11.7, is an abstraction. There are many other ways of implementing this abstraction. A Graph_T operation is translated into one or more operations on the underlying ADTs.

There are three parts to the implementation. The first section deals with building the Graph_T. In the second we look at the operations for marking vertices. Lastly the implementation of Traveller_T is outlined.

11.4.1 Building the Graph_T

Going back to the definition in Section 11.2.3, we need a set of vertices and a set of arcs. How do we store them? We need to be able to traverse both sets. One answer is to have a binary search tree (BST) of vertices and a BST of arcs. How this is done is dependent on the support offered by the language of implementation. In the subset of C++ we are using, this entails having two separate codings of the BST, one for `ArcBST_T` in `arc_bst.h/.cpp` and one for `VertBST_T` in `vert_bst.h/.cpp`. However, this can be done quite quickly because the data and procedure structures are exactly the same of course. We just use our editor's search and replace facility, and a little care! In fact it is such a mechanical process that many languages have a feature called *pure polymorphism* built in. This means, for example, that you just write the code for the BST once and then declare a BST to store integers, another one to store student records and so on. In fact C++ does offer this facility in the form of `templates` but this is an advanced object-oriented feature that we are not assuming for this book.

In fact it is useful to have a second `BST_T` for the arcs ordered by the initial vertex key – that is, the key of the vertex whence the arc comes. As we shall see this entails a small change to the code.

Once again we use the `void` pointer for information hiding, so in `graph.h` we have

```
typedef void  *Graph_T;
```

The 'real' data structure is in `graph.cpp` as shown.

```
typedef struct {
  VertBST_T   VertBST;
  ArcBST_T    ArcBST,
              FromArcBST;
  VertBST_Iterator_T  VertIterator;
  ArcBST_Iterator_T   ArcIterator,
                      FromArcIterator;
  int  NumVerts,
       NumArcs;
} GraphRec_T, *GraphRec_Ptr_T;
```

So the `Graph_T` is based on three `BST_Ts` and associated iterators. Two of the `BST_Ts`, `ArcBST` and `FromArcBST`, will hold exactly the same items but ordered on different keys – `ArcBST` on the key of the arc, and `FromArcBST` on the key of the vertex the arc is from. How is this to be done? The answer is, as in Chapter 9 and `clubs.cpp`, to pass a function that selects the sort key – rather than the sort key – as a parameter. Here is part of the code for adding an arc to the `Graph_T`.

```
ArcBST_Insert_R(Get_ArcKAPRecKey, NewKAPRec,
                GraphRec_Ptr->ArcBST);


ArcBST_Insert_R(Get_ArcKAPRecInitialKey, NewKAPRec,
                GraphRec_Ptr->FromArcBST);
```

A slight liberty has been taken here. The two key selector functions return different types, ArcKey_T and VertKey_T respectively. These are both really ints, so the whole thing works. Note the contrasts with the BST_T that we started with.

```
BST_Insert_R(Element_T Rec, BST_T &BST) {
  Key_T Key;
  ........................
    Key = Get_KAPRecKey(Rec);
  ........................
    if (Key < Get_KAPRecKey(Parent->Element)) {
```

The process of building a Graph_T then comes down to operations on the three trees. To understand how each operation works just see how the relevant tree or trees are manipulated, as well as the other fields, such as the count of vertices.

Finally we have Load_Graph_From_File. This is implemented as a procedure which first prompts for the name of the Graph_T, <gname>. It then attempts to open and read <gname>.ver, which is a text file containing the vertex records for <gname>. If this succeeds, then it attempts to open and read <gname>.arc, which contains the arc records for <gname>. If this is successful then the Graph_T <gname> has been loaded. Any failure results in a 'rollback' and the argument Graph_T to Load_Graph_From_File is empty.

Exercise

1   For each operation for building Graph_T, read the pre- and post-condition specifications in the source files and then see how the implementation for each meets the specification.

11.4.2 Marking vertices

The idea of marking is that we can use the iterator to traverse the set of vertices, marking or unmarking any as we wish. Here is the specification and implementation of Set_CurrentMark.

```
// PRE   NOT Q_EmptyGraph(Graph)
// POST Q_CurrentVertMarked(Graph')
void
Set_CurrentMark(Graph_T Graph) {
  GraphRec_Ptr_T GraphRec_Ptr;
  VertKAPRec_T VertKAPRec;

  GraphRec_Ptr = (GraphRec_Ptr_T) Graph;
```

```
    VertKAPRec = Get_CurrentVert(
            GraphRec_Ptr->VertIterator);
    Mark_Vert(VertKAPRec);
    Update_CurrentVert(
            VertKAPRec, GraphRec_Ptr->VertIterator);
}
```

Three new procedures are needed. Mark_Vert and UnMark_Vert are implemented in vstore.h. Here is Mark_Vert, with UnMark_Vert being the same except that the obvious line is changed.

```
// PRE   TRUE
// POST VertKAPRec' is marked
void
Mark_Vert(VertKAPRec_T &VertKAPRec) {

  VertKAPRec.Q_Marked = TRUE;
}
```

A new iterator procedure Update_CurrentVert has been provided. Here is its specification and implementation.

```
// PRE   Q_Iteration_Started(Iterator)
//       AND
//          Get_VertKAPRecKey(VertKAPRecUpdate) =
//          Get_VertKAPRecKey(Get_CurrentVert(Iterator))
// POST Get_CurrentVert(Iterator) =
//          VertKAPRecUpdate))
// NOTES PRE (ii) required to maintain key ordering
void
Update_CurrentVert(VertKAPRec_T VertKAPRecUpdate,
VertBST_Iterator_T Iterator) {
  VertBST_ItRec_Ptr_T ItRec;

  ItRec = (VertBST_ItRec_Ptr_T) Iterator;
  ((VertNode_Ptr_T) ItRec->Current)->Element =
      VertKAPRecUpdate;
}
```

Once again, we see that, although we can take existing ADTs, such as BST_T and KAPRec_T, as the basis of the implementation of a new type, like Graph_T, it may be necessary to extend the specification and implementation of the original ADTs. This provides motivation for the idea of inheritance in object-oriented design and programming, where a class (type) is based on another class (type) with some extra functionality added.

11.4.3 Implementing `Traveller_T`

Having built the `Graph_T` we can traverse it, using the iterators, but this is not a very flexible way of exploring its connectivity. `Traveller_T` is an associated ADT that gives the facility for algorithms, defined on `Graph_T`, to pick their way through the `Graph_T`. We have already seen the specification. How we implement it is going to be very much influenced by the `Graph_T` implementation used. Before starting on this section look back to Figure 11.7, which shows abstractly what some of the operations are meant to achieve. Once again recall that the actual implementation is mainly in terms of `BST_T`s.

`Traveller_T` is an opaque type. So, in `graph.h` we find

```
typedef void *Traveller_T;
```

The 'real' implementation is based on the following data structure:

```
typedef struct {
   VertKey_T  VertKey;
   VertBST_T  VertTreeRoot;
   ArcBST_T   ArcTreeRoot,
              CurrentArcTreeRoot;
   BOOLEAN    Q_NoArcs,
              Q_AtLastArc;
} TravellerRec_T, *TravellerRec_Ptr_T;
```

A `Traveller_T` once created for a particular `Graph_T`, has to be able to refer to the vertices and arcs, other than the ones where it is located, of that `Graph_T`. So we pass across `VertTreeRoot` and `ArcTreeRoot`, the vertex and 'from' arc trees of the `Graph_T`. `VertKey` is just the key of the vertex where the `Traveller_T` 'is at'. `CurrentArcTreeRoot` is the tree, whose root is the arc, if any, from the `Traveller_T`'s vertex which is 'being considered'. If there is no such arc – that is the `Traveller_T` is at a dead end – then this is an empty tree. Refer back to Figure 11.7 for a diagram. If `Q_NoArcs` is set to TRUE the `Traveller_T` is at a dead end. `Q_AtLastArc` is set to TRUE if the arc being considered, from the vertex where the `Traveller_T` is at, is the last one in the set being considered.

Since all the 'from' arcs are kept in a `BST_T`, `FromArcBST` of the `Graph_T`, then to move from the arc being considered to the next one to be considered, we have to find the 'next' arc with the same initial vertex value. Although the arcs are labelled a, b, c and d in Figure 11.7 and we move from a to b to c then back to a, the first, this is just to illustrate the idea of 'next' and 'first'. What we require is that there is some ordering of all the arcs from a given vertex. It so happens that this is given implicitly by the process of putting the arcs into the `FromArcBST` field of `Graph_T`. Because the initial vertex key is the sort key and for any initial vertex there may be more than one arc, as in Figure 11.7, then the sort key is not unique.

In Chapter 9, Section 9.4, we discussed searching through the set of records with the same non-unique key. This is the basis for the two following procedures defined on the ArcBST_T.

```
// PRE   TRUE
// POST IF ArcBST contains records with key Key
//         RETURNS tree with first record as root
//       ELSE
//         RETURNS the empty tree
ArcBST_T
Find_First_R(int (*Get_Key) (ArcKAPRec_T), int Key,
      ArcBST_T ArcBST) {
  ArcNode_Ptr_T Arc_Ptr;

  if (ArcBST == NULL) {
    return(ArcBST);
  }
  else {
    Arc_Ptr = (ArcNode_Ptr_T) ArcBST;
    if (Key < Get_Key(Arc_Ptr->Element)) {
      return(Find_First_R(Get_Key, Key,
            (void *) Arc_Ptr->Left_Ptr));
    }
    else {
      if (Key > Get_Key(Arc_Get_Root(ArcBST))) {
        return(Find_First_R(Get_Key, Key,
              (void *) Arc_Ptr->Right_Ptr));
      }
      else {
        return(ArcBST);
      }
    }
  }
}

// PRE   TRUE
// POST IF record with from key Key
//       is in ArcBST apart from the root
//         (different from Find_First_R)
//         RETURNS tree with that record as root
//       ELSE
//         RETURNS the empty tree
ArcBST_T
Find_NextDuplicate(int (*Get_Key) (ArcKAPRec_T),
        int Key, ArcBST_T ArcBST) {
  ArcNode_Ptr_T Arc_Ptr;

  Arc_Ptr = (ArcNode_Ptr_T) ArcBST;
  return(Find_First_R(Get_Key, Key,
        (void *) Arc_Ptr->Right_Ptr));
}
```

Find_First_R has the same structure as Q_ArcBST_Present_R but returns the sub-tree, the key of whose root is the first encountered equal to Key, instead of TRUE, if Key is present, or returns the empty tree instead of FALSE, if Key is not present.

Find_NextDuplicate uses the property, discussed above, that the next, if any, occurrence of Key must be in the right sub-tree of the tree whose root contains the current occurrence of Key. Thus this amounts to a call of Find_First_R on the right sub-tree.

So this extension to the basic underlying BST_T of the ArcBST_T gives the facility to work through all the arcs sharing the same initial vertex. Now we can code the 'arc considering' procedures for Traveller_T as follows:

```
void
Go_To_FirstArc_From_Vertex(Traveller_T Traveller) {
  TravellerRec_Ptr_T TravellerRec;

  TravellerRec = (TravellerRec_Ptr_T) Traveller;
  TravellerRec->CurrentArcTreeRoot =
      Find_First_R(Get_ArcKAPRecInitialKey,
      TravellerRec->VertKey,
      TravellerRec->ArcTreeRoot);
  TravellerRec->Q_AtLastArc =
    Q_EmptyArcTree(Find_NextDuplicate(
    Get_ArcKAPRecInitialKey,
    TravellerRec->VertKey,
    TravellerRec->CurrentArcTreeRoot));
}

void
Go_To_NextArc_From_Vertex(Traveller_T Traveller) {
  TravellerRec_Ptr_T TravellerRec;

  TravellerRec = (TravellerRec_Ptr_T) Traveller;
  TravellerRec->CurrentArcTreeRoot =
    Find_NextDuplicate(Get_ArcKAPRecInitialKey,
    TravellerRec->VertKey,
    TravellerRec->CurrentArcTreeRoot);
  TravellerRec->Q_AtLastArc =
    Q_EmptyArcTree(Find_NextDuplicate(
    Get_ArcKAPRecInitialKey,
    TravellerRec->VertKey,
    TravellerRec->CurrentArcTreeRoot));
}
```

To move along the arc we have Move_To_Vertex_Along_Current_Arc.

```
void
Move_To_Vertex_Along_Current_Arc(Traveller_T Traveller) {
  TravellerRec_Ptr_T TravellerRec;
```

```
    TravellerRec = (TravellerRec_Ptr_T) Traveller;
    TravellerRec->VertKey =
      Get_ArcKAPRecFinalKey(Arc_Get_Root(
        TravellerRec->CurrentArcTreeRoot));
    TravellerRec->CurrentArcTreeRoot =
      Find_First_R(Get_ArcKAPRecInitialKey,
        TravellerRec->VertKey,
        TravellerRec->ArcTreeRoot);
    TravellerRec->Q_NoArcs =
      Q_EmptyArcTree(
        TravellerRec->CurrentArcTreeRoot);
    if (!TravellerRec->Q_NoArcs) {
      TravellerRec->Q_AtLastArc =
        Q_EmptyArcTree(Find_NextDuplicate(
          Get_ArcKAPRecInitialKey,
          TravellerRec->VertKey,
          TravellerRec->ArcTreeRoot));
    }
  }
```

Note how Traveller_T needs always to have the roots of the vertex and from arc trees of the Graph_T it is travelling.

Exercise

1   For each operation for Traveller_T, read the pre- and post-condition specifications in the source files and then see how the implementation for each meets the specification.

11.5 Using the Graph_T

To demonstrate the use of the Graph_T we have a small application implemented in graphdem.h/.cpp. A sample Graph_T called Roads, consisting of places and roads between them, is provided. The vertex and arc files are Roads.ver and Roads.arc. Figure 11.8 shows the skeleton of Roads as vertex and arc keys. If you run the application, first use the l, (l)oad graph from file, option and load Roads. Then t gives the (t)raveller option, which asks for the key of a vertex in the Graph_T, which, in this case, you have just loaded from Roads. 92 is such a vertex.

To demonstrate an advanced graph algorithm we have option h, c(h)eck path. This calls a procedure which searches for a path between two vertices, printing it out if it exists, and reports failure if not. Here is part of the output when we ask it to find a path between vertex 3 and vertex 49.

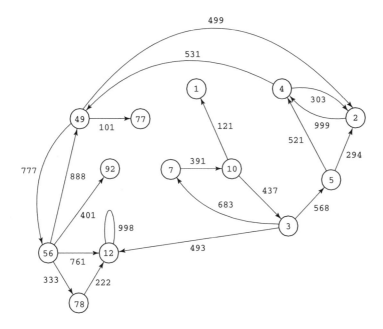

Figure 11.8 Roads showing the keys of vertices and arcs.

```
Next  traveller request [0] ==> h
Please input the Start vertex key ==> 3
Please input the End vertex key ==> 49

  ARC 683 called Raglan_Road to VERTEX 7 called Chorley
  ARC 391 called London_Road to VERTEX 10 called Atlantis
  ARC 121 called Yellow_Brick_Road to VERTEX 1 called
    Marsport
    NOT Path vertex DEAD END 1 called Marsport
  ........................
  ARC 303 called St_Giles to VERTEX 2 called Rome
    NEXT VERTEX is 2 called Rome and is marked
  ARC 531 called Wilmslow_Road to VERTEX 49 called El_Dorado
  END OF PATH 49 called El_Dorado
    Path vertex  4 called Bywater
    Path vertex  2 called Rome
    Path vertex  5 called Camelot
  START vertex  3 called Poictesme
  Path found
```

Figure 11.9 shows the progress of the search. The letters a to j show the various arcs tried in finding the path. This is known as a *depth first search*. The search goes as deep as it can, stopping only if successful or if it can go no further, in which case it backtracks to the last place where there were still unexplored arcs

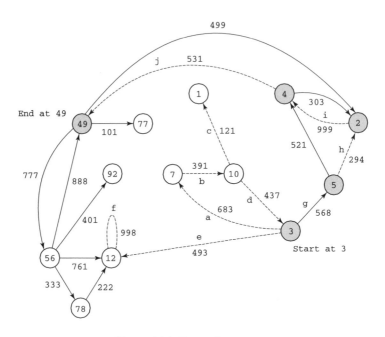

Figure 11.9 Traversing Roads.

to choose. At any stage of the exploration, you have reached some vertex V along a path from the start vertex S. So if you can find a path from V to the end vertex E, then you have the two components of a complete path from S to E. To see if there is a path from V to E, mark V as visited and then consider each of the successor vertices of V that are not marked as visited. If there is a path from any of those to E then there is a path from V to E. If there is not, V is not on any possible path to E, because there is no way from V to E, so backtrack to the last vertex where there are unexplored arcs. If there is a path from V to E, then note that V is on the path. Noting that V is on the path might mean just printing to screen as here, or maybe storing it in a data structure – see the Exercises at the end of this section. Since we are trying to find a path in terms of finding a simpler path this should alert you to the fact that recursion is one way we can do this!

Marking vertices as visited avoids getting into a cycle. A marked vertex may be one that is not on a path and has been marked by a failed depth search. Or it may be on the path that you are currently trying to build. For example, there is a cycle 7->10->3->7 in Roads. In this case 3 is on the path we are trying to build so it is pointless going back there.

How do we *backtrack* (get back) to the choice points where there are still alternatives to consider? We could push unused choices onto a stack, to be Popped off when the last chosen fails. Or, as we have done before, we could use recursion and force the system to maintain the stack for us.

Here is the algorithm for Seeking a path from StartVert to EndVert.

```
Seek_R(Start, Traveller, End, Q_PathFound)

    Mark Start
    IF Start = End
      SET Q_PathFound TO TRUE
    ELSE
      SET Q_PathFound TO FALSE;
      IF Start is not a dead end
        FOR each successor vertex U to Start
          IF U is not marked
            Seek_R(U, End, Q_PathFound)
            IF Q_PathFound
              Note U as on path
              RETURN
```

This needs to be elaborated since we are using a Traveller_T to explore. Examine the code for Seek_R to see how Traveller_T is used for this. Note that we use ReSet_Traveller because each time it is sent off in another call to Seek_R, its internal state will be changed in some way. ReSet_Traveller puts it back to the vertex it was on and the arc it was considering as it went into Seek_R. The actual implementation of Seek_R incorporates output as well to show the progress of the search, as shown in the run above. Seek_R is called by (non-recursive) Seek_Path.

Exercises

1   Run graphdem using the Roads files. Add some new vertices and arcs to the Roads file. Examine the full Seek_R code noting the output put in alongside the code from the basic algorithm above.

2   Add a new property to the arcs in the Roads example. This is the length of the road in kilometres. You will need to change the IO operations for ArcDataRec_T. Look at Print_VertexDetails in graphdem.h/.cpp. Implement Print_ArcDetails with the obvious semantics in graphdem.h/.cpp and use it in Seek_R.

3   Instead of displaying the vertex keys, store them in a VertSequence_T, a Sequence_T adapted for VertKAPRec_Ts, which is passed over as a parameter to Seek_R. Thus the signature of Seek_R will be

```
void
Seek_R(VertKey_T StartVertKey, Traveller_T Traveller,
VertKey_T EndVertKey, BOOLEAN &Q_PathFound, Route
VertSequence_T)
```

The first VertKAPRec_T in Route will be for the first vertex, the second for the second and so on. Seek_Path will call Seek_R with a global variable as the Route parameter.

Implement another procedure Print_Route(Route VertSequence_T) which will just print the vertex details for all the KAPREc_Ts in Route in order. You will need to add a new case to the switch statement etc.

4   Repeat Exercise (3) but for ArcKAPRec_T, using ArcSequence_T, a Sequence_T adapted for ArcKAPRec_Ts. Implement a new function Find_Length_Root(ArcRoute ArcSequence_T) which returns the length, in kilometres, of the route along the arcs in ArcRoute. Amend Print_Route so that it prints out the vertex details alternating with the arc details, and the length of the route.

5   The implementation of Graph_T would be inefficient for large numbers of arcs and vertices. One obvious problem is that, when considering arcs, we have to look through the whole FromArcBST component of GraphRec_T. This is liable to be 'stringy' because of the non-unique key value, in this case the InitialVertKey component of the ArcKAPRec_T. An alternative is a NonUBST_T specifically for non-unique keys. For each key value there is just one node, but that node contains an ArcSequence_T field, called Arcs say, for all the ArcKAPRec_Ts with that key value. So insertion is just an extension of that for a unique key BST_T. If there is no node with that VertKey_T value for the initial vertex of an arc, then one is created, as before, but within that the Arcs field is initialised and the ArcKAPRec_T added to Arcs. Otherwise there is already a node with the VertKey_T value and the ArcKAPRec_T added to the Arcs field. Design and implement this change without changing the specification of Graph_T or the code in graphdem.h/.cpp.

6   A further improvement would be to hold the Arcs field, discussed in Exercise (5), in the corresponding VertDataRec_T itself, saving the bother of working out a BST_T at all. Design and implement this change without changing the specification of Graph_T or the code in graphdem.h/.cpp. This is known as an *adjacency list* implementation.

7   Of course it would be even better to implement the Arcs field in Exercise (6) as an ArcBST_T. Design and implement this change without changing the specification of Graph_T or the code in graphdem.h/.cpp. One problem is that when you add the first arc to the Arcs field, you need access to be able to change this field. You can get a copy, change it and then physically replace the original with the updated copy. This may require extending one or more of the component ADTs.

8   In this exercise we change problems from Roads to Trains. Suppose that we are trying to take a train from A to B. In this case the arcs will be journeys – e.g. an arc might represent the fact that there is a train departing from Oxford at 10.05 a.m. arriving at Manchester at 1.15 p.m. We can find if there is a feasible trip from A to B in much the same way as Seek_R does, except that clearly we cannot go from A to X to B if the only journeys from X to B all depart before we arrive at X. We shall add two new fields to ArcDataRec_T, called DepartTime and ArriveTime of type

Time_T. Time_T has two components, Hours and Minutes, of type int.
As well as the obvious operations on Time_T, such as
Read_Time_From_File, Write_Time etc., there are three comparison
operators, Q_Earlier, Q_SameTime and Q_Later. Here is the specification
of Q_Earlier.

```
// PRE   TRUE
// POST IF Time1 is before Time2
//         RETURNS TRUE
//       ELSE
//         RETURNS FALSE
BOOLEAN
Q_Earlier(Time_T Time1, Time_T Time2);
```

The specifications of Q_SameTime and Q_Later are left to you. You then
need to look again at Seek_R and adapt the algorithm to take into account
this new constraint that a train must arrive at a station before the next one
on the trip departs from that station. Assume for simplicity that the whole
trip has to be done in one 24-hour period. You will need to set up new
.ver and .arc files of course!

11.6 Dijkstra's algorithm: an advanced graph traversal example

In this section we look at a more advanced graph traversal operation which is an
exemplar of the type of operations that we require to solve real-world problems
which use the graph representation. Once again, existing ADTs will be used and
extended to solve the problem.

11.6.1 What we want to do

As we have seen, graphs can be used to represent many real-world problems. We
have used the example of communication between places with roads. Our first
algorithm was to see if there was a path between any two places. A more useful
operation would be to find the shortest distance between two places. Even with
our small example it is not obvious which path between 3 and 49, say, is the
shortest, because branching means that the number of possible paths can grow
very quickly with the number of vertices in the graph. We need a systematic way
of working through the possibilities.

Before we look in more detail at a systematic way of finding the shortest path
from A to B, note that we need in effect to find the shortest path to any vertex in
the graph that is on a path between A and B. We could use our algorithm from
before to check out which vertices are on paths from A to B, but in practice we
may as well find the shortest distance from A to each vertex, since the processing

time is about the same. But some vertices may not be reachable from A, so what does the shortest path mean here? For simplicity we say that the shortest path between two vertices, which are not the initial and final vertices respectively of any path, is infinity.

One immediate change is to our ArcDataRec_T, with consequent changes to various functions and procedures that use it.

```
typedef struct {
   ArcKey_T Number;
   char *Name;
   VertKey_T InitialVertKey,
         FinalVertKey;
   int  Weight;
} ArcDataRec_T;
```

We also add a Weight field to ArcKAPRec_T and some relevant operations. Note that Weight need not be a distance. It could be times for example, so that we might use the same algorithm to find the shortest journey time.

Our file of arcs, roads.arc, now has an extra data item added to each record. The revised code is in ch11\examples\dijsdemo.

11.6.2 Relaxation

Suppose that we have been exploring some of the paths and for some of the vertices, n_1, n_2, ... n_k, in the graph we have established *provisional* shortest paths from some source vertex S. That is to say for each n_i, $1 \leqslant i \leqslant k$ that our procedure has established there is a path of that length from the source S to n_i. Each of the other vertices has its 'shortest path' set to infinity to show that there is, as yet, no path, let alone a shortest path, established between S and that vertex. So we can associate with each vertex either a shortest path value or a value representing infinity, here ∞. Figure 11.10 shows the situation at some stage. Vertex 45 is being considered. The currently known shortest path from S to 45 has length 209. There is an arc of length 18 to vertex 35, to which the shortest

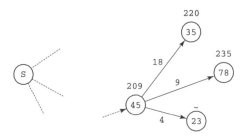

Figure 11.10 Before considering vertex 45 to see if any of its successors can have their shortest path from S updated.

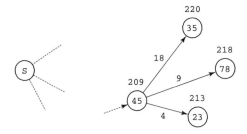

Figure 11.11 After considering vertex 45 to see if any of its successors can have their shortest path from S updated.

known path from S has length 220. Another arc of length 9 goes to vertex 78, which has a known shortest path from S of 235. Finally an arc of length 4 goes to vertex 23, which, so far, has no known path. This is indicated by the ~ symbol, which we are taking to show infinity.

If we consider vertex 35 first, we can see that taking the current shortest path to 45 and then going along the arc to 35 would give a path of length $209 + 18 = 227$. But this is not useful since we already have an established path of length 220, so we can rule out the 227 length path. However, taking vertex 78, it is clear that the path from S to 45 with the hop from 45 to 78, giving a path of length $209 + 9$, is an improvement over the current shortest path to 78 of length 235. Finally no path has yet been found from S to 23. So the path from S to 45 followed by the hop to 23 gives a path of length $209 + 4 = 213$, and the shortest, because the only one, found so far. The revised situation is shown in Figure 11.11.

This process is called *relaxation*. In fact there were three relaxations, one for each arc. Relaxation is an operation that is used in many graph searching algorithms. We shall want relaxation to do a little more than this and store the key of the previous vertex as well. Because we shall be dealing with the VertKAPRec_T we extend its specification to include the following new operations.

```
// PRE   TRUE
// POST Get_PathWeightUB(VertKAPRec')  = PathWeight
void
Set_PathWeightUB(VertKAPRec_T &VertKAPRec,  int PathWeight);

// PRE   TRUE
// POST RETURNS upper bound on shortest path to
//       Get_VertKAPRecKey(VertKAPRec)

int
Get_PathWeightUB(VertKAPRec_T VertKAPRec);
// PRE   TRUE
// POST Get_PathPred(VertKAPRec')  = PredVertKey
void
```

```
Set_PathPred(VertKAPRec_T &VertKAPRec,  VertKey_T
PredVertKey);

// PRE   TRUE
// POST RETURNS key value of predecessor of
//         Get_VertKAPRecKey(VertKAPRec)
VertKey_T
Get_PathPred(VertKAPRec_T VertKAPRec);
```

The first two operations deal with the weight of the shortest path so far. They contain the upper bound on the shortest path – hence to suffix UB. The next two operations deal with keeping the key of the predecessor on the shortest path so far. The struct for VertKAPRec_T has accordingly to be extended with two new fields PathWeight, of type int, and PredVertKey, of type VertKey_T, to implement these operations.

Now we can specify Relax.

```
// PRE   Q_ArcPresent(ArcKey, Graph)
// POST IF Get_PathWeightUB(ToVertKAPRec) >
//          Get_PathWeightUB (From VertKAPRec) +
//          Get_ArcKAPRecWeight (ArcKAPRec)
//          Get_PathWeightUB(ToVertKAPRec') =
//          Get_PathWeightUB (From VertKAPRec) +
//          Get_ArcKAPRecWeight (ArcKAPRec)
//          Get_PathPred(ToVertKAPRec') =
//          Get_VertKAPRecKey(From VertKAPRec)
//          AND Q_Updated'
//        ELSE
//          NOT Q_Updated'
// WHERE
//    ArcKAPRec = Retrieve_Arc(ArcKey, Graph)
//    InitialVertKey =
//      Get_ArcKAPRecInitialKey(ArcKAPRec)
//    FinalVertKey = Get_ArcKAPRecFinalKey(ArcKAPRec)
//    FromVertKAPRec = Retrieve_Vert(InitialVertKey, Graph)
//   ToVertKAPRec = Retrieve_Vert(FinalVertKey, Graph)
void
Relax(ArcKey_T ArcKey, Graph_T Graph, BOOLEAN &Q_Updated);
```

Checking this against the example above, you should be able to see that all this does is to update the shortest path information and then make a note of the predecessor vertex key, which we did not bother with in the example but was 45. Because the specification is so tight and expressed in terms of ADT operations, we find that the code is more or less the same as the specification, and can be found in ch11\examples\dijsdemo.

Relaxation is a single operation to be used in a variety of algorithms that systematically explore a graph initialised for such exploration. The next two sections deal with initialisation of a graph, and then a particular algorithm for graph exploration.

11.6.3 Initialisation

We need to set all the path weights to infinity and the key of the previous vertex to a null value. The second of these is straightforward. We reserve a special value, here −1 on the assumption that we will not have negative key values, called `NullVertKey` and `#defined` in `vstore.h`. To deal with infinity we note that relaxation will not cause a cycle, as shown in Figure 11.12. If we are relaxing the arc from y to x, where we have previously been through x, and then through 0 or more further vertices, shown as dotted circles, then the shortest path to y, p12, must be at least as great as the shortest path to x. So p12 ⩾ p11. Since the arc length 1 must be non-negative we must have p12 + 1 ⩾ p11. Relaxation will not occur and so vertex x will not acquire a shortest path predecessor y that has x as a predecessor. This is an invariant property of the relaxation procedure applied to a graph with no *negatively weighted arcs*.

We use this property to get a virtual infinity. Since there are no cycles then each arc can appear at most once in any stored shortest path. So no path can have a length greater than that of the sum of the lengths of all the arcs. Since infinity is larger than any integer we can count to, we take virtual infinity to be greater than the sum of all the arc lengths by just 1. So, to the declaration of `GraphRec_T` we add

```
int VirtualInfinity;
```

and then to `Create_Graph()` we add

```
NewGraphRec_Ptr->VirtualInfinity = 1;
```

and finally, to `Add_Arc` we add

```
GraphRec_Ptr->VirtualInfinity =
  GraphRec_Ptr->VirtualInfinity + Get_Weight(Arc);
```

A new `Graph_T` operation is required to access `VirtualInfinity`.

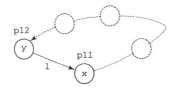

Figure 11.12 Relaxation cannot produce cycles in finding shortest paths if all arc weights are non-negative.

```
// PRE   TRUE
// POST RETURNS sum of all path weights in Graph + 1
int
Get_VirtualInfinity(Graph_T Graph);
```

This is the specification and implementation of the initialisation operation.

```
// PRE   Q_VertPresent(VertKey, Graph);
// POST For all VertKAPRec st
//         Q_VertPresent(Get_VertKAPRecKey(VertKAPRec), Graph)
//         IF SourceVertKey <> Get_VertKey(VertKAPRec)
//           Get_PathWeightUB(VertKAPRec') =
//           Get_Virtual_Infinity(Graph)
//         ELSE
//           Get_PathWeightUB(VertKAPRec') = 0
//           Get_PathPred(VertKAPRec') = NullVertKey
void
Initialise_Single_Source(Graph_T Graph, VertKey_T
      SourceVertKey) {
  BOOLEAN Q_Finished;
  int  VirtualInfinity;
  VertKAPRec_T VertKAPRec;

  VirtualInfinity = Get_VirtualInfinity(Graph);
  Go_To_FirstVert(Graph);
  Q_Finished = FALSE;
  for(;!Q_Finished;) {
    VertKAPRec = Get_CurrentVertKAPRec(Graph);
    if (SourceVertKey ==
        Get_VertKAPRecKey(VertKAPRec)) {
      Set_PathWeightUB(VertKAPRec, 0);
      Set_PathPred(VertKAPRec, NullVertKey);
    }
    else {
      Set_PathWeightUB(VertKAPRec, VirtualInfinity);
      Set_PathPred(VertKAPRec, NullVertKey);
    }
    Update_GraphVert(VertKAPRec, Graph);
    if (Q_LastVert(Graph)) {
      Q_Finished = TRUE;
    }
    else {
      Go_To_NextVert(Graph);
    }
  }
}
```

This sets things up for systematic processing to find the shortest path from the source, whose key is SourceVertKey, to any other vertex to which there is a path. We now turn to one method of systematic processing.

11.6.4 Dijkstra's algorithm

Dijkstra's algorithm finds the shortest paths from a source vertex to all other vertices reachable from that source. This is the specification.

```
// PRE   Q_VertPresent(SourceVertKey, Graph)
// POST  For each vertex VertKey in Graph
//       Get_PathWeightUB(VertKAPRec') is the weight of
//       the shortest path from Source to VertKey
//       AND Get_PathPred(VertKAPRec') is key of
//       predecessor of VertKey on that path
// WHERE
//    VertKAPRec = Retrieve_Vert(VertKey, Graph)
```

It can be stated very shortly.

```
1  Initialise_Single_Source(Graph, SourceVertKey)
2  SET ToBeProc, the set of VertKAPRec_Ts to be
   processed TO
     the set of all VertKAPRec_Ts in Graph
3  FOR NOT Q_EmptySet(ToBeProc)
4    V ∈ ToBeProc is such that
       for all other U ∈ ToBeProc
       Get_PathWeightUB(V) ≤ Get_PathWeightUB(U)
5    FOR all U such that
       there exists an ArcKAPRec_T A
       AND Get_ArcKAPRecInitialKey(A) =
         Get_VertKAPRecKey(V)
       AND Get_ArcKAPRecFinalKey(A) =
         Get_VertKAPRecKey(U)
6      Relax(Get_ArcKAPRecKey(A), Graph)
7    Remove V from ToBeProc
```

So every time the outer FOR is performed, one vertex moves from being unprocessed to being processed, which guarantees that the algorithm will complete. The processing consists of just performing relaxation on each arc out of the vertex being processed. This means that every arc in Graph gets relaxed sooner or later, although this does not mean that every arc necessarily gets updated.

We already have Initialise_Single_Source and Relax worked out. The major remaining problem is how to implement ToBeProc. We could just implement it as a Sequence_T, but we would spend a long time looking through for the vertex with minimal shortest path. Another way to implement ToBeProc would be as a VertBST_T keyed by the shortest path attribute. That way the vertex with the shortest path of all would always be the first and could be accessed by using an Iterator_T with Start_VertIteration. The only problem with this is that Relax may cause the shortest paths for one or more vertices to change.

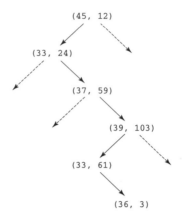

Figure 11.13 Path weight as a non-unique key.

This can be overcome by deleting any vertex whose shortest path changes from Proc and reinserting again, having set its new shortest path value. In turn, this raises the problem that using the shortest path as key may give rise to duplicate key values. However, we know the general approach to this from Sections 9.4 and 11.4.3. Figure 11.13 shows what might occur. This shows a VertBST_T, and the first and second elements of the ordered pair in brackets at each node are the PathWeight and VertKey attributes respectively. If we wanted to delete (33, 61), then we follow the usual BST_T procedure, using the primary key of PathWeight, until we get to (33, 24). Since the secondary key of VertKey does not match we carry on searching. Because 'greater than or equal to' goes to the right, then we resume the search in the right-hand tree, using the primary key.

The process of deletion has two stages. First, find the node to be deleted. Then delete it, readjusting the tree as required. So we write a new deletion procedure for VertBST_T, based on a primary but non-unique key selected by Get_PKey, and a secondary unique key, selected by Get_SKey. Here is the prototype.

```
// PRE  VertBST is primary ordered by Get_PKey()
// POST if VertBST contains Rec such that
//         Get_PKey(Rec) = PKey
//         AND Get_SKey(Rec) = SKey
//         VertBST has Rec deleted
void
VertTwoKeysBST_Delete_R(int (*Get_PKey) (VertKAPRec_T),
   int (*Get_SKey) (VertKAPRec_T), int PVertKey,
   int SVertKey, VertBST_T &VertBST);
```

The full procedure can be found in VertBST.h/.cpp but here is the code for the search for the VertKAPRec_T to be deleted.

```
if (PVertKey < Get_PKey(Vert_Ptr->Element)) {
  VertTwoKeysBST_Delete_R(Get_PKey, Get_SKey,
     PVertKey, SVertKey,
     (VertBST_T)  Vert_Ptr->Left_Ptr);
}

else {
  if (PVertKey > Get_PKey(Vert_Ptr->Element)) {
    VertTwoKeysBST_Delete_R(Get_PKey, Get_SKey,
       PVertKey, SVertKey,
       (VertBST_T)  Vert_Ptr>Right_Ptr);
  }
  else {
    if (SVertKey != Get_SKey(Vert_Ptr->Element)) {
      VertTwoKeysBST_Delete_R(Get_PKey, Get_SKey,
         PVertKey, SVertKey,
         (VertBST_T)  Vert_Ptr->Right_Ptr);
    }
```

Note than in the prototype for Relax, we have an extra parameter Q_Updated. This is used for performance purposes to reorganise the actual data structure used for ToBeProc for efficient retrieval.

Here is the code for Dijkstra's algorithm.

```
void
Dijkstra(Graph_T Graph, VertKey_T SourceVertKey) {
  Initialise_Single_Source(Graph, SourceVertKey);
  VertBST_T ToBeProc;
  VertBST_Iterator_T Iterator;
  VertKAPRec_T  VertKAPRec,
       ToVertKAPRec;
  VertKey_T InitialVertKey,
       FinalVertKey;
  ArcKey_T ArcKey;
  Traveller_T Traveller;
  BOOLEAN Q_Finished;
  ArcKAPRec_T ArcKAPRec;
  int ToPathWeight;
  BOOLEAN Q_Updated;

  ToBeProc = Extract_And_Copy_Verts(Get_PathWeightUB, Graph);
  Iterator = Create_VertIterator();
  Start_VertIteration(Iterator, ToBeProc);
  VertKAPRec = Get_CurrentVert(Iterator);
  InitialVertKey = Get_VertKAPRecKey(VertKAPRec);
  Traveller = Create_Traveller(InitialVertKey, Graph);
  Print_Weights_And_Preds(Graph);
  for (;!Q_EmptyVertTree(ToBeProc);) {
    Start_VertIteration(Iterator, ToBeProc);
    VertKAPRec = Get_CurrentVert(Iterator);
```

```
      InitialVertKey = Get_VertKAPRecKey(VertKAPRec);
      Start_Traveller(Traveller, InitialVertKey);
      if (!Q_Dead_End(Traveller)) {
        Q_Finished = FALSE;
        for (;!Q_Finished;) {
          ArcKAPRec =
            Get_CurrentTraveller_ArcKAPRec(Traveller);
            ArcKey = Get_ArcKAPRecKey(ArcKAPRec);
          FinalVertKey =
            Get_ArcKAPRecFinalKey(ArcKAPRec);
          ToVertKAPRec = Retrieve_Vert(FinalVertKey, Graph);
          ToPathWeight =
            Get_PathWeightUB(ToVertKAPRec);
          Relax(ArcKey, Graph, Q_Updated);
          if (Q_Updated) {
            ToVertKAPRec =
              Retrieve_Vert(FinalVertKey, Graph);
            VertTwoKeysBST_Delete_R(Get_PathWeightUB,
              Get_VertKAPRecKey, ToPathWeight,
              FinalVertKey, ToBeProc);
            VertBST_Insert_R(Get_PathWeightUB,
              ToVertKAPRec, ToBeProc);
          }
          if (Q_No_More_Arcs(Traveller)) {
            Q_Finished = TRUE;
          }
          else {
            Go_To_NextArc_From_Vertex(Traveller);
          }
        }
      }
      VertTwoKeysBST_Delete_R(Get_PathWeightUB,
        Get_VertKAPRecKey,
        Get_PathWeightUB(VertKAPRec), InitialVertKey,
        ToBeProc);
    }
    //tidy up
    Destroy_Traveller(Traveller);
    Destroy_VertIterator(Iterator);
  }
```

Note that the extra parameter, Q_Updated, which appears in the specification of Relax but not in the call in the original Dijkstra algorithm, is introduced because we want to know if we have to carry out the deletion/insertion of any VertKAPRec_T that has changed.

11.6.5 A picture of what Dijkstra's algorithm achieves

The graph for the roads example is executed as shown in Figure 11.14, showing the weights of the arcs.

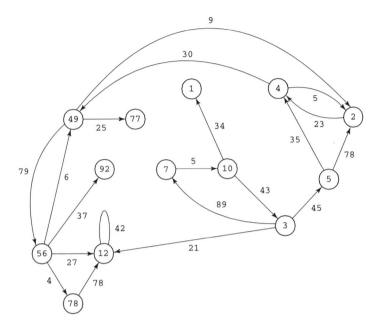

Figure 11.14 The roads example showing the arc weights.

If you compile and run ch11\examples\dijsdemo\dijsdemo, loading the roads example again, then choosing the Dijkstra option with 'd', then 'd' again with 2 as the source vertex, you will eventually end with this. There are various displays on the way to show progress.

```
Vertex 1 path weight 716 predecessor -1
Vertex 2 path weight 0 predecessor -1
Vertex 3 path weight 716 predecessor -1
Vertex 4 path weight 23 predecessor 2
Vertex 5 path weight 716 predecessor -1
Vertex 7 path weight 716 predecessor -1
Vertex 10 path weight 716 predecessor -1
Vertex 12 path weight 159 predecessor 56
Vertex 49 path weight 53 predecessor 4
Vertex 56 path weight 132 predecessor 49
Vertex 77 path weight 78 predecessor 49
Vertex 78 path weight 136 predecessor 56
Vertex 92 path weight 169 predecessor 56
```

This shows the final path weights. In this case VirtualInfinity is 716. Dijkstra's algorithm has identified a tree, whose root is 2. The shortest path to any other vertex can be found by starting from that vertex and just moving from parent to parent until you find 2. You have traced the path in reverse. Figure 11.15 illustrates this.

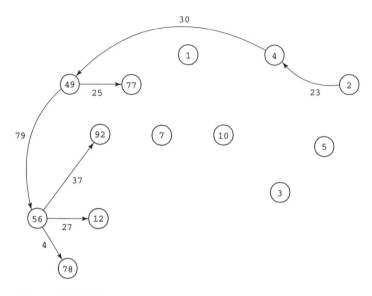

Figure 11.15 The roads example showing the shortest path tree.

This is but one of a large number of algorithms defined on graph structures for a variety of problems arising in the fields of networks, operations research, artificial intelligence and information systems, to name a few major examples. This small case study illustrates how we can start from the statement of the algorithm as given in a textbook on graph theory and then design an implementation, using or extending existing ADTs.

Exercises

1   Run dijsdemo using the Roads files and try out various source vertices.
2   Once Dijkstra's algorithm has been run, each VertKAPRec_T in Graph has PredVertKey set for the previous vertex on the shortest path from the chosen source, or to NullVertKey if there is no such previous vertex. Design and write a procedure, together with appropriate 'wrapper' procedure for user interaction, that will return TRUE if a shortest path has been found and FALSE if there is no such path.
3   Design and write a procedure, together with appropriate 'wrapper' procedure for user interaction, that will print out the shortest path from the source to any vertex. The procedure will have a pre-condition that a shortest path has been found. The 'wrapper' must check this using the procedure from Exercise (2).

4   Design and write a procedure, together with appropriate 'wrapper'
    procedure for user interaction, that will return the shortest path from the
    source to any vertex in a Sequence_T. Again the procedure will have a
    pre-condition that a shortest path has been found and the 'wrapper' must
    check this using the procedure from Exercise (2).

11.7 Summary

In this chapter we have covered the following:

- The graph structure of vertices and arcs has been introduced by example,
  definition and specification.
- The specification of the ADT Graph_T has building, query and traversal
  operations.
- The Traveller_T has been specified for exploring a Graph_T.
- Graph_T and Traveller_T types have been implemented, mainly using
  BST_Ts.
- A simple path-finding algorithm was given as an example of a higher-level
  operation on Graph_T.
- Dijkstra's algorithm was described and then implemented, using and
  extending the existing ADTs.

CHAPTER 12

What next?

12.1 Introduction

In this chapter I shall summarise what we have done in the last 11 chapters, and then discuss where you might continue from here, introducing some further reading.

12.2 A review

The approach to data structures in this book has been that of the abstract data type (ADT). ADTs at one level provide data structures for ADTs at the next higher level. In this way we have started out with a few simple ADTs – the built-in array, the Sequence_T and the BT_T – and then developed more specialised ADTs – such as the Stack_T from the Sequence_T – or compound ADTs – such as the Graph_T – or auxiliary ADTs – such as the Iterator_T for the BST_T. ADTs are concerned with correctness and are indifferent to matters of efficiency. But having got our ADT working as we want, we can then set to work to make it more efficient by removing intermediate levels of ADT, as we did with the Stack_T, coding it directly in terms of pointers and nodes. It may be that nothing is gained because 'smart' compilers do this automatically, using in-line coding to transform non-recursively coded function and procedure hierarchies.

Recursion has been covered as a natural way to look at many structures and processes. Despite its initially counter-intuitive appearance, it provides a useful problem-solving technique in situations where the non-recursive or iterative approach does not obviously provide a solution. The recursive solution may then indicate a non-recursive solution. This was seen, for example, in the Hanoi problem, when a pattern emerged from using the recursive solution. If the generality of the pattern was proved then it gave rise to a very simple non-recursive solution. However, this simple non-recursive solution was not at all obvious from the initial problem statement.

It was through the use of recursion that we were able to refine the specification of the BST_T in terms of the ordinary BT_T to give concise recursive implementations of the procedures. Once we had 'got a feel' for the ADT, through the recursive implementation, we could transform the implementation into a non-recursive one. Both these examples are cases where 'smart' compilers might find it impossible to use in-line coding transformations.

Searching and sorting provided a number of good examples of common and important algorithms on data structures, mainly linear data structures, but searching and sorting are implicit in the work on the BST_T.

The last ADT was the Graph_T, providing a versatile data structure for real-world problems in every field. Having implemented it, using a number of other ADTs, we then implemented a simple searching algorithm for it. Then we saw how we could adapt some of the underlying ADTs to provide a base for implementing a typical example of more intricate graph searching algorithms, namely Dijkstra's algorithm.

Throughout, the emphasis has been on reasoning about specification, design, testing and, if as is often unfortunately required, debugging. The number of data structures covered is small but I hope that the lessons learned will equip you to tackle problems more particular to your future academic or industrial work. The real-world applications have been limited but it should be obvious by now that, for example, if you can quicksort an array of 100 integers into order, then there is no further intellectual challenge in quicksorting an array of 50,000 records for employees, each containing a hundred or more data fields of various types, as long as there is a key data field.

Although C++ has been used, no special tricks are essential parts of the implementations. For example, the use of the void pointer is to provide information hiding, which can be handled in much the same way, although with different syntax of course, in Modula-2 and most implementations of Pascal. I shall talk about Java later but the same is true for that language. When we get to higher-level code then the differences are small enough to make 90% of translation a careful use of the search-and-replace facility in a text editor. For example, the following fragment from the Dijkstra algorithm

```
for (;!Q_EmptyVertTree(ToBeProc);) {
  Start_VertIteration(Iterator, ToBeProc);
  VertKAPRec = Get_CurrentVert(Iterator);
  InitialVertKey = Get_VertKAPRecKey(VertKAPRec);
  Start_Traveller(Traveller, InitialVertKey);
  if (!Q_Dead_End(Traveller)) {
```

becomes in Pascal

```
while not Q_EmptyVertTree(ToBeProc) do
begin
  Start_VertIteration(Iterator, ToBeProc);
  VertKAPRec := Get_CurrentVert(Iterator);
  InitialVertKey := Get_VertKAPRecKey(VertKAPRec);
  Start_Traveller(Traveller, InitialVertKey);
  if not Q_Dead_End(Traveller) then
  begin
```

12.3 Further work

For students continuing with programming there are four main areas of further work from the material covered in this book.

12.3.1 Further data structures

The first is to investigate further data structures, in particular in the tree family. For example, we have not looked at B trees, B+ trees, heaps or general trees. A good place to start with this is *Intermediate Problem Solving and Data Structures: Walls and Mirrors* by Paul Helman, Robert Veroff and Frank Carrano (Benjamin Cummings 1991, 2nd edition). Space prevented these topics being covered but I shall add implementations of the B tree and B+ tree with an introduction to the website in due course.

12.3.2 Using data structures

All the examples of using data structures are fairly simple, yet even so you have the building blocks for some quite substantial applications without even considering further data structures. One way to really consolidate the work here is to do a project that requires a great deal of updating, manipulating and retrieving data. This might be for a real-world problem or one that you specify yourself. An obvious opportunity is in your undergraduate project. (All code from the website can be used and amended as you wish, the only stipulation being that you declare such use, so as to be in line with your university or college plagiarism regulations.)

12.3.3 Using algorithms

Most of the algorithms of any complexity have appeared in Chapter 10 on sorting and searching. If you look in any book on discrete maths or graph theory you will find any number of algorithms defined on various structures, particularly the graph. A good book for this is *Mathematical Structures for Computer Science* by Judith Gershing (W.H. Freeman & Company 1999, 4th edition). Good exercises are those taking the abstract statement of the algorithm, such as Dijkstra's algorithm as usually stated, and developing the pseudo-code then the C++ code that is applicable to our ADT Graph_T. Although they are not primarily either discrete maths or graph theory books, two other excellent books for this are *Foundations of Computer Science* by Alfred Aho and Jeffrey Ullman (Computer Science Press 1992) and *Introduction to Algorithms* by Thomas Cormen, Charles Leiserson and Ronald Rivest (MIT Press 1990). Space has prevented us exploring proofs about algorithm and structures to any extent but you are advised to look at, for example, the proof of why Dijkstra's algorithm works. Proofs of property invariance under certain operations may lead to greatly simplified algorithms.

12.3.4 Object-oriented programming

I have held back from *classes* and other *object-oriented* features of C++ as discussed in the Preface. There are two good reasons for this. First, it means that C programmers, and those Pascal and Modula-2 programmers willing to put in a little extra work at the start, can use this book without too much trouble. Second, I hope that now you know what classes are intended for! The class feature is just language support for an ADT. It extends the record feature so that you can have procedures and functions, called methods in OO speak, as items alongside the data items. So, instead of writing

```
BST_Insert(DataRec, Dbase);
```

you have

```
Dbase. BST_Insert(DataRec);
```

This neatens things up but it goes further. Where we adapted ADTs, either by specialisation – for example, specialising the `Sequence_T` to `Stack_T` – or extension – for example, adding `VertTwoKeysBST_Delete_R` as a new procedure to `VertBST_T` for Dijkstra's algorithm – then with an object-oriented language we can use a feature called *inheritance* to develop new classes, like the old one in some ways but different in others.

It is essential to realise that the whole point of object-oriented programming is to provide language support for the design and implementation of computer programs. Object-oriented languages do not let you do more in principle.

An excellent introduction to the theory and practice of object-oriented programming is *Object Oriented Software Construction* by Betrand Meyer (Prentice Hall 1997). This uses Eiffel, which is a far superior although less popular language than C++. The fact that it uses Eiffel, even though you may not know it, helps tremendously. Eiffel was designed as an object-oriented language, which means that the language is meant to support the practice of object-oriented software construction.. Hence it 'fits around' that practice rather like the language of a mature science like physics fits around doing physics. This means that the points are made that much more clearly than they would be using C++. For example, the use of type parameters in Eiffel is clear and simple, whereas the use of templates in C++ can get in the way of explaining what they are meant to do. Meyer is quite clear about what classes and objects are for. This is not about buzzwords or the 'hottest thing happening'. Read this and you will understand what classes and objects are for! Of course you will then know want you want to do with classes, so you may want to see how it is then done in C++. I recommend

Introduction to Data Structures and Algorithms with C++ by Glenn Rowe (Prentice Hall 1997).

In fact, you will probably have an easier time moving to the use of Java rather than C++ classes. If you are keen to start working with Java, get a good introductory book, such as *The Essence of Java Programming* by Glenn Rowe (Pearson Education 1999), together with *Java in a Nutshell* by David Flanagan (O'Reilly 1997, 2nd edition). Having read Meyer's book try reimplementing some of the examples from this book in Java. I suggest you work out how to use the various graphical user interface components in the Abstract Windowing Toolkit (AWT) early on. It makes life a whole lot easier!

12.4 Last words

Well, that's it! In the words of Sir Winston Churchill you are now at the 'end of the beginning'. Programming is like painting (houses not pictures). The secret is in the preparation!

Index